Children in New Religions

Children in New Religions

EDITED BY

SUSAN J. PALMER

CHARLOTTE E. HARDMAN

Rutgers University Press

New Brunswick, New Jersey, and London

Library of Congress Cataloging-in-Publication Data

Children in new religions / edited by Susan J. Palmer and Charlotte E. Hardman
p. cm.
Includes bibliographical references and index.
ISBN 0–8135–2619–1 (alk. paper). — ISBN 0–8135–2620–5 (pbk. : alk. paper)
1. Cults. 2. Children—Religious life. I. Palmer, Susan J. II. Hardman, Charlotte.
BP603.C48 1999
200'.83—dc21 98–30474
CIP

British Cataloging-in-Publication data for this book is available from the British Library

Parts of Helen Berger's essay, "Witches: The Next Generation," appeared in her book *A Community of Witches: Contemporary Neo-Paganism and Witchcraft in the United States* (Columbia: University of South Carolina Press, 1998). Used with permission of the author and publisher.

Manufactured in the United States of America

To our children: Sandor, Sylvia, Sophie, and Helen

Contents

ACKNOWLEDGMENTS

Susan J. Palmer wishes to thank the Social Science in the Humanities Research Council and the Society for the Scientific Study of Religion for the research grants they awarded to assist her studies in childrearing in new religious movements. Charlotte E. Hardman expresses her gratitude to the Small Grants Committee of Newcastle upon Tyne. We both want to acknowledge the invaluable help that Bruno Geslain gave Palmer in helping her apply for grants and in printing out the manuscript. Also, we could not have met the deadline without Vivian McKoy's secretarial skills and Clare Robert's help with the index.

We wish to thank Martha Heller at Rutgers for her amazing empathy in understanding and directing the course of this study. Also, we are grateful to Tom Robbins, David Bromley, Eileen Barker, James T. Richardson, and James Lewis for encouraging us in this project and helping us track down authors. We wish to acknowledge the open attitude and generosity of the new religious parents who trusted us sufficiently to let us meet and interview their children. Finally, we want to thank the children themselves.

Children in New Religions

INTRODUCTION

Alternative Childhoods

SUSAN J. PALMER AND CHARLOTTE E. HARDMAN

The study of children in new religious movements (NRMs) is a largely uncharted terrain with intriguing opportunities for future researchers. This new frontier has formed as the result of the maturation of many alternative religious communities that found root in the counterculture of the United States and Europe. The period from the late 1960s to the early 1970s was remarkable for its spiritual experimentation and the proliferation of new religious organizations. Since the mid-1970s, the number of children in many of these movements has been steadily rising. The second generation is now coming of age, and in some NRMs the children even outnumber their parents.

The social context of these movements has changed considerably since the 1970s. For one thing, the children of NRMs are in a very different situation from their parents, many of whom made the choice as single adults to "drop out" of mainstream society and embrace radical religious goals. Having rejected their own parents' marital patterns, preprogrammed career choices, and materialistic lifestyles, these former rebels are currently preoccupied with raising a second generation to carry on their religious traditions and must confront the dilemma of how to transmit their own values to their children. But the second generation's attitude toward the larger society is very different from that of their parents. Members of this generation were born into religious communities they took for granted and have grown up assimilating their budding subcultures, many of these children gazing with curiosity at the surrounding society that it was never their choice to reject. As the researcher becomes better acquainted with studying these second-generation youths, the potential future shapes and dreams of these movements begin to come into focus.

Our volume explores four important areas of interest that have emerged from our research: the enormous impact that children have on a young movement, how movements socialize their children, what issues of religious freedom arise as a result, and how children in NRMs construct meaning. In part 1, Helen

Berger explores the ways in which Witches and Pagans have sought to adapt their ritual practices and nature-oriented lifestyles to accommodate their little "Witchlings." Burke Rochford has gleaned insights into the future of the Hare Krishna movement by interviewing its teenagers who are adjusting to public high schools and sorting out what aspects of their parents' faith they will retain and what they will leave behind. In contrast to this NRM's gradual reintegration into society, Amy Siskind's history of the Sullivanian Community demonstrates how a radical, impractical, and adult-centered approach to parenting can hasten a group's involuntary demise by provoking a public reaction that is devastating to the group's morale. These studies explore the issues of how NRMs socialize their second generation, how they integrate children into the commune, whether they involve them in missionary activity, and how they protect them from, or expose them to, the surrounding secular world. A comparison of these patterns tells us a great deal about the different ways charismatic movements mature over time, and what factors or strategies affect their survival.

The chapters in part 2 focus on how new, experimental notions of childhood that reflect sacred ideologies affect the second generation. Over two decades these communities have hammered out their own unique models of child development, education and morality. In contrast to loss of control by the International Society for Krishna Consciousness of its youth, the Word of Life congregation in Sweden, according to Simon Coleman, has successfully held onto its children, who are valued as essential components of the nuclear family and are encouraged to cultivate their own charismatic gifts. His study also addresses the "passive socialization" versus the "active makers of meaning" debate that flows through this volume: that is, the extent to which children are "indoctrinated" or "freely choose" these alternative worldviews. Most adult societies tend to stereotype children and their "childish" activities, forgetting the enormous power that the children's valued objects, games, and rhymes hold for them in their own, autonomous worlds. In Word of Life, the culturally defined boundary between adulthood and childhood is rendered ambiguous by the group's clear distinction between physical maturity and spiritual maturity. Coleman addresses the interesting paradox of a community that, while partially denying the autonomous symbolic world of the child, at the same time fosters charisma and spiritual potential in its children, and he investigates how the group's ritual and verbal forms act to reinforce this role adaptability and personhood ambiguity. Elizabeth Puttick's study of a school in England based on the mystical, antinomian teachings of the late Indian guru Osho raises the question of whether this radically individualistic approach has resulted in a "religious" education in spite of Osho's ideology of personal freedom from any kind of institution or authority. Judith Coney shows how Sahaja Yoga founder Sri Mataji Nirmala Devi, who is highly critical of Western society, aims to preserve the innocence of "her" children and make them conform to an ideal that demands separating them from their parents and absorbing them into the fictive, idealized family of Sahaja Yoga. Coney highlights the problems of translating an ideal into practical reality within a sectarian environment, which raises the sensitive issue of the renunciation of family ties, a common feature of communal and apocalyptic religions. Gretchen Siegler's study of how a Christian commune of this type in California socializes its young suggests that a community that strives for a healthy balance between collective and family life has a better chance of surviving. Massimo Introvigne describes children's participation in festivals, art, and ritual at Damanhur, a large magical-theosophical commune in northern Italy famous for its subterranean temple, and he traces Damanhur's struggle for social legitimacy.

These ethnographies are important, since we live in an era marked by dramatic transformations in the structure of the family due to the baby boom; birth control and reproductive technology; the feminist, sexual, and gay liberation movements; and the prolonged "cult of youth." New religions can offer us fresh perspectives on mainstream society's experimental and pluralistic approaches to childrearing.

In part 3, scholars and lawyers tackle questions of religious freedom. Susan Palmer's legal history of a Vermont-based commune that sustained a 1984 government raid on its children explores three frontier myths embedded in our culture. These myths, she argues, which fuel our deep-seated fears of family mutation and fragmentation, are projected onto "cults." But frontier myths also explain our nostalgic attraction toward utopian communities that remind us of simpler times. James Richardson traces the early efforts of the anticult movement to exert social control over "cults" and notes that with the decline of the "brainwashing" theory, a new rationale was needed to limit the power of what were regarded as dangerous and inauthentic religions. The conspicuous presence of children in communities that are marginal, mysterious, and perceived as weird and threatening has provided a new weapon for the anticult movement, resulting in the frequent and fashionable accusation of child abuse in all its ugly manifestations. Michael Homer explains the historical background of the courts' recent decisions regarding custody of children in NRMs in the United States and in Europe by reviewing outstanding cases involving minority religions that have tested the precarious balance between freedom of religion and the best interest of the child. Anthony Bradney examines the attitudes of courts and judges in Britain toward parents who are involved in unconventional religions (often deemed socially unacceptable) and how intense commitment to their faith (perceived as immoderate, even fanatical) has affected their chances of winning custody and care of their children.

Part 4 takes up the issue of how we understand children in NRMs. No self-respecting researcher today would disregard the voices of women, but they rarely bother to listen to children. If we do not take seriously their own versions of reality and realize that children are active in the construction and determination of their own lives, how can we possibly begin to assess their well-being inside controversial communities or analyze their impact on the futures of new religious movements? Charlotte Hardman's comparison of children's concepts of morality in The Family, Transcendental Meditation, and Findhorn acknowledges children as competent social agents and creators of meaning. This approach to children as subject and creators of culture "muted" by adult dominance has been developing slowly in the United Kingdom since the 1970s (Opie and Opie 1969; Hardman 1973; Prout and James 1990; Toren 1993) and challenges the hackneyed, prevailing view that children in "cults" are "total victims" (Singer 1996). Many of our researchers into these sectarian communities have stumbled across something resembling a children's subculture, constructed from ideas, contraband music, secret pacts, and shared values that do not belong to the adult world of meaning surrounding them. Hardman's study suggests that, even though these subcultures are more distinct and articulated in some types of NRMs than in others, unless researchers are willing to sit down and "hear the children," our understanding of a movement will be incomplete.

These ethnographical insights into the "alternative childhoods" fostered inside spiritual communities fill a lacuna in the growing microsociology of NRMs that is not surprising given the barriers to research. Studying children in NRMs presents researchers with a methodological challenge requiring value-free reflexivity, so that a researcher's own cultural expectations do not impinge on the process. In a highly politicized field where custody battles are waged, it is difficult for the researcher to avoid being drawn into territorial skirmishes between "cult apologists" and anticultists. Sociologists requesting permission to engage in field research and participant observation strike a vulnerable zone. Groups undergoing investigations by public health officials or local school boards are not particularly receptive to the cold, scientific questionnaires and surveys that could eventually be used against them. Many of these movements are engaged in the intense process of experimentation, adapting their socialization processes and disciplinary measures to fast-growing, demanding ranks of toddlers, children, and teens. This process is often chaotic. Mistakes will be made that will be reviewed and corrected as new rules are set in place. The improvisational nature of this process means that the groups are reluctant to invite in outsiders to study them. Once their schools are mature and have proved successful, of course, then they will welcome public relations and conduct tours for visitors.

These "successful" schools, however, require another kind of caution, since there has always been a distance between PR and real research, between a private school's brochure and the experiences of its students. NRMs have produced reams of fascinating utopian literature on how to give birth and rear children, but once the researcher begins to interview mothers, fathers, teachers, and children, she or he will find striking discrepancies between the idealized, religiously based portraits of family life and the messy complexities of real-life relationships.

Studying childhood has always been a daunting task. Historians complain of formidable obstacles in the field of social history. Joy Parr (1982:8) writes: "In general, it is not easy to find out about childhood and family life. We are dealing largely with activities in the private . . . realm." She points to the scarce documentary sources, since families in previous centuries living in close proximity felt no need to compose letters or were illiterate. Generalizations made by earlier historians about the European family have come under attack, since "childhood and family change all the time, not a little, but a lot" (Parr 1982:7). Parr's observations remind us that we know very little about how members of NRMs raise their young. What we are beginning to realize is that their patterns of parenting are many and their differences cannot be underestimated. We find a wide gamut from groups that do not acknowledge age distinctions, to groups with elaborate rule-bound age sets; from groups that consider kids to be boring little nuisances, to groups that cultivate charismatic qualities in their young, place them on a higher scale of purity, or endow them a key role in the anticipated Endtime. Many of the communities described in this volume are child-centered and most interesting for our purposes because they have developed the most radical, highly elaborated, and religiously based family patterns.

In any North American town that hosts a new religious community, rumors usually circulate concerning its children. By providing real, documented information on specific groups, we hope to deconstruct some of the negative stereotypes concerning parents and children in cults. There have, of course, been several well-publicized tragic incidents involving children in unconventional religions. Two hundred sixty children died in Jonestown in 1978. The Solar Temple's mass suicides/homicides in 1994 in Cheiry and Salvan, Switzerland, and in 1995 in Vercours, France, claimed the lives of seven children and three teenagers. In Quebec, the baby of an apostate couple, believed by Solar Temple leaders to be the newborn Antichrist, was ritually murdered by two Templars (Bedat, Bouleau, and Nicolas 1996).

Individual cases of neglect, abuse, or infanticide have occurred in unconventional religions, as in the larger society, but they tend to excite far more media attention. There were several notorious cases in the 1980s. In 1983, a twelve-year-old Black Hebrew boy from the Michigan-based House of Judah was killed by a blow on his spine during an overzealous application of the leader's ideas on corporal punishment; his mother was convicted of manslaughter and the leader, William Lewis, of conspiracy to enslave children (Singer 1996:254). In 1988, an eight-year-old girl was beaten to death in Ecclesia Athletics Association, a Christian youth camp near Portland, Oregon. Fifty-three children were removed by the authorities, and the leader, Eldridge Broussard (also the child's father), was charged with conspiring to deny the civil rights of children by holding them in involuntary servitude (Mullins 1988).

However, many children from nonconventional faiths have been killed accidentally through the bungled efforts of the law enforcement officers, the Federal Bureau of Investigation (FBI) and the Bureau of Alcohol, Tobacco, and Firearms to *rescue* children and exert control over "dangerous cults." The son of white supremacist Randy Weaver was fatally shot in the back at Ruby Ridge. Branch Davidian leader David Koresh's eighteen children probably died of suffocation and poisoning when the highly flammable CS tear gas was injected into the walls of the group's compound in Waco, Texas, or they may have been crushed by the falling debris caused by FBI armored trucks bombarding compound buildings. Five children died in 1985 when the Philadelphia city police bombed the headquarters of the black radical "back to nature" commune MOVE (Goldberg 1996). Moreover, five mothers in MOVE claimed that police officers had beaten them during their pregnancies, causing miscarriages and the death of one infant, Life Africa, who had never been issued a birth certificate, so her existence could not be proved in court.

Aside from these tragic events, there is no evidence to support the notion that children raised in unconventional religions are statistically more at risk than children in secular society. Indeed, the Institute for the Study of American Religion (Melton 1986:255, 258) found that most child abuse charges were related to conservative evangelical Christian churches that practice biblically based chastisement. The current widespread concern over the fate of children in new religions will probably not subside until the mystery and rumors obfuscating the issue are put to rest by more case studies, such as ours, that are based on social-scientific methods that demonstrate the remarkable diversity of family patterns in NRMs and place their alternative models of childhood within a wider historical and cultural perspective.

The brainwashing controversy of the 1970s and 1980s raised the problem of whether joining a cult involved authentic religious motives or whether it was the unwholesome result of the ineluctable forces of brainwashing and techniques of "mind control." Since 1988 when the American Psychological Association dismissed brainwashing theories as lacking in scientific rigor, allegations of brainwashing have been repeatedly rejected by U.S. judges as inadmissible in court. Also since 1988, allegations of child abuse occurring in cults have escalated.

Although the individual's right to choose her or his own religion—no matter how apparently bizarre—is generally recognized today, the rights of first-generation converts to "impose" their religious beliefs and way of life on their own progeny is at stake. For those born and raised in an NRM, the public wonders, is there room for individual freedom of choice in making a religious commitment? When an Amish father and an Iroquois mother instruct their children in sacred songs and prayers, they are perceived by the outside world as passing on quaint and valuable traditions. When Unificationists, Scientologists, or Krishna devotees worship in family groups or enroll their children in their alternative schooling programs, outsiders tend to view the process as one of "indoctrination." An April 1995 conference organized by the European anticult movement and called "Sects and Sickness" (held in Uppsala, Sweden) highlighted the "problem" of the psychological damage perpetrated on children through "cult indoctrination." Sweden is a nation that strongly upholds an individual's freedom in religious matters, but a committee was formed during the conference to lobby for new laws that would limit the freedom of parents to transmit their own faith to their progeny. The rationale was that religious instruction infringes on a child's right to *choose,* and the assumption was that religious beliefs (irrational by nature) are potentially damaging to the child's psychological health. If these laws come into effect, unrest might follow among Sweden's many Muslim immigrants, who enjoy the respect and tolerance that Sweden offers but tend to produce large families and certainly intend to raise their children in *al Islam.*

As we enter the next century, the question of how children are reared will become one of increasing concern. Science fiction writers envision a world of sterile, aging adults (P. D. James's *The Children of Men;* J. G. Ballard's *The Grey People*). Children appear as genius-heroes and Christlike redeemers in apocalyptic sci-fi, as in Orson Scott Card's *Ender's Game* or Whitley Streiber and James Kunetka's *Nature's End.* Female detective fiction writers such as Ruth Rendell and P. D. James have begun to explore the twisted passions of thwarted maternal love as a source of violence, in contrast to the well-worn sex, power, and money murders that prevail in the novels of Ian Fleming or Mickey Spillane. The popular media are replete with reports of secular child abuse, incest, and infanticide; indeed, the issue of child abuse has become a veritable obsession of our time.

This widespread concern over the well-being of children in the larger culture renders nightmarish accounts of kids in cults all the more believable. If pedophilia and rapist stepfathers are rife in the suburbs, the (uncritical) newspaper reader might argue, is it not reasonable to assume that even worse abuse is perpetrated on children inside those mysterious groups where brainwashed fanatics espouse alien belief systems and venerate megalomaniacal messiahs? The public's tendency to believe the horror stories of anonymous apostates quoted in poorly researched media reports, and to dismiss the defensive testimonies of current "cult members," has exacerbated the "tribal wars" that are currently erupting around child-centered NRMs. These are wars fought through ongoing custody battles, local school board inspections, social services investigations, and deviance labeling in the media.

Ironically, mirror images of these public attitudes abound in the utopian literature issuing from NRMs. These convey dark portraits of the amoral, loveless, television-taught and drug-ridden lives of children in the mainstream. Historian Frank Manuel (1967:70) remarks, "The utopia may well be the most sensitive indicator of where the sharpest anguish of an age lies." To study the NRMs' self-conscious efforts and experiments to heal the maladies besetting the modern family—the broken marriages, the generation gap, the unsupervised dating, the absentee fathers, the violent, bleak, impersonal neighborhoods—is to look into mirror fragments, albeit distorted and magnified, that reflect our own passionate familial concerns.

The "alternative childhoods" found in NRMs have implications for our ways of thinking about more "traditional" forms of the family. Indeed, looking at how children are raised in marginal spiritual groups will expand our ways of thinking about the social, psychological, moral, educational, and legal dimensions of family life. A cross-cultural study of the various schools of child development studies, from Aristotle to Jean-Jacques Rousseau, from Rudolph Steiner to Margaret Mead, indicates the degree to which conceptions of childhood can vary. The historical theory of Philippe Ariès that childhood as we now know it is an institution originally created in the nineteenth century and not part of the human condition has been refuted by recent social historians, but there is a general consensus that the Western world tends to set children apart from adults to an exaggerated degree. Among NRMs there is a wide range of responses to this issue: from nostalgic recreations of Victorian nurseries, to claustrophobic parodies of the 1950s nuclear family in Christian fundamentalist sects, to the avant-garde, autonomous miniadults of the gnostic orders. The ethnographies that follow might amuse, refresh, or appall us, but hopefully they will help us assess our own less intentional, pluralistic patterns of parenting with more objectivity and humor.

References

Bedat, A., G. Bouleau, and B. Nicolas. 1996. *Les chevaliers de la mort: Enquête et révélations sur l'Ordre du Temple Solaire.* Geneva: L'Illustre TFI Editions.

Goldberg, D. 1996. "City Found Liable in Attack on MOVE." Special to *Washington Post,* June 25.

Hardman, C. E. 1973. "Can There Be an Anthropology of Children?" *Journal of the Anthropological Society of Oxford* 4(1): 85–99.

Manuel, F. E. 1967. "Toward a Psychological History of Utopias." In Frank Manuel, ed., *Utopias and Utopian Thought.* Boston: Beacon Press.

Melton, J. G. 1986. *Report on the ISAR Survey of Cult-Related Violence.* Santa Barbara, Calif.: Institute for the Study of Religion.

Mullins, J. 1988. "Cult That Made Headlines After Shocking Death of Girl." *The Enquirer,* November 8.

Opie, I., and P. Opie. 1969. *Children's Games in Street and Playground.* Oxford, U.K.: Oxford University Press.

Parr, J. 1982. *Childhood and Family in Canadian History.* Toronto: McClelland and Stewart.

Prout, A., and A. James, eds. 1990. *Constructing and Reconstructing Childhood.* Basingstoke, England: Falmer Press.

Singer, M. T., with J. Lalich. 1996. *Cults in Our Midst: The Hidden Menace in Our Everyday Lives.* San Francisco: Jossey-Bass.

Toren, C. 1993. "Making History: The Significance of Childhood Cognition for a Comparative Anthropology of Mind." *Man* (NS) 28: 461–478.

Part I

How Children Change Movements

Impact on the Future

Chapter 1

Witches

The Next Generation

Helen A. Berger

This is the first generation of kids really being raised as Pagans. All the people I know have been raised [as] Christians, Jews, nothing, or something else and then found Wicca. (Beth interview 1997)

Beth, a woman in her thirties, mother of three children, and an initiated Witch for eight years, is concerned about the education and incorporation of this second generation into the religion.[1] When I interviewed her in January 1997, she and her husband were in the process of hiving off—that is, breaking from the coven in which they had been trained—to start a family-oriented coven. Beth envisions her coven as providing an opportunity for Neopagan children to learn about Neopaganism and join with their parents in the celebration of the seasons and in the practice of magic.

Beth's desire to provide a place for Wiccan children and their parents to celebrate together is part of a larger trend that I have witnessed during my ten-year participant observation of Witches on the northeastern seaboard of the United States: the transformation of Wicca in the United States to accommodate the development of a second generation.[2] Robert Balch (1988) and James Richardson (1985) have noted that the inclusion of children in new religions changes the organization and practices of the groups. However, little empirical research has been done on the specific ways in which the demands of child rearing and of children themselves transform new religions.

This chapter is a case study of the effects of children on Wicca in the United States. Unlike many of the religions discussed in this volume, Wicca does not have a charismatic leader or a central organization to determine orthodoxy or child-rearing practices. Furthermore, as Wicca emphasizes individual choice in all matters, there is no organizational, religious, or ideological imperative to have, or restrain from having, children. The decision by Witches to have children has been made on an individual basis. Similarly, no central organization or doctrine determines child-rearing techniques, although a growing body of literature is developing to guide parents in raising children in a Neopagan home. Many of the changes I have witnessed in the religion have occurred on an ad hoc basis as parents and groups respond to the increased number of children in their midst. Nonetheless, the unintended consequences of children being born into the American Wiccan community is the development within this amorphous religion of a clearer definition of its boundaries, greater routinization, increased sexual conservatism, and a growing concern about being viewed as a legitimate religion.

Neopaganism and Witchcraft

Although the distinction between the two terms *Witch* and *Neopagan* is not firm, Witches are usually viewed as the more committed members of the larger Neopagan movement. Adherents' self-definition as either a Witch or a Neopagan is normally accepted by others in the religion. Most Neopagans, however, take the label *Witch* (Neitz 1991; Orion 1995). I use the terms *Witch, Wiccan,* and *Neopagan* to describe the members of this religion. Although there are distinctions among these three terms, most of the adherents who write about their experiences as parents use them interchangeably.

Witches speak of themselves as members of the "old religion." They maintain that they are returning to, or re-creating, a pan-European, pre-Christian faith in which the world is viewed as enchanted. Scholars note, and many Witches acknowledge, that Wicca was created by Gerald Gardner in the 1940s in Great Britain (Kelly 1992; Adler 1986). Wicca, as Gardner presented it, is a gentle nature religion that venerates the Goddess of fertility and the horned God. There are eight Sabbats throughout the year that correspond to ancient agricultural festivals. Rituals are used both to celebrate the Sabbats and to "raise energy" for magical workings.

In the 1960s, Witchcraft migrated to the United States, where it has grown and taken on a particularly American flavor. The religion initially appealed to members of the counterculture who were interested in alternative consciousness, medical treatments, therapies, and lifestyles. Mysticism, ecological concerns, women's rights, and antiauthoritarianism were incorporated into this new religion. Furthermore, an elective affinity developed between Neopaganism and fantasy groups, the Society for Creative Anachronism, and science fiction groups (Ben-Yehuda 1985; Neitz 1991).[3] The veneration of the Goddess(es), as well as the Gods, within Witchcraft has made the religion appealing to women in the second wave of feminism. The 1970s saw the development of feminist Witches or women's spirituality groups that were composed only of women and that venerated the Goddess but not the Gods. Many of the women who joined these groups had no knowledge of the link between their practices and Wicca as developed by Gardner (Finley 1991). A split developed and continues to exist between all-women's groups and groups that are inclusive of men and women, although at festivals, on the Internet, and through books there are an increased interaction and cross-fertilization between these two types of groups. I focus here exclusively on inclusive groups, as they are most likely to involve entire families.

Most of the adherents of Witchcraft are white, middle class, well educated, and disproportionately female (Kirkpatrick, Rainey, and Rubi 1986; Orion 1995). The religion is still gaining adherents. Neopagans do not on the whole proselytize, because they believe that each individual must find his or her own path to spiritual understanding (Adler 1986). Individuals come to the religion through several avenues. Some people learn about the religion through friends, others through reading a book or an article about Neopaganism and Witchcraft, and still others through attending a class at an adult education center or occult bookstore. However, children who are raised in this new religion, much like children raised in traditional religions, are less spiritual seekers than passive recipients of their families' traditions.

The Place of Children

A debate has developed within Wicca about the appropriateness of including children in the religion. The debate goes to the heart of how the religion will be defined. A tension exists between the religion's being conceived as a spiritual path or paths that each person can choose to follow and as the "old religion" that unifies a community. This ambiguity was not initially obvious as it was only one element of the more general and amorphous nature of the religion. However, the contradiction between the two conceptions of Wicca has become more striking as children are brought into the religion.

This debate is occurring in the same venues as those that are used by Neopagans to exchange ideas on how to run a coven, or create a ritual—that is, in books, journal articles, and discussions on computer networks. Although no consensus has been reached, the terms and the language of the debate are defined within this literature. Concerns have been raised about both the method and appropriateness of bringing children into this new religion. Writing in a Neopagan journal, Michael Sontag (1994:13) voices his apprehension that the religion will become diluted if children are raised as Neopagans and Witches: "By bringing people on to the magickal path, as opposed to them finding the path themselves, we run the risk of finding ourselves dealing with an increasingly apathetic magickal community."

Sontag worries that the Neopagan community could eventually suffer from the same problems he perceives among organized religions—a preponderance of participants who are only nominally involved. He asserts that the community would be better served by a focus on the personal growth and initiation of spiritual seekers than by training of children. Although Sontag's misgivings about the effect of children on the religion are shared by others, these concerns are more often voiced by people who are childless. Most parents are more concerned about their children than about the effect their children may have on the religion.

Neopagan parents want to avoid for their offspring the negative experiences they endured as children when their parents forced them to attend religious services that bored them. They want their children to have the freedom to follow their own path. As one Neopagan mother writes, "When I think of the next generation, I do not think of it in terms of Pagan or Magick, but in terms of individuals each finding their own unique path through the world—no matter what that might be" (Stanford-Blake 1994:21). Thus, Neopagan child-rearing techniques reflect the ideology of openness and antiauthoritarianism that permeates this religion.

Holly Teague (1994), a Neopagan mother who advocates that children be free to find their own spiritual path, describes her experience with her daughter. Teague initially took her young daughter out into the woods to create a sacred circle. As children are believed to be more spiritually open, Teague presumed that her daughter would intuit the four directions (east, north, west, and south) and the elements (air, earth, water, and fire) that correspond to them. She discovered that, even though her daughter did begin by equating north with the earth, she did not "correctly" identify the elements that correspond to the other three directions. Although initially the mother was disappointed, she came to see that it was more important to permit her child to enjoy working in a magical circle than to ensure that she did it in the "correct" way. Instead of telling the child what to do, Teague waited to be asked before instructing her daughter. Since the child was uncertain of the procedures, she frequently turned to her mother for help and was gently guided in the art of casting a circle. Teague writes about this incident as a primer for other parents on techniques they could use to foster their children's self-development.

Another parent, Jaq Hawkins (1994:2), wants his children to freely choose their own spiritual path. Yet he modifies that wish by asserting: "I've asked myself what I would do if my child fell in with the 'wrong' crowd at the delicate age of fifteen and joined a cult of Jesus freaks. It's a frightening thought, and one I have no answer for as yet."

Although parents may hope that their own path is chosen by their children, most Neopagan parents are willing, at least in principle, to accept that as their children grow to adulthood they may choose another religion or secularism. As Ashleen O'Gaea (1993:24) discloses, "I fantasize that Explorer [her son] will marry a nice Wiccan girl and raise bouncing Wiccan babies—but he might not."

Parents, furthermore, worry about involving their children in a nontraditional religion. Susan Curewitz, one of the leaders of EarthSpirit Community, the largest Neopagan organization in New England, was surprised when she learned from a group of teenagers that their parents chose not to raise their children as Pagans, fearing that their children would suffer repercussions in schools (Curewitz 1989:26). Jenet (1994d:9), the editor of *The Labrynth,* a newsletter for Pagan families, reiterates this concern. She suggests that parents be careful using the word *Witch,* or speaking of Gods and Goddesses, particularly if they live in the Bible Belt or in areas where there are many fundamentalist Christians, lest they evoke hostility in the surrounding communities. Children will nevertheless be influenced by their parents' beliefs, as O'Gaea (1993:39) maintains: "Unless you never speak to your kids and never do anything religiously different from your Christian family or neighbors, unless Wicca has not changed your life at all, you are raising your children to the craft."

More important than the parents' ambivalence is the issue of how children are forcing this religion to confront its own process of maturation. As Ceisiwr Serith (1994:ix) contends: "As the young Pagan movement starts to leave its adolescent years behind and its members raise children, the problem becomes more acute. Are we to remain a religion of converts? Or will we be able to develop an organic form of Paganism for our children?" Creating an "organic form" of Neopaganism will result in a less individualized religion that can be taught to children and in which children are included. However, it will also increase the probability of the religion's continued existence. Nancey Finley (1991) predicts that feminist Witchcraft will die out because of its amorphous structure. Religions such as the Shakers declined, at least in part, because they were completely dependent on converts (Kephart 1982). With the birth of "Witchlings," as the Witches jokingly call their own children, this new religion can become firmly entrenched in the United States, albeit in an altered form.

To teach the religion to children involves the creation of traditions. As Jenet (1995b:14) asserts: "In order to leave a Pagan legacy for our children, we need traditions to pass on. In order to have meaningful traditions we will have to make them ourselves." The creation of traditions is part of the process of routinization. Because children enjoy repetition, rituals are likely to become systematized. I have already seen elements of this as groups that at one time created new rituals for every Sabbat have begun to repeat the rituals. One Witch justifies the reuse of old rituals: "They become more magically powerful with repetition." They also become less spontaneous and less individually tailored (Berger 1995).

Children and Rituals

Within Wicca all adult initiates are trained to be priests or priestesses who can create and lead a ritual. There are no passive observers, as everyone present must actively participate in the ritual. The inclusion of children in Wicca is forcing parents and covens whose members have children to reconsider the notion of a religion composed completely of priestesses and priests but no laypeople. Furthermore, changes are occurring in rituals themselves to both accommodate children and acknowledge their life cycles.

Neopagan rituals appear welcoming to children because they can actively participate instead of being required to sit still and listen to a sermon. Witches embrace a belief that adults possess an "inner child" or "younger self" through which they can access the divine within themselves, or what is called the "higher self." Children are believed to more easily access the divine as they have not yet fully developed a rational, talking self. However, rituals that are designed to access the younger self are created for adults. It is they who can concentrate on guided meditation and understand dialogue phrased partially in Elizabethan English. As Lisa Manor (1994:15) notes: "How much more do we forget the needs of children attending our magickal rites? More often than not, if they are not shuttled off to a different room to be supervised by the unfortunate of the month, they shuttle and murmur their way through the mechanics of a ceremony in which they have little interest or understanding."

Because few children have been involved in the movement until recently, rituals and training have been formulated for adults. But teaching children about Paganism requires a different form of training than that used for adults. Jenet (1994c:13) cautions against subjecting children to "Paganism 101 at a lower reading level."[4] Neopagan adults have been trained in ritual practices, as well as a variety of skills—such as raising energy, practicing astral projection, performing magic, and using medicinal herbs—through classes, workshops, books, and magazines.

Witches read widely about Wicca, Neopaganism, and ancient and contemporary Pagan cultures. Two journals for Neopagan children are being published, *How About Magic* (HAM) and *Witches and Witchlings.*[5] The number of children's books with a Neopagan theme is growing. Parents purchase these books and journals to help their children understand elements of Neopagan practice and feel part of a community. The readings, however, are secondary to involving children in ritual practice.

Such involvement often breaks the concentration of adults. I recently attended an initiation ritual for two women into MoonTide coven, whose members have three children under the age of two. Gordon, a large and active eight-month old, attended with his mother. The youngest child, Lisa, who had turned one month old that day, was also present. Lisa's mother, Abby, was the high priestess for the ritual. As the ritual began, Abby gave Lisa to her father, who put her in a carrier, which he hung around his chest. Throughout the ritual Abby became distracted as her baby cried. As soon as the essential part of the ritual was completed, she reached for her newborn and began breast-feeding. Gordon, in the meantime, was being passed from woman to woman to stop him from reaching for the candles on the altar. The moment the ritual ended, the candles were blown out and then moved to prevent Gordon from hurting himself. This coven is committed to creating a family-oriented religion in which the participation of children is welcome. However, other groups, particularly those in which only one couple or member has a child, are less tolerant of the distraction of children.

Serith (1994:8), a strong advocate of the integration of children into the religion, suggests that they not be included in rituals geared for adults. "A mistake often made by Pagan parents is to bring the children into Wiccan rituals or, at the least, to compose rituals based closely on what is done by a coven. This arises from a misunderstanding of the role of Mystery Religions in culture."

According to Serith, covens are the modern equivalent of a mystery religion. He contends that in traditional pagan societies mystery groups were always reserved for adults because children not only would disrupt rituals but also would not benefit from them. He asserts that in these societies children would be included in some community rituals and all family rituals. Serith urges Neopagans to integrate their children into the religion through both family rituals and daily life practices.

In family celebrations children are often invited to cast the circle or invoke one of the directions. If the child is old enough, she or he is solicited to read a part of the ritual. Those rituals created with the inclusion of children in mind are shorter and worded in language that children can read or at least easily understand. Elements such as music, dance, and pageantry, which appear in all Neopagan rituals, are easily adapted for children. Children's rituals are less formal, but to help develop a sense of tradition, they are also more consistent. The goal for children is different than that for adult initiates. Parents want their children to become comfortable with rituals and with basic principles of Paganism. As Althea Northage-Orr (1994:6) contends, "A love of and affinity for ritual, like the ability to read, is best cultivated early on."

Children are taught to put their lives in tune with the cycle of the year through the celebration of the Sabbats. Many of these Neopagan celebrations correspond to Christian or secular holidays. As Neopagans frequently note, this is not an accident; many Christian celebrations were devised to coincide with older pagan holidays. For instance, Christmas and Easter fall close to the more ancient celebrations of Yule and the spring equinox, respectively. Bringing evergreens into the home in the middle of the winter, a German pre-Christian practice, is common in Christian countries. Spring fertility symbols of chicks, eggs, and rabbits have become incorporated into the celebration of Easter. Similarly, the integration of some Pagan celebrations, such as the dancing of the Maypole for Beltane (May 1), has been absorbed into popular culture. This helps to facilitate the normalization of some Neopagan practices. However, many of the basic differences between Neopagans and more mainstream Americans also become evident.

Neopagans view death as part of the cycle of life, and most believe in reincarnation. Death is seen as necessary for renewal and as a period of rest. The notion of death as a time of renewal is presented by Deirdre Pulgram Arthen (1992) in her children's book *Walking with Mother Earth.* In this simple tale, Mother Earth is met by Lord Death, who is portrayed as a handsome and kindly man. He convinces Mother Earth that she needs a rest. But Mother Earth asks: "'What of my children if I go with you? They cannot survive without my love. I cannot destroy them.' The Lord of Death replied, 'They will not be destroyed. When you leave, their spirits will go deep within to rest as well. When you return, so too will they, refreshed with new life'" (Arthen 1992:25)

Death is celebrated at the Sabbat of Soheim (Halloween). Because of the emphasis on rebirth and renewal, the holiday is not morbid; rather, it provides an avenue for children to mourn pets, relatives, and friends who have died. Although this holiday has much in common with Halloween, its focus is very different. Neopagan children make jack-o-lanterns, dress up in costumes, and go trick-or-treating, but they also participate in family rituals about death and mourning.

To involve children in the Sabbats, parents engage offspring in activities that evoke the spirit of the season and the upcoming holiday. Arts and crafts projects are devised to help align children with nature and to make them aware of the spiritual significance of the season. For example, at Imbolc (February 1), which celebrates the growing strength of the sun and the approach of spring, parents may teach their children to make candles that can be used in ritual (McArthur 1994). Imbolc is celebrated by the lighting of a large number of candles to symbolize the increase in the amount of sunlight each day. One Wiccan mother told me that, instead of a formal Imbolc ritual, she and her husband participate in an informal celebration of the holiday with their children. The electric lights are turned off, the house is illuminated with candles, and the parents tell their children stories, such as the myth of the quickening of the sun king in the great mother. The children in turn are invited to tell stories and to reflect on the ending of winter and coming of spring. Making candles is part of the fun and the symbolism of the holiday for the children.

Rites of Passage

Rites of passage, such as welcoming ceremonies and rituals to denote the transition from childhood to adulthood, are being created by Neopagans. The welcoming rite—referred to as a Wiccaning, a Saining, or a Paganing—serves a threefold purpose: first, to introduce the child to the deities and ask for their help and protection as the child grows; second, to give the community an opportunity to meet and bless the child; and third, to bring the child into his or her first sacred circle. Welcoming rituals do not commit the child to Pagan Goddesses and Gods or to a particular spiritual path. However, there appears to be an ambivalence on the parents' part concerning the prospect of their child's leaving the religion.

Sainings vary from group to group more than any other Wiccan ritual I have attended. In all instances the child is introduced to the four directions, given good wishes and words of wisdom by the participants, and awarded Goddess parents.[6] However, other aspects of the ritual vary widely. At one Wiccaning I attended in a state park, the ritual used the child's placenta and birth blood, which had been stored in the family freezer. The afterbirth was placed by the father, Allen, in a hole that had been prepared in the center of the circle. Addressing the child, Erik, Allen told him that this umbilical cord had sustained him for nine months when he was attached to his mother. Now there was a new rope, a white one, that would spiritually attach him to the mother of us all, Mother Earth. A white silken rope was dipped in the child's birth blood. Erik was anointed with his own birth blood, which dripped down his father's arm and splashed on the silk baptismal gown. Although I have read about birth rituals involving blood

(Curewitz 1990; Campanelli 1994; McArthur 1994), Erik's was the only welcoming ritual in which I saw it used. Other welcoming rituals I have attended have taken place in either the parents' or the high priestess's home, and perhaps the use of blood was not deemed appropriate within the confines of a family home. Furthermore, some birthing centers and hospitals may not allow the parents to appropriate the afterbirth. Some covens or parents may be less comfortable handling the afterbirth.

At Erik's Wiccaning each person who attended was asked to give the child a wish or an empowerment for his future. Participants chose a piece of ribbon, which they charged with their wish for the newborn. One by one each person tied the ribbon to a branch held by Erik's mother. Because the branch was viewed as magically charged with our wishes, it was taken home and saved for Erik. At another welcoming ritual I attended, the child's next rite of passage was anticipated at her Saining. Prior to the ceremony each participant was asked to write some words of wisdom for the newborn, Lisa. During the ritual Lisa's mother collected the cards, promising to preserve them unread until Lisa's puberty rite.

Puberty rites are being developed by Neopagans to address the lack of a clear demarcation between childhood and adulthood in present-day America. As Jenet (1994a:3) asserts: "When there is no longer a common extracurricular rite of passage for early adolescents, less savory common experiences have an open field for entry. Parents can hope that today's students have decided not to join in popular culture's rite of passage in gangs, drugs or guns."

Because of the long period that offspring remain dependent in contemporary society, some Neopagans are developing two separate rituals to denote different stages of maturity. The first ritual occurs around the time of puberty and the second when the child graduates from high school or is preparing to leave home. These rituals mark the transition from childhood to adolescence or adulthood for both the parents and their progeny.

Puberty rites are gender specific, unisex rituals. As Serith (1994:10) maintains: "Only a man can make man, and only a woman can acknowledge a women." The distinction between the acknowledgment of womanhood and the "making" of manhood is reflected in the puberty rites of Neopagans. These rites more than other rituals highlight the ambiguous status of gender roles within Wicca. In *Dreaming the Dark*, Starhawk (1982:75) contends, "There is no underlying feminine nature, no underlying masculine nature—there is the reality of what we experience, in our differing bodies, in the differing impact culture has on each sex. . . . The Goddess, the Gods are our potential." However, even Starhawk, in talking about the Goddess and the Gods, reverts to gender-specific images. The God is the hunter; he dies and is reborn. The Goddess is the earth, eternal. Unlike Starhawk, some Witches, while acknowledging that we all have both male and female aspects within us, sharply delineate male and female natures. Although all Witches whom I have met have a commitment to feminism, there is an essentialist element that permeates the religion, which can be most clearly seen in the rites of passage.

The girl's ritual underscores her metamorphosis into womanhood. In one rendition of this ritual, a woman who represents the east, the element of air and of intellect, says to the young woman:

> Know that as a woman
> Once in the month when your blood flows
> Or the Moon is full, your mind will be
> Open and receptive to things unseen.
> Learn to see with the mind's eye,
> and listen to the wind
> Heed your inner voice
> To be a woman is to gain Wisdom.
> (Campanelli 1994:43)

The rituals for boys, like those for girls, focus on the spiritual, as well as physical, changes the boy experiences.[7] Boys are expected to endure an ordeal prior to being recognized as men. The notion of men proving themselves through an ordeal is common among indigenous groups. Although symbolically Wiccan boys are expected to face their mortality, in reality they are never placed in any danger. The ordeal may be as simple as spending a night alone in a tent in the woods, with the boy's father or other men close enough to hear if there is a problem. The lack of real risk may mitigate the boy's experience of a psychological transformation into manhood. Zack Darling-Ferns, the founder of *HAM,* reflecting on his puberty rite, asserts: "I felt that the rite of passage let me into the men's circle and the whole male aspect of magic. But I never really felt I was a man until the truck fell on me. My rite of passage didn't do that" (quoted in Judith 1993:85). The experience Zack felt resulted in his transition into manhood was an accident in which he almost died.

Similarly, the girls' rites of passage may or may not result in their feeling like women. The rituals do celebrate and affirm the changes that are occurring in their bodies. However, within the larger society there is little validation of the new status of either females or males. The children remain in middle school, economically dependent on their parents, and socially unprepared to begin a family. Furthermore, the dispersion of Neopagans throughout the country means there is no stable face-to-face community to acknowledge the new adult on a daily basis and ensure that the parents change their behavior toward their minor offspring.

The rituals, however, are helping create a community, even if they may not ultimately define a passage from youth to adulthood. It is a community of people who are loosely linked but who share at least the outlines of a common body of rituals. Furthermore, the inclusion in the sacred circles of extended kin and friends—many from outside Wicca—to celebrate the family's life passages affirms Wiccans in their practices.

Sex and the Pagan Child

What constitutes a healthy notion of sexuality for children and youths in our society is being questioned in parents' magazines, schools, and even law courts. As heirs to the counterculture, the Neopagan community is on the whole sexually permissive—accepting open sexuality, homosexuality, bisexuality, and nontraditional family forms such as group marriages and open marriages. Witches exalt both homosexuality and heterosexuality as magical acts. However, Neopagan parents are concerned that their children be neither pressured into premature sexuality nor taken away from them by social agencies that view their attitude toward sex as too radical. At the same time, these parents maintain the importance of presenting sex to their children in a positive light. This ambivalence is expressed in a growing uneasiness among Neopagan parents about the actual expression of sexuality in rituals and at festivals. As Jenet (1994b:4) notes: "Now that I am a parent, the traditional Beltane games that are frequently of a playful sexual content make me a bit nervous. . . . Sexuality is a powerful tool, an emblem of the union that sparked the Universe, and as a tool it can be misused, abused and neglected, but well used it brings joy to our lives. . . . It is an enormous challenge to teach our children a healthy view of sexuality."

Rituals, particularly those that occur in the spring at either the equinox or Beltane, have a sexual flavor, because fertility is being celebrated. At Beltane the Goddess and God are invoked in their roles as consorts. The rituals focus on fertility in nature and among people. The symbolic expression of sexuality can be quite explicit. At one Beltane ritual I attended, at which no children were present, men and women formed into two winding circles facing each other. People whirled by one another, kissing or attempting to kiss the new person who faced them. The atmosphere was charged. At one point everyone in the room took off their robes and stood sweaty and naked in the makeshift temple of the high priest and priestess's home. At another Beltane ritual attended by two children about five and eight years old, there was no nudity. However, again there was a sexually charged atmosphere during the ritual. The man invoking the green man, or male aspect, was dressed in a short green robe open at the sides, so that as he moved his underpants were revealed. He went around the circle kissing all the women and challenging the men in the group. It was a playful moment, with women moving away and mocking being chased or complaining that the green man had bad aim when he kissed. He was carrying a staff and jokingly challenged the other men in the circle to compare the size of their staffs with his. He then joined the priestess, who was invoking the Goddess in the center of the circle, in a dance that implied a sexual union. In mundane life, the green man and the priestess were soon to be married, and their dance was clearly lustful. However, as they both remained dressed, the dance was only symbolic of the sexual union.

Festivals are gatherings of large groups of Neopagans, usually at campsites in rural areas for a week or weekend in the spring, summer, and, sometimes, early fall. These gatherings provide an avenue for networking, sharing magical and spiritual information, and developing friendships and romances. Nudity at rituals, sunbathing, and dancing around a open fire at night are accepted behaviors at festivals. There is both an awareness and a concern within the community about the transmission of AIDS. At one festival, multicolored condoms were made available throughout the campsite for anyone who might want one. Many of the children availed themselves of the condoms, blowing them up to use as balloons or filling them with water to throw at one another.

Neopagan parents, most of whom have participated in the campsite dances and in open sexuality, are reevaluating the appropriateness of that environment for their children. A forty-year-old woman expressed her concern that her fourteen-year-old daughter might be "hit up" at a festival they were about to attend. The child had reached puberty, and though still a minor, she looked like a woman. As more Neopagan children reach puberty, more adults are concerned about protecting them from unsolicited sexual advances.

Neopagans are attempting to define what is a healthy sexual atmosphere for children. In "Youth and Maiden Lovemaking," Darling-Ferns (1990), who was then fourteen years old, presented his view of responsible sex for Pagan youths. He (1990:10) began the article, "A lot to being Pagan is being a good lover. My attitude is, why not start sooner [rather] than later?" He advocated that youths learn to practice responsible sex, which he described as having four aspects: (1) the practice of safe sex through the use of either condoms or "outercourse"; (2) the use of birth control to avoid unwanted pregnancies; (3) sex occurring only between two consenting parties; and (4) both partners' respecting the other's privacy by keeping the details of their sexual encounter between themselves. Since Darling-Ferns was writing as a youth to other young people, he cautioned that would-be lovers consider parental approval or disapproval before embarking on a romantic union. He noted that most Neopagan parents are supportive of their adolescent children's sexuality, but that some parents, especially non-Pagans, may be more conservative.

Darling-Fern's article was controversial among Neopagan adults. Some Neopagan adults were apprehensive that the article might give the impression that minors were being encouraged by the community to have sex (Judith 1993:83). The issue of children and sex is a difficult one for Neopagans. When the religion primarily involved adults, dealing with sexuality was relatively easy. Consenting adults are legally free to revel in their sexuality. The potential for problems to arise was always there, but they were problems among adults.

The appropriateness of sexual behavior, however, is an issue that is magnified when children are involved. Pagan parents fear that courts or child protection agencies may remove children from their homes because of Neopagan sexual practices or open nudity. Custody hearings or decisions about foster children make this anxiety particularly acute. Anne, a tall, lithe woman with two lively children, is fighting her former husband to maintain custody of their son and daughter. She has had to defend her religious practice, as well as the open sexuality within the religion. Her husband was a Witch who left the religion shortly after ending the marriage. His legal brief for custody of the children accused Anne of corrupting his minor children by providing them with Pagan coloring books that depicted nude Goddesses. Anne has been required to show in court that her religious practices will not harm her children. She has been enjoined by the court from including her children in Wiccan rituals.

Most parents do not want their children pushed into premature sexuality. Like many liberal parents, Neopagans confront the problem of defining when their children are adults. Anodea Judith (1993), in her interview of three adolescents who were raised as Neopagans, found that both of the young women she spoke to felt social pressure within the community to become sexually active, although they also claimed that their communities' sexual openness had given them a healthier attitude toward sex than their peers.

As more Neopagan youths reach puberty, the controversy about sexuality will become more acute. The notion of sex as both beautiful and magical is so embedded in rituals and in the attitudes of a large segment of the community that I suspect it will remain. However, as more children begin to mature within the Wiccan community, rituals and festivals may have fewer instances of open sexuality. The tone of the festivals has to some degree already become quieter. Although young adults may enjoy drumming and dancing throughout the night, young parents are anxious that the campsites be quiet enough for their children and themselves to sleep.

Magical Children

Pagan children are raised among people who speak "with a different rhythm" (Luhrmann 1989). Mysticism, magic, and immanence within nature are all active parts of the way in which individuals conceptualize and interpret their lives. Among Neopagans the mundane—going shopping, happening on a sale, planting a garden—is defined in mystical terms. For Witches, there are no coincidences; things occur either as a sign from the Goddess or as part of the pattern of life. As O'Gaea (1993:25) contends: "Nearly everything we do at home can be done with Wicca in mind. From rearranging a room to brushing hair, everything can be a spell. . . . And if we share mundane blessings with our children it will become second nature to them."

Within Wicca, all of life and its activities becomes imbued with spirituality. Joan (interview 1989), who had been raised in a Wiccan family and was pregnant with her first child when I interviewed her, noted that although the child would grow up knowing about all religions and have the option of choosing whichever religion she or he wanted, the child would be raised "understanding the healing aspect and communicating with the animals and nature and taking on the [magical] responsibility—the child will be raised with that everyday of its life and that will be very natural; and the child will know that is from the craft."

Susan, the high priestess of the MoonTide coven, is starting a nursery school for Pagan children that she hopes to expand into a day school. She told me that the Goddess had guided her in this decision. Initially, she had not wanted to become involved with educating young children, having already raised a family of her own, but "the Goddess hit me on the side of the head with the proverbial two-by-four and I knew this was something I had to do." She came to believe the creation of a school was necessary to protect Neopagan children from becoming psychically and magically crippled.

Susan contends that she and other Neopagan adults were harmed as children in "nominally" secular schools. Imps, spirit guides, and god forces that the child spoke to were reinterpreted in the schools as imaginary friends. Susan argues that we were all trained to ignore and reinterpret psychic experiences as either coincidences, imagination, or psychological displacement. She asserts that Pagan adults must now spend their time and energy trying to revitalize their psychic and magical abilities, which they were naturally attuned to as children. Susan feels that the next generation must be saved from being thwarted as their parents have been.

According to Susan, the public schools, which claim to be secular, actually incorporate Judeo-Christian ideals and celebrations. For example, children make Christmas cards and sing Christmas carols in school. Halloween is a time to decorate the classroom with pictures of disfigured women, who are referred to as Witches, dressed in black and flying on broomsticks. Susan feels that on the whole public schools are harmful to Neopagan children.

Every Neopagan parent to whom I have spoken has expressed similar sentiments. One Pagan on the Internet notes: "I didn't like seeing my stepdaughter coming home parroting the cowan [secular], no blatantly Xian [Christian] . . . stuff she was exposed to at school. . . . Think what our childhoods might have been like if we'd been brought up by people that didn't force us to disbelieve the guidance of the spirits" (Magical Rat 1994).

Although children are believed to be born in synchrony with the spiritual world, their natural ability can be either developed or impeded. Parents use a number of techniques to help their children develop their magical abilities, including meditation, rituals, and other forms of raising energy. To overcome the larger society's skepticism about magic, parents use concrete examples to demonstrate to their children that magic does work. For instance, O'Gaea (1993) points out to her son his successful use of his psychic powers when he was thinking or talking about a friend and that person then telephoned.

Some aspects of the mystical and magical beliefs and practices of Neopagans have resonance in more mainstream religions. Catholics light candles to ask saints to intercede on their behalf. Fundamentalist Christians speak of Christ's guiding them or being part of their everyday life. However, even with these similarities there remains a fundamental difference between espousing Witchcraft and participating in Christianity. Herbert Danzger (1989) notes that being a Christian, even a fundamentalist or a devout one, is a form of "hyperconformism" in America. Christians tend to regard Witchcraft and magic with disdain or fear, attitudes that affect all Neopagans and complicate the issue of children's involvement in Wiccan practices.

Because Neopagans live in the secular world, their children are required to bifurcate their lives into the magical, enchanted world of Wicca and the secular society. Most Neopagan adults compartmentalize their lives successfully. Magic and mysticism do not become directly or openly incorporated into their professional or mundane lives. Many remain in the "broom closet" in the larger society. Even those who are open about their religion do not normally conduct rituals or enter trances at work. Children, particularly younger children, who are trained to participate in meditation and magic may have a more difficult time compartmentalizing. Jenet (1995a:10) remarks that "as parents who are Pagan and Wiccan we need to teach our children a series of 'know-hows' primarily in order to know how to live in two worlds."

Eluba (interview 1990), the mother of two Pagan children, similarly notes, "If you have them [children] in normal schools, they have to lead a double life." However, she goes on to suggest that, although this creates some difficulty for the children, she thinks that "the skills that being part of a Pagan community are imparting to them will be invaluable to them as they grow up—when they are grown up, they will be nourished and encouraged."

Conclusion

In an interview (1987) I conducted with Jane, Erik's mother, prior to her pregnancy, she defined Paganism as "the [celebration of the] cycle of the seasons and the full moon rituals and working with symbol and ritual and those sorts of things. And it is wonderful." She was differentiating Paganism from Witchcraft, which she saw as a more disciplined practice of magic used for transformation. Neopagan children are born into a community that celebrates nature through rituals and ecological practices. The children are encouraged to recycle, create gardens, and pick up trash.

Many aspects of Neopagan children's upbringing are the same as that of other middle-class American children. Neopagan parents try to teach their children self-respect, respect for others, and respect for the ecosystem. However, Neopagan children are encouraged by both their parents and the Neopagan community to develop their magical personas and psychic abilities through rituals and other mystical practices.

Almost every Witch I have spoken to has raised concerns about the negative stereotypes that surround the term *Witch*. This problem is intensified for children. Joan (interview 1989), an adult raised in a Wiccan family, speaking of her childhood, remarks, "Kids at that age—still in grammar school—are nasty anyway, looking for someone to be the scapegoat, like the fat kid or the one with braces, and for us it was the Witches." A generation later, things have not changed significantly. Eluba (interview 1990) notes: "In some ways it's been incredibly difficult for them [her children]. Children are nothing if not little animals of peer pressure, and being different is difficult no matter who you are."

Because Neopagan parents worry that their children may suffer discrimination, more than other participants these parents are concerned that their religious practice be seen as legitimate. The growth of the number of children being born to adherents is forcing a very decentralized community to start rethinking and redefining itself. Witchcraft and Neopaganism, which grew out of the counterculture, are becoming more conservative. Tradition, continuity, and restrained sexuality become more important as children enter the circle.

Notes

1. This is a pseudonym. I have used fictitious names for people and covens throughout, except when referring to authors of published works or when noting otherwise. Some authors have published under their craft or magical names. Others use only their first names when publishing in Neopagan journals. I use the name as it appears in print. Furthermore, to protect and maintain the anonymity of my informants, I have in some instances altered small details of their lives.
2. During the first two years of my fieldwork, I participated in the rituals, classes, and meetings of a coven that was in the process of formation. I also attended rituals of ten other covens, took a class on Witchcraft at the Cambridge Adult Education Center, and participated in Neopagan festivals and events in the northeastern United States. I conducted more than forty formal, taped interviews with participants of this new religion. All quotes from these interviews are cited with the pseudonym of the person interviewed and the date of that interview. I informally interviewed over one hundred Neopagans whose ideas and thoughts I later recorded in my field notes.
3. Luhrmann (1989) notes a similar interest in fantasy and science fiction literature among British Witches.
4. Pagans jokingly refer to introductory courses on the craft offered at occult bookstores or adult education centers as Wicca or Witchcraft 101.
5. *HAM* (obviously a play on Dr. Seuss's children's book *Green Eggs and Ham*) was developed as a journal for Pagan children by an adolescent Neopagan whose father is the editor of *Green Egg,* one of the oldest Pagan journals in the United States. *HAM* was initially distributed by *Green Egg.*
6. The term *godparents* or *guardians* is also used.
7. Based on written accounts and descriptions by my male informants of boys' puberty rites.

References

Adler, M. 1986. *Drawing Down the Moon.* Rev. ed. Boston: Beacon Press.

Arthen, D. P. 1992. *Walking with Mother Earth.* West Boxford, Mass.: D and J Publications.

Balch, R. 1988. "Money and Power in Utopia: An Economic History of the Love Family." Pp. 185–222 in J. T. Richardson, ed., *Money and Power in New Religions.* Lewiston, N.Y.: Edwin Mellen Press.

Ben-Yehuda, N. 1985. *Deviance and Moral Boundaries.* Chicago: University of Chicago Press.

Berger, H. A. 1995. "Routinization of Spontaneity." *Sociology of Religion* 56(1): 49–61.

Campanelli, P. 1994. *Rites of Passage: The Pagan Wheel of Life.* St. Paul, Minn.: Llewellyn.

Curewitz, S. 1989. "Pagan Rites of Passages: Puberty." *FireHeart* (spring-summer): 24–26, 56.

———. 1990. "Pagan Rites of Passages: A Celebration of Birth." *FireHeart* 5: 8–10, 54.

Darling-Ferns, Z. 1990. "Youth and Maiden Lovemaking." *How About Magic* 1(4) (Litha): 10.

Danzger, M. H. 1989. *Returning to Tradition.* New Haven, Conn.: Yale University Press.

Finley, N. J. 1991. "Political Activism and Feminist Spirituality." *Sociological Analysis* 52(4): 349–362.

Hawkins, J. 1994. "What Do We Teach Our Children?" *Mezlim: Practical Magick for Today* 4: 1–3.

Jenet. 1994a. "Becoming Men and Women." *The Labrynth* 2(1) (Imbolc): 2–3.

———. 1994b. "Track 1." *The Labrynth* 2(2) (Beltane): 4–5.

———. 1994c. "Track 5." *The Labrynth* 2(2) (Beltane): 11–13.

———. 1994d. "Track 3." *The Labrynth* 2(3) (Lammas): 8–9.

———. 1995a. "Track 3." *The Labrynth* 3 (Imbolc): 10–11.

———. 1995b. "Track 5." *The Labrynth* 3 (Imbolc): 14.

Judith, A. 1993. "Between the Worlds: Late Adolescence and Early Adulthood in Modern Paganism." Pp. 75–92 in C. S. Clifton, Ed., *Modern Rites of Passage: Witchcraft Today.* Book 2. St. Paul, Minn.: Llewellyn.

Kelly, A. A. 1992. "An Update on Neo-Pagan Witchcraft in America." Pp. 136–151 in J. R. Lewis and J. G. Melton, eds., *Perspectives on the New Age.* Albany: State University of New York Press.

Kephart, W. 1982. *Extraordinary Groups: The Sociology of Unconventional Lifestyles.* 2d ed. New York: St. Martin's Press.

Kirkpatrick, G. R., R. Rainey, and K. Rubi. 1986. "An Empirical Study of Wiccan Religion in Postindustrial Society." *Free Inquiry in Creative Sociology* 14(1): 33–38.

Luhrmann, T. M. 1989. *Persuasions of the Witch's Craft: Ritual Magic in Contemporary England.* Cambridge, Mass.: Harvard University Press.

Magical Rat. 1994. Internet communication: netgroup:Alt.Pagan. December 14.

Manor, L. D. 1994. "Welcome to the Hundred Acre Wood." *Mezlim: Practical Magick for Today* 4: 15–16.

McArthur, M. 1994. *WiccaCraft for Families.* Langley, B.C.: Phoenix Publishing.

Neitz, M. J. 1991. "In Goddess We Trust." Pp. 353–372 in T. Robbins and D. Anthony, eds., *In Gods We Trust.* New Brunswick, N.J.: Transaction.

Northage-Orr, A. 1994. "Working with Children." *Mezlim: Practical Magick for Today* 4: 6–9.

O'Gaea, A. 1993. *The Family Wicca Book.* St. Paul, Minn.: Llewellyn.

Orion, L. 1995. *Never Again the Burning Times: Paganism Revived.* Prospect Heights, N.J.: Waveland Press.

Richardson, J. T. 1985. "The Deformation of New Religions: Impacts of Societal and Organizational Factors." Pp. 163–175 in T. Robbins, W. Shepard, and J. McBride, eds., *Cults, Culture, and the Law.* Chico, Calif.: Scholars Press.

Serith, C. 1994. *The Pagan Family: Handing the Old Ways Down.* St. Paul, Minn.: Llewellyn.

Sontag, M. 1994. "Children, Magick, and Realism." *Mezlim: Practical Magick for Today* 4: 12–13.
Stanford-Blake, D. 1994. "Pagan Parenting: My Perspective." *Mezlim: Practical Magick for Today* 4: 21.
Starhawk. 1982. *Dreaming the Dark.* Boston: Beacon Press.
Teague, H. 1994. "Children: The Next Generation." *Mezlim: Practical Magick for Today* 4: 19–20.

CHAPTER 2

Education and Collective Identity

PUBLIC SCHOOLING OF HARE KRISHNA YOUTHS

E. BURKE ROCHFORD JR.

I spent three years in a public high school and now I'm attending college. It's really tough to do the spiritual thing in these circumstances. Cause you go to school and you can't ignore it, what everyone else is doing. They're doing different things than you're use to, and it's hard not to worry about being accepted. This is what happens when gurukula *kids go to the nondevotee schools. When the Krishna Consciousness part of their life is not affecting them more than the other part, in consciousness. They're not burned out on Krishna Consciousness. They're just not interested. It no longer makes any sense to them. It makes no sense in that place [public high school]. (Words of one second-generation Hare Krishna devotee 1992)*

Richard Niebuhr (1929) noted long ago that the process of educating the young plays a determinative role in the development of religious communities, especially sectarian ones. In being attentive to the educational requirements of children, the religious enterprise undergoes a fundamental change in the direction of denominationalism. The result is that "as generation succeeds generation, the isolation of the community from the world becomes more difficult" (Niebuhr 1929:19–20).

Although educating and socializing those born into the faith does represent a pivotal moment in the career of any religious movement, it is by no means certain that secularization results, as Niebuhr suggests (Wilson 1987:41, 1991:108). Rather, effective socialization distinguishes successful religious movements from those that fail (see Stark 1987:24–25).

The historical record amply demonstrates that religious communities have met with varying degrees of success in their efforts to retain the young into adulthood (see, e.g., Bainbridge 1982, Foster 1991, on the Shakers' adopted children; Barthel 1984, on Amana; Kraybill 1989, on the Amish; Carden 1969, Mandelker 1984, on Oneida). In general, it appears that religious communities successfully secure the commitment of their young by simultaneously socializing them into the values and lifestyle of the group, while limiting, or neutralizing, countervailing influences of the conventional culture (Kraybill 1977). Moreover, as Rodney Stark suggests, enduring religious communities and movements provide their young with useful and significant things to do, thereby building group commitment and loyalty (1987:25). Expanding on this idea, I (Rochford 1995c, 1997) argue that the fate of succeeding generations within communally organized sectarian groups such as the Hare Krishna depends on the existence of a functioning *oppositional religious culture.* Without it, young people lack the very basis for a life within the group and out of necessity become dependent in various ways on the mainstream culture.

This chapter focuses on the efforts of the International Society for Krishna Consciousness (ISKCON), more popularly known as the Hare Krishna movement, to educate and socialize its second generation. I begin by detailing ISKCON's attempts historically to educate and socialize its youngest members. I describe how ISKCON's traditional system of education was organized and functioned and the factors that transformed it in the early 1980s, leaving the majority of the movement's children to attend outside schools. Next, I consider the consequences of ISKCON youths being "yoked together" with unbelievers within the context of a public high school environment. Specifically, I consider how ISKCON youths negotiated the public school setting and how these negotiations influenced their collective identity as ISKCON members and Krishna devotees. The findings demonstrate that the transition into public schooling did undermine the ISKCON collective identity of most second-generation youths but had far less of an impact on their identity as Krishna devotees. I conclude by linking the findings presented to broader issues of social movement culture, collective identity, and ISKCON's development as a religious movement.[1]

A History of Schooling Within ISKCON

In 1968, only two years after founding the Hare Krishna movement, Srila Prabhupada began to lay plans for establishing a Krishna-conscious school. Because Prabhupada saw the school system in America as doing little more than indoctrinating "children in sense gratification and mental speculation, he called the schools 'slaughterhouses'" (Goswami 1984:1). The ultimate goal of the *gurukula* (place of the guru) was to train students in spiritual life so they could escape the cycle of birth and death. Although academic subjects were taught in the gurukula, its primary purpose was to teach children sense control and practices of renunciation. By being obedient and self-controlled, a young devotee could become self-realized in Krishna Consciousness (Goswami 1984:34–37).

Given the purpose of the gurukula, children were removed from the care of their parents as early as age four or five. Because of the naturally strong ties between parent and child, Prabhupada saw little hope that a child could learn self-control within the family context. As one parent and former teacher explained: "It's understood that the parent is lenient and easily influenced by the child because of the ropes of affection. So this is why it is best if a *gurukula* teacher is instructing them" (Rochford 1997).

Children attended the gurukula on a year-round basis, with occasional vacations to visit with parents. They resided in *ashramas* (places of residence) with six to eight other children of similar age and sex. An adult teacher lived in the ashrama supervising the children and tending to their daily care.[2] As this implies, children and their parents lived more or less separate lives. (For a more detailed description of the traditional ashrama-gurukula, see Goswami 1984.)

ISKCON's system of education changed dramatically in North America during the early 1980s because of the movement's changing economic circumstances. Up until this period, the distribution of religious literature (i.e., *sankirtana*) generated sufficient revenue to support ISKCON's communal lifestyle. By 1980, however, book distribution had declined to less than one-quarter of its North American peak (Rochford 1985:175). As a result of these developments, the gurukula underwent major changes, and by 1986 ISKCON's two remaining ashrama-gurukula projects in central California and upstate New York had closed.

Today, the majority of ISKCON's children in Canada and the United States attend non-ISKCON schools or are home-schooled. In 1992, the chair of ISKCON's North American Board of Education estimated that approximately 75 percent of all elementary school–aged children and 95 percent of all secondary-level students attend non-ISKCON schools (Rochford 1997). Most attend public schools.

Traditionally the ashrama-based gurukula served as *the* institution responsible for enculturating ISKCON's youngest members (Goswami 1984; Rochford 1992, 1997)—that is, transferring the movement's spiritual and material culture to the next generation. To ensure successful cultural transmission, the gurukula was structured to maximize boundary maintenance, thereby limiting the possibility of cross-cultural exchange between young devotees and the surrounding conventional culture. The gurukula was thus expressly structured to limit *acculturation,* the "intercultural transfer of values and behaviors between groups" (Kraybill 1977:2). Given that the traditional gurukula system has largely disintegrated since the mid-1980s, with the majority of ISKCON's young people being educated outside the movement, the question arises as to what effect this has had on ISKCON's second generation and on ISKCON as a whole.[3]

The Public High School and the Negotiation of Identity

Young people raised within a sectarian religious community may well find their commitment and beliefs challenged by associating with nonbelievers in the context of a public school environment. As one ISKCON mother whose daughter attended a Catholic high school comments: "Association, Prabhupada [ISKCON's founder] said, is 95 percent. You put these kids in with a bunch of rotten apples, like in the public school, this is what you get, a rotten apple. . . . Kids are taking drugs, they're having sex, they're taking intoxication, they're stealing. It's the norm for a kid to have a boyfriend at 13. What do you expect to happen?"

Social science theories of adolescence often argue along much the same lines. Whether with respect to "normal" adolescent development or juvenile delinquency, peer relationships are viewed as playing a vital role in shaping adolescent socialization and development. The transition from childhood to adolescence, for example, is often depicted as a loosening of the symbolic "umbilical cord" that links parent to child in favor of peer and friendship ties (Muuss 1988:308). The school provides one key setting where adolescents interact and peer socialization occurs.

For youths raised within a sectarian community, the public high school stands as a "reality-disrupting," and even potentially "reality-transforming," social environment (Berger and Luckmann 1967:159). Such a setting, to use Peter Berger and Thomas Luckmann's (1967:159) apt phrase, represents a "'laboratory' of transformation." As this term implies, the public school setting is socially and ideologically antagonistic to the socioreligious world of persons raised in an unconventional religious community.

Although logical sociologically, this view effectively reduces social actors to little more than passive objects shaped by the structure, goals, and activities associated with institutional life. Such a perspective obscures the ways that individuals remain active agents in making choices and constructing their own identities (Burke and Reitzes 1991:244; Rochford 1995a:154). It also risks wrongly portraying unconventional religious beliefs as inherently fragile and readily subject to disconformation (see Snow and Machalek 1982).

Donald Kraybill's (1977) investigation of Mennonite public high school students is informative in this regard. Compared to youths enrolled in Mennonite high schools, those attending a public high school were no different in their religious commitments. Kraybill (1977:35) concludes: "The public high school environment does *not* erode attitudes toward religious orthodoxy" (emphasis added). Kraybill's study suggests the need to look more closely at the specific social processes that work for and against assimilation and changes in religious identity. Given these considerations, the question of how, and if, a public school environment affects the identity of Hare Krishna youths must remain an empirical one.

Interaction, Identity, and Consciousness

A person's identity "establishes *what* and *where* the person is in social terms" (Stone 1981:188). According to Debra Friedman and Doug McAdam (1992:169), a social movement's collective identity is "that identity or status that attaches to the individual by virtue of his or her participation in movement activities." As these definitions suggest, social identity—whether collective or individual—is shaped by ongoing interaction and identification with others. Role transitions and related shifts in identity thus depend on the relative significance of both existing and emergent social networks in people's everyday lives (Silver 1996:2).

The literature on religious conversion has focused attention on the interrelationship among interaction, identity, and changing consciousness. Empirical studies have identified social interaction and affective social bonds as keys to the conversion process. John Lofland and Rodney Stark (1965) have found that conversion remains incomplete in the absence of ongoing and intensive interaction between potential converts and committed believers. Along the same lines, David Snow and Cynthia Phillips's (1980:444) investigation of Nichren Shoshu concludes "that conversion in general is highly improbable in the absence of affective and intensive interaction." In the words of Berger and Luckmann (1967:157), "These significant others are the guides into the new reality." Conversion thus takes place when a person comes to believe what friends believe (Lofland and Stark 1965).

Social ties play a role in the conversion process in yet another way. Conversion is more likely to occur if ties to the people supporting the *previous* identity and worldview are neutralized. Such attachments represent countervailing sources of commitment capable of undermining the conversion process (Lofland and Stark 1965; Rochford 1985:79–83, 87–122). The need to counteract these out-group ties appears especially relevant for conversion to communally organized religious groups, especially those defined as "peculiar" or "threatening" (Snow and Phillips 1980:441–442).

Given these empirical and theoretical considerations, it seems reasonable to hypothesize that ISKCON youths who successfully establish close relational ties with conventional high school students will undergo a change in identity, becoming more assimilated into American mainstream culture. This may even involve a process of "deconversion" (Jacobs 1987) as their Krishna-conscious worldview loses salience in everyday affairs. Conversely, those who eschew ties with non-ISKCON students in favor of devotee relationships are unlikely to undergo a change in collective identity.

The findings in table 2.1 report on how ISKCON youths negotiated the public high school environment and the consequences thereof. As indicated, a substantial majority of the ISKCON students did establish meaningful social ties with their nondevotee classmates. Moreover, these relationships appear to have formed at the expense of ties with other devotee youths and their religious involvement and beliefs.

Approximately three-quarters of the ISKCON youths who attended a public high school developed close friendships with nondevotees, visited the homes of these friends, and dated nondevotees during their high school years. Of equal significance, only a small minority (15 percent) associated primarily with other devotee students while in school. Less dramatically, somewhat less than half (42 percent) admitted withdrawing from their relationships with devotee young

TABLE 2.1 *ISKCON Youths' Negotiations in Public High School Setting (N = 53)*

Negotiated involvements	Percentage	(no. of youths)
Social relationships		
Spent time visiting homes of nondevotee friends	75	(40)
Developed close friendships with nondevotee students	77	(41)
Dated nondevotee classmates	72	(38)
Associated mostly with other devotee students when in school	15	(8)
Became less involved with other devotee youths	42	(22)
Involvement in school/youth culture		
Was involved in popular kids' culture	60	(32)
Was involved in (school) sports	53	(28)
Religious involvement and commitment		
Became less interested in attending temple activities	53	(28)
Experimented with breaking some regulative principles	74	(39)
Began to question Krishna-conscious beliefs	51	(27)

people more generally. Thus, although most interacted with and established friendships with nondevotee students, roughly an equal proportion did and did not withdraw from interpersonal relationships that kept them tied to the world of ISKCON and Krishna Consciousness.[4]

As the data in table 2.1 reveal further, many ISKCON youths were involved in the social worlds of their classmates. A majority participated in various aspects of contemporary "kids'" culture (i.e., listening to popular music, drinking alcohol, smoking marijuana, and generally keeping up with trends in the conventional youth subculture). Half played high school sports, several distinguishing themselves as star athletes.

With respect to their religious involvement, over half became less interested in attending religious activities at their local ISKCON temple. A similar number began questioning their Krishna-conscious beliefs. Particularly striking is that three-quarters admitted to breaking one or more of the movement's regulative principles, behavioral standards that define ISKCON's religious way of life.

If we compare ISKCON youths who did and those who did not become involved in nondevotee friendships, we gain a more precise picture of the influence of nondevotee attachments, although few actually rejected such ties (N = 12). As shown in table 2.2, those ISKCON youths who established nondevotee friendships were much more likely to become involved in aspects of conventional youth culture and to break some of the movement's regulative principles. Even though the differences are not statistically significant, it is worth noting that ISKCON students with nondevotee friendships more often withdrew from relationships with other devotee youths, became less interested in attending temple services and activities, and were more likely to question their Krishna-conscious beliefs. Consider the statement of one young woman who attended a public high school: "I was into partying, going out. I was curious and so I got

TABLE 2.2 *Nondevotee Friendship Patterns for ISKCON Youths by Selected Measures (N = 53)*

Nondevotee friendships	Was involved in kids' culture	Became less involved with devotee youths my age	Became less interested in attending temple activities	Broke some regulative principles	Questioned Krishna-conscious beliefs
Have close nondevotee friendships	73% (30)[a]	44% (18)	56% (23)	83% (34)[b]	56% (23)
Have no close nondevotee friendships	17% (2)	33% (4)	42% (5)	42% (5)	33% (4)

[a]$p < .001$ [b]$p < .01$

into it. When I was fifteen, I experimented with drinking, going to parties. I had my first boyfriend, all of that. I felt that I had to be part of the whole scene, or I wouldn't be accepted. If I went around 'Hare Krishna, Hare Krishna,' you know, who would be my friend?"

Given the significance of nondevotee friendships, it is important to consider some of the ways that these ties were forged. As suggested by the young woman just quoted, dating provided one means by which ISKCON youths formed relational ties with their nondevotee counterparts. This was especially true for women devotees in my sample, 82 percent (N = 27) of whom dated nondevotee classmates, as compared to 55 percent (N = 11) of their male counterparts.[5] Sports played a significant role in the integration of both men and women into nondevotee friendship networks. Only two of the twenty-eight youths who played sports failed to establish close friendship ties with their nondevotee classmates. The role that sports played in establishing friendships is suggested by the comments of a second-generation male devotee who attended a public high school in West Virginia: "The most difficult thing for me was to fit in [at the local high school] because of the way I acted and dressed—it just wasn't 'up to par.' I wasn't really 'cool' like the other dudes. I was a mess until I played football and did well, which created many friends."

Identity Work and Identity Change

The foregoing findings suggest that most ISKCON youths did, in fact, became integrated socially into the public high school culture, establishing close nondevotee friendships and becoming involved in popular adolescent culture.[6] Although revealing, these findings ultimately leave us with little understanding of what actually transpired when devotee youths encountered the social world of the public high school. How, and why, for example, did some ISKCON youths become socially integrated into nondevotee networks while others escaped, or perhaps resisted, such involvements? Moreover, how did differing levels of involvement and integration into the nondevotee world influence the collective movement identity of ISKCON youths? To answer these questions, we must delve further into the nature of the relations between ISKCON youths and their nondevotee student counterparts. In particular, we must grasp how being a Hare Krishna itself shaped the identity negotiations that took place within the context of the public high school. Two issues were particularly relevant to the identity work that took place.

First, ISKCON youths became public high school students with little practical knowledge of the social world they were about to enter. Not only was this environment antagonistic to what they believed and who they were; it also remained unknown in its particulars. Second, ISKCON youths entered the public high school with a highly stigmatized personal identity. To be a Hare Krishna was (and is) to be viewed by others as "deviant," "crazy," "dangerous," or, in Erving Goffman's (1963:5) words, "not quite human." This was all the more true during the 1980s, when anticult sentiment was particularly virulent in North America. It was during this period that most of the ISKCON youths in this study were attending high school or approaching high school age. Because of the dual challenge posed by having "stigma potential" (Schneider and Conrad 1993) while having little working knowledge of the conventional world, ISKCON youths found themselves preoccupied with the problem of social acceptance (see Goffman 1963:8–9) and undertook several strategies to deal with it.

Commonsense Knowledge and the Problem of Social Acceptance

The problem of gaining social acceptance, and avoiding victimization, was a troublesome proposition for ISKCON youths in ways that rarely confront people with stigma potential. Having been raised apart from the dominant culture, within a totalistic community, ISKCON youths lacked even the most basis knowledge about what their nondevotee classmates claimed as "common culture." As Harold Garfinkel (1967:76) suggests, such an understanding is a prerequisite for group participation and claims to group membership. As one particularly astute devotee youth commented about his transition into the public high school: "I had large gaps in my culture-specific knowledge. I had no skills." The following statements point to the content that defined these "gaps":

> I couldn't relate to these kids. I wasn't seeing anything the same way. From age eleven, when we thought of men, we thought of marriage. Nothing was lighthearted and funny. I had to *learn* to laugh, how to have a sense of humor. As a girl we were taught to be chaste—therefore we never learned to ride even a bicycle, and so when I was put into PE class, it was one of the most embarrassing moments for me. I didn't know what third base was or what to do when the ball came to me.

> I think the most difficult thing was that I didn't know how to deal with these people [nondevotee students]. . . . I didn't know anything about the way people grew up. I never saw any [of the] TV shows they were talking about, etc.
>
> This may seem strange, but the names of the students were confusing at first because they weren't Indian, and I had never heard them before.
>
> *Sister 1:* We [she and her sister] didn't even know what "the finger" was. And we got into fights because we didn't know who Michael Jackson was. We were so lost.
> *Sister 2:* It was so hard, so hard for us to deal with karmies [nondevotees].

For many, the "dis-ease" they felt within the environment of the public high school provoked confusion and even a sense of "anomic terror" (Berger and Luckmann 1967:103).

> I was scared. I didn't know how to deal with my fellow classmates. I was very uptight. I thought I was so different from them because we had been raised to believe they were bad people. Mainly I was terrified that everyone knew how I was raised.
>
> I did not fit in at all! It was a major change. In the ashrama we were kept so segregated from the nondevotees and never taught much [about] the outside world. When we were, it was always negative. I was very afraid and felt totally out of place. I felt everyone noticed how strange and different I was.

To deal with the structural strain associated with attempting to cope with an unfamiliar and even hostile world, ISKCON youths undertook what amounted to a "secret apprenticeship" (Garfinkel 1967:147). Such a strategy allows actors to simultaneously mask incompetencies while permitting the "environment to furnish . . . the answers to its own questions" (Garfinkel 1967:147). My respondents mentioned two interrelated roles—being shy and being a loner—that were particularly amenable to such an apprenticeship, although these youths tended to view each as a personality trait rather than a strategy of social adaptation.

A number of the second-generation devotees I interviewed observed that they, and their devotee peers, were often shy and withdrawn within the school environment:[7]

> At first I was shy. A lot of the devotee kids are shy, but I was extremely shy. . . . You have to understand we didn't know how to relate. This was all new to us.
>
> I was shy and extremely self-conscious. I found that going to school

> with these "strangers" made me very uncomfortable. Dealing with girls was difficult and the most embarrassing aspect. . . . But I adjusted after a while and learned how to relate to this new "species" of human.

> When I first entered public school, I was very shy. I had a lot of catching up to do with the latest trends, and cliques were something new to me.

Some youths were loners within the public school environment, remaining largely uninvolved with their nondevotee classmates. As the following statement suggests, the loner role had strategic value: "Even though I was around them [the other students] I kept myself pretty isolated. I felt very alone. I wanted to be open about myself, but it was too risky. I just didn't want to have the pressure on. I didn't know anything about these kids. I wanted to stay on the side[lines]. That way I could check them out."

Taking on the role of loner, or being shy, allowed ISKCON youths to gain a marginal degree of acceptance within the adolescent world of the high school without their devotee status becoming a public issue. Not only could they learn the ropes of adolescent culture from within these roles, but they could also create social distance between themselves and the very culture they were seeking to understand. Although for most students this strategy appears to have been only temporary, for others being shy or a loner formed the basis of a stable social role that allowed them to escape integration into student friendship networks: "I didn't want to get too close to them because I know that when you hang out with party animals, you become one yourself. So I believe in association; that if I associate with devotees, I will become a devotee. So I chose to stay on my own."

Stigma and the Problem of Social Acceptance

Goffman (1963:3) in his classic work on the topic defines stigma as "an attribute that is deeply discrediting. An individual who is stigmatized, be it on the basis of "abominations of the body," "blemishes of character," or the "tribal stigma of race, nation or religion[,] possesses a trait that can obtrude itself upon attention and turn those of us whom he meets away from him, breaking the claim that his other attributes have on us. He possesses a stigma, an undesired differentness from what we had anticipated" (Goffman 1963:4–5).

ISKCON youths who attend non-ISKCON schools do so fully aware of their movement's public reputation as a deviant "cult." They are cognizant as well that as "outsiders" (Becker 1963) they are vulnerable to being shunned or even harassed. As one devotee youth commented, "When I first went to public school, I was afraid the kids wouldn't like me because of the devotees' reputation." And, in fact, some ISKCON youths did face stigmatization and rejection at the hands of nondevotee students and teachers.

> The transition was very hard. I wasn't used to being ridiculed for who I was. I fought because that was all I could do.

> The embarrassment when the nondevotees made fun of me was real hard to take. Some of the teachers' insolence towards us also. Just trying to become another person at school was so difficult. Every time something went wrong, we devotee students were always accused of doing it.

Because of the stigma attached to being a Hare Krishna, most ISKCON youths were intensely self-conscious as they anticipated the transition to the local public high school. Because of the ever-present potential for rejection and harassment, many studiously avoided mentioning their ties to ISKCON or Krishna Consciousness.

> I felt a bit nervous about saying, "I am a Hare Krishna," because they [nondevotee students] would call me bad names. The bad names will start coming right away. People will make fun of us.

> *Devotee Woman 1:* I mean if people were to find out what your religion was, they're like "Oh my God!" So it's better not to tell them what your religion is, so they can get to know you as a person.
>
> *Devotee Woman 2:* Like you can't say, "Hi, I'm Sally and I'm a Hare Krishna." Because you will never make friends. We had to keep it—not a secret but [pause] . . .
>
> *Devotee Woman 1:* There are such stereotypes about us. I must admit for a while I was embarrassed to admit that I was a Hare Krishna.

The 1992–1993 Second-Generation Survey lends further support to the concerns expressed in the foregoing comments. Fifty-three percent of those who attended a public high school agreed that they were at least "somewhat embarrassed at being a devotee" on entering high school. Others, although not embarrassed by their devotee identity, nonetheless sought to avoid being stigmatized and hid their Krishna identity from their classmates. Overall, six in ten (61 percent) admitted "try[ing] to avoid revealing the fact that I was a devotee" on entering the public high school.

As these findings suggest, interactions between devotee youths and their classmates involved ongoing identity work, at least during the initial period of their transition into the public school environment. The challenge interactionally was one of information control, or managing self-presentation to avoid revealing their collective identity as Hare Krishnas. As potentially *discreditable* persons, ISKCON students engaged in the ongoing "concealment of creditable facts" (Goffman 1963:42). As such, they were committed to the project of *not being different.* To be "ordinary" allowed for the possibility of gaining acceptance. As one devotee woman who attended a public high school in Denver commented: "It was kind of odd because I felt like an oddball. . . . And of course I never, never told anyone that I was a Hare Krishna. . . . The thing was I didn't go around with my head covered or anything like that. I was just into the whole scene there. They really didn't know anything—that I was different from a normal student, any other student coming to school."

To avoid conveying information that might reveal their actual identity, ISKCON youths engaged in a number of interactional strategies directed toward gaining acceptance as conventional students.[8] Below I briefly consider several of these practices. I then turn to how the work of "passing" (Goffman 1963) practically facilitated the integration of ISKCON youths into conventional networks and the social world of their nondevotee peers.[9]

Stigma and Self-Presentation

The demands of social life routinely require people to convey information about themselves in the process of interaction. On the one hand, this social requirement allows actors to make claims about who they are, and on the other hand, it provides others with the "raw materials" to construct "working" identities for those who are otherwise unfamiliar. Such signs, of course, can communicate status or prestige, as well as draw attention to deviant, or debasing qualities of a person's identity. Goffman (1963:43–44) refers to the latter as *stigma symbols,* and they constitute the focus of "stigma management," or passing. Essentially, a potentially *discreditable* person engages in identity work directed toward neutralizing, or otherwise keeping hidden from public view, discrediting information about his or her self. By so doing, this person preserves the basis of social acceptance.

To avoid revealing their actual social identity, ISKCON youths undertook a variety of self-presentation strategies that effectively rendered their identity as Hare Krishna members invisible. These strategies were specifically crafted with an eye toward gaining acceptance from their classmates.[10]

Dress. In research on appearance and the self, Gregory Stone (1981:202) concludes "that the self is established, maintained, and altered in social transactions as much by the communications of appearance as by discourse." Through our appearance we mobilize specific self-definitions in the minds of those with whom we interact. It is in this sense that our appearance serves as a public announcement of our identity (Stone 1981:193). As one second-generation ISKCON woman (Devi Dasi 1994:41) put it: "Wearing a sari helps me stay pious and remember Krsna. . . . It helps remind me and others that I'm a devotee of Krsna, in the same way a policeman's uniform helps him remember his service and reminds citizens he's an agent of the law."

Almost without exception, ISKCON youths attended their local public high school dressed in clothing that mirrored that worn by their nondevotee classmates. Such an appearance was a statement of their "ordinary" student status. Up until this point, most ISKCON youths had spent their lives attired in traditional religious garb: a *dhoti* for men or a *sari* for women.

Only in one instance did a second-generation youth report having gone to school wearing clothing that openly acknowledged her Hare Krishna identity. The young woman in question did so only at the insistence of her stepfather, whose motives are clear from her comments: "We went to junior high—public.

But my stepfather wouldn't let my brother and I wear normal clothes—made [name of brother] keep his *shika* [clump of hair on the back of an otherwise shaved head], me wear a long dress. But worst of all we were not allowed to associate with other kids our age because he was afraid of our contamination by nondevotees. So in other words, no friends." In Goffman's terms, this young woman's stepfather explicitly wanted her and her brother to face discreditation at the hands of their nondevotee classmates. By so doing, he sought to negate any possibility that they would become friendly with nondevotee students, thereby avoiding potential threats to their devotional way of life. Such actions by parents, however, appear to have been rare.[11]

Name Changes. The devotional names of ISKCON youths represented a significant threat to their efforts to gain acceptance as conventional students. On entering the public high school, devotee youths routinely Anglicized their devotee names (e.g., Caitanya became Chris) or, if they had one, reverted to their legal Christian name. The following exchange suggests the implications of using a devotee name and the resulting pressures to seek an acceptable alternative:

> *Man 1:* Feeling different, being teased about my name made for a difficult adjustment to the public high I went to.
> *Man 2:* Everyone had difficulty with my spiritual name. Eventually I took a Christian name. It just made things a lot easier for me.

Very often the use of Christian and Anglicized names moved beyond the boundaries of the school environment as devotee youths referred to one another by these names even within the ISKCON community. I observed teenagers on many occasions, and in different ISKCON communities, make reference to one another using Christian names, or obviously Anglicized devotee names. The act of changing their names in the direction of conventionality represented a fundamental symbolic break from the world of ISKCON.

Vegetarianism. Diet was one element of the lives of ISKCON youths that worried them most as they made the transition into public education. Given a lifetime of strict vegetarianism, eating meat was not an option.[12] Even though American attitudes toward vegetarianism have become increasingly favorable, ISKCON youths saw this aspect of their lifestyle as one that made them particularly vulnerable, since it promised to invite curiosity and questioning from other students.

> Being a vegetarian . . . was one of the things I tried to keep hidden. I excluded myself from social actions with other students and would not eat near anyone else.

> I was vegetarian. The kids thought my bread, lettuce, tomato, and cheese sandwich was weird and wouldn't taste it. Explaining why I didn't eat

> meat was the most difficult. It was like you weren't human if you didn't eat it.

As the following comment by one ISKCON youth suggests, being a vegetarian on occasion did raise suspicion and identity challenges: "Even people who asked me: 'You're a vegetarian. You do this. You do that. Are you a Hare Krishna by any chance?' 'No. Are you kidding?' Just a flat out-lie."

Association with Other ISKCON Youths. The possibility of a discreditable person's identity being revealed is heightened when she or he associates with others who share the same stigma. As Goffman (1963:47) suggests, "to be 'with'" someone reveals information about social identity because we all usually assume that people associate with others like themselves.

Being in the presence of other devotee young people while at school involved two potential risks. Because not all ISKCON youths were as equally skilled in techniques of passing, and because a few apparently had little or no regard for protecting their ISKCON identity, being with other devotees invited the possibility of public exposure and increased the likelihood that a devotee would let down her or his own guard. The devotee might, for example, slip into distinctive ways of speaking and acting that appeared "out of character" to nondevotee peers. For these and other reasons, the vast majority of the ISKCON youths consciously avoided devotee contacts when in school, instead favoring those with nondevotee students (see Table 2.1).[13] As one second-generation devotee who graduated from a public high school in Los Angeles stated:

> *EBR:* Were there other devotee kids at the high school when you went?
> *D:* Oh yeah. Lots of them.
> *EBR:* Did you hang out together?
> *D:* No, not really. . . . I wasn't really that interested in being with them [devotee kids]. I was just trying to deal with all that was happening [at the high school]. That was enough [for me]. I didn't want other [nondevotee] kids to know who I was anyway.

Passing, Social Relationships, and Identity

The findings reported in table 2.3 suggest how concerns about stigma and attempts to pass influenced the ways that devotee youths adapted to the high school environment, as well as to ISKCON. The findings indicate that ISKCON youths who remained less concerned about their Krishna identity more readily integrated socially into the high school milieu. Conversely, those who were embarrassed and/or sought to hide their ISKCON identity more often withdrew from the devotee community.

In nearly every case, youths who felt embarrassment at being an ISKCON devotee sought to avoid revealing their Krishna identity within the high school setting. These youths were also less likely to establish close friendships with

TABLE 2.3 *ISKCON Youths' Responses to Stigma by Selected Measures (N = 53)*

Stigma response	Avoided revealing devotee identity	Developed close friendships with nondevotee students	Was involved in kids' culture	Became less involved with devotee youths my age	Became less interested in attending temple activities	Broke some regulative principles	Questioned Krishna-conscious beliefs
Embarrassed at being a devotee							
Yes	89% (25)[a]	64% (18)	50% (14)	50% (14)	75% (21)[a]	71% (20)	57% (16)
No	28% (7)	92% (23)[b]	72% (18)[c]	32% (8)	28% (7)	76% (19)	44% (11)
Sought to avoid revealing ISKCON identity							
Yes		72% (23)	59% (19)	53% (17)[b]	69% (22)[a]	69% (22)	56% (18)
No		86% (18)	62% (13)	24% (5)	29% (6)	81% (17)	43% (9)

[a]p < .001 [b]p < .05 [c]p < .10

nondevotee peers, although nearly two-thirds did so in spite of these feelings. In addition, those embarrassed by their ISKCON identity were less involved in popular "kids' culture" and were far less interested in taking part in temple activities. Feelings of identity embarrassment were not, however, related significantly to involvements with other devotee young people, breaking the movement's regulative principles, or questioning Krishna-conscious beliefs.

Attempts to avoid revealing an ISKCON identity were not associated significantly with developing nondevotee friendships, which suggests that efforts by ISKCON youths to pass and gain social acceptance were largely successful. However, avoidance was associated with being less involved with other devotee young people and less interested in taking part in temple activities. These latter findings raise a more fundamental question about identity and self-presentation. If ISKCON youths were involved in passing strictly as a strategic device, we might reasonably expect that their ISKCON ties and involvements would remain more or less stable. To avoid other devotee youths and to lose interest in attending community activities at the temple suggest that something far more significant occurred for many ISKCON youths. As previously suggested, individual identity and collective identity are grounded in social relations. To the extent that ISKCON youths responded to stigma potential by withdrawing from devotee relationships and community life in favor of ties with nondevotee classmates, the social basis for their identity changed.

TABLE 2.4 *Collective Identify of ISKCON Youths According to Public High School Attendance*[a]

	Collective identity							
Public high school attendance	Active core/ congregational ISKCON member		Little/no involvement but devotee		No longer ISKCON member or devotee		Total	
Attended	10%	(4)	67%	(28)	24%	(10)	101%	(42)
Did not attend	33%	(7)	57%	(12)	10%	(2)	100%	(21)

[a]Significant at < .05

Table 2.4 compares the collective identity of ISKCON youths who did and those who did not attend public high schools at the time of the second generation survey in 1992–1993. The findings presented include only those ISKCON youths who *completed* high school.[14] As indicated, those who attended a public high school were much less likely to declare an ISKCON collective identity either as a core or congregational member. Moreover, one-fourth of those who did attend a public high school rejected both ISKCON and Krishna Consciousness as a meaningful part of their identity. Nevertheless, the data in table 2.4 make clear that relatively *few of either group* actively identified with ISKCON. In fact, the majority of second-generation youths from both groups rejected an ISKCON collective identity, although most continued to define themselves as Krishna devotees (i.e., believers and followers of Krishna Consciousness).

These findings suggest that the role transition associated with attending a public high school did influence the ISKCON collective identity of second-generation youths but had far less effect on their identity as Krishna devotees. ISKCON youths may have traded their ISKCON collective identity for the sake of gaining social acceptance from their nondevotee peers, but most held on to their religious identity even if they became less involved in the practices and lifestyle of Krishna Consciousness. Thus, few can be said to have undergone deconversion. Rather, the majority found ways to socially and cognitively bridge the religious world of Krishna Consciousness with mainstream American culture.

Conclusion

This study raises a broader question about the role of culture in communally organized sectarian movements. The growth of family life requires cultural and institutional development if a religious sect has any hope of remaining insulated from the influences of the surrounding society. Without a functioning religious culture to support the needs of family life, a sect faces inevitable change in the direction of secularization (Rochford 1995a, 1997). This study points to one way this can happen. Lacking an internal system of secondary education,

ISKCON parents faced the uncomfortable decision of sending their children to schools outside the movement. This set off a complex set of negotiations resulting in identity challenges and change for the second-generation youths involved. Significantly for ISKCON, youths found themselves exchanging their ISKCON collective identity in the interest of gaining social acceptance from nondevotee classmates. The result was that second-generation youths became less involved in ISKCON and less identified with ISKCON's purposes and goals.

Yet the findings presented suggest still other consequences associated with ISKCON's lack of cultural innovation. As we saw in table 2.4, even those ISKCON young people who did manage to escape being educated in a public high school nonetheless remained largely uninvolved in ISKCON, the majority rejecting an identity as either a core or congregational ISKCON member. This suggests the presence of yet other sources of estrangement for ISKCON's second generation.

Young people growing up in ISKCON ultimately have little basis for making a life for themselves within the context of ISKCON's North American communities. Opportunities for employment and/or other meaningful activities that could serve to integrate ISKCON's young people are sorely lacking. In a recent presentation to ISKCON teachers, parents, and second-generation youths, the chair of ISKCON's North American Board of Education made this very point. In his talk, appropriately titled "All Dressed Up with No Place to Go," he argued that even those ISKCON young people who had been educated entirely within the movement's school system lacked any real hope of making a life for themselves within ISKCON. The future remained bleak for all of ISKCON's second generation given the sheer lack of paid work opportunities *within* the movement's communities (Dasa 1994). Unable to secure their lives within ISKCON, young people are following in the footsteps of their parents' generation, seeking life options outside the movement's ranks (see Rochford 1995a, 1997).[15]

Without a culture supportive of family life, ISKCON is certain to face continuing change and transformation. Its communal structure has already largely disintegrated in North America (Rochford 1997), depriving ISKCON of the foundational social arrangements that support its traditional sectarian way of life. As first- and second-generation devotees alike continue to "make peace with the world" in an effort to make a life for themselves and their families, their ISKCON collective identity will progressively lose relevance and meaning in their everyday lives. Without committed followers, ISKCON will find it more difficult to mobilize members in the interest of realizing group goals and purposes. As we approach the twenty-first century, ISKCON's future stability and vitality as a religious organization remain very much an open question.

Notes

1. The Hare Krishna movement originated in India and was brought to this country in 1965 by A. C. Bhaktivedanta Swami, or Srila Prabhupada, as he is called by ISKCON members. ISKCON is dedicated to spreading Krishna Consciousness throughout the

world and has communities and preaching centers on every continent. At its height in the mid-1970s, ISKCON had approximately five thousand core members residing in its communities worldwide. During the 1980s, the movement's expansion was fueled primarily by the involvement of a substantial number of East Indian immigrants living in America and elsewhere (e.g., Western Europe). More recently, the movement has successfully recruited members in Eastern Europe and the former Soviet Union. The aim of the Krishna devotee is to become self-realized by practicing *bhakti yoga* (devotion to God). Central to this spiritual process are chanting Hare Krishna and living a lifestyle free of meat, intoxicants, illicit sex, and gambling. For a discussion of the movement's historical roots in India, see Brooks (1989) and Judah (1974). For a more detailed history of ISKCON's development in America, see Rochford (1985, 1989, 1995a, 1995b, 1997, 1998a, 1998b).

2. In more general terms, ashrama refers to living arrangements that are structured to facilitate spiritual activities and growth (i.e., where Krishna Consciousness remains at the center of everyday life).
3. Data for this study were collected over a five-year period (1990–1995). The data presented are derived from interviews, participant observation, and a survey of second-generation ISKCON youths in North America. Open-ended interviews were conducted with forty-seven second-generation ISKCON youths. Most of these interviews (N = 30) were with devotee men and women in their late teens and twenties; seventeen interviews were with high school-age students attending ISKCON secondary schools in Alachua, Florida.

   The primary source of data for this study is derived from a survey conducted in 1992–1993 that included eighty-seven second-generation ISKCON youths from North America. The survey targeted older members of ISKCON's second generation. The average age of my respondents was between eighteen and nineteen years, with a range from thirteen to twenty-seven years of age. Three-quarters (74 percent) of those surveyed were born within the movement. The remainder accompanied one or both parents into the movement, most at an early age. All respondents had previously attended one or more ISKCON schools or were doing so at the time of the survey. All but two at some point had attended an ashrama-based gurukula. The average number of years attended was 6.7, with a range of 1 to 13 years.

   Approximately two-thirds of my respondents were enrolled in school at the time of the survey: 38 percent were students at a junior college or four-year college/university, 10 percent attended a public high school, 13 percent were students at an ISKCON secondary school, 2 percent were being home-schooled, and 1 percent were students at a religious high school not affiliated with ISKCON. Of those surveyed, 36 percent had spent at least some time as a student in a public elementary school, 39 percent in a public junior high, and 61 percent in a public high school.
4. In a handful of cases that I am aware of, young people were openly rejected by some ISKCON adults when they made the transition into public education. Their parents also faced criticism. As we might expect, this rejection served only to weaken further the ties between the affected young person and the ISKCON community.
5. Researchers have found that the identity of women making the transition into college is strongly influenced by the "culture of romance" (see Holland and Eisenhart 1990; Silver 1996:12).
6. We might reasonably question the extent to which there is an adolescent subculture distinct from the dominant culture. Whatever the empirical status of an adolescent

subculture, it still remains aligned with the conventional culture. Adults and adolescents do, after all, share the same "home-world" (Berger and Luckmann 1967), even though they may inhabit different sectors of that social reality. In this way, the culture found within the public high school provides both a window and a potential pathway into the conventional society for ISKCON youths.

7. Unfortunately, I have no systematic way to determine just how extensive either one of these forms of adaptation actually was. I became aware of them only after beginning to analyze my data.
8. Each of the ISKCON youths who attended either a private or religious high school (N = 6) took measures to avoid revealing his or her ISKCON identity. Attending school outside the neighborhood appears to provide certain advantages for concealing an ISKCON identity. Peer relationships can be more easily avoided, given the distance students typically live from one another. Moreover, these relationships are more readily subject to self-presentation strategies directed toward concealment. For example, one ISKCON mother whose daughter attended a Catholic high school told me that she had held birthday parties and other social gatherings for her daughter at a park near the ISKCON community where she lived. By contrast, a local public school is a *community* institution and hence interactions between classmates naturally spill over into the neighborhood. This very fact makes concealment difficult to sustain over the long run for ISKCON youths attending local public schools.
9. It appears that a limited number of ISKCON youths actively sought to become integrated into the outside culture on entering the public high school. I have found three cases where ISKCON youths saw the public high school as a stepping-stone toward leaving ISKCON. One of two reasons was cited: either the young person had experienced abuse—psychological, physical, or sexual—during his or her days in the gurukula (Rochford 1998b), and/or one or both parents had defected or had otherwise suffered mistreatment by ISKCON authorities.
10. One exception to this can be found in ISKCON communities located in rural locations, where effectively managing an ISKCON identity becomes difficult, if not impossible. In one ISKCON farm community located in rural Pennsylvania, for example, devotee youths entered the local public high school with the full knowledge of the locals that they were Hare Krishnas. ISKCON students were routinely ostracized and found themselves at the bottom of the school social hierarchy. They established friendships—to the extent they did so—with working-class youths, who were themselves situated at the lower rungs of the status system. ISKCON parents have painfully revealed how these young devotees often became involved in drinking alcohol, taking drugs, and expressing a general resistance to learning. In short, they began to take on the habits and attitudes of their newly acquired working-class friends.
11. By the early 1980s, it was common for *first-generation* ISKCON members to wear conventional attire when venturing outside the devotee community to work or run errands.
12. Of the eighty-seven second-generation ISKCON youths surveyed, only seven indicated that they had ever consumed meat. Of these, only three regularly ate meat.
13. Some ISKCON youths (especially young men) did report hanging out together, but apparently only after their nondevotee classmates became aware of their ISKCON identity. Having been discredited, being with other devotee students became one means of defense against threats of harassment and/or rejection by other students.

14. I excluded those still in high school to highlight how role transitions initiated during the high school years influenced subsequent identification with ISKCON and Krishna Consciousness. It should be obvious that influences beyond the public high school experience may have played a significant additional role in shaping respondents' identification with ISKCON and Krishna Consciousness. Unfortunately, my data do not allow me to determine precisely the separate influence of high school and post-high school factors on collective identity.
15. Beginning in 1992, there was an initiative to provide apprenticeship and employment opportunities for second-generation ISKCON youth. "Project Future Hope" represents a joint effort by first- and second-generation devotees to create opportunities for ISKCON's young people. The program allows ISKCON youths to learn and work in an environment with other devotees rather than going outside the movement. Until recently, the program suffered from inadequate funding and only token support from movement leaders. As a result, the potential of Project Future Hope has not been realized. This may be changing, however, as ISKCON leaders in North America committed funds and other resources to Project Future Hope in 1996.

References

Bainbridge, W. 1982. "Shaker Demographics, 1840–1900: An Example of the Use of U.S. Census Enumeration Schedules." *Journal for the Scientific Study of Religion* 21: 352–365.

Barthel, D. 1984. *Amana: From Pietist Sect to American Community.* Lincoln: University of Nebraska Press.

Becker, H. 1963. *Outsiders.* New York: Free Press.

Berger, P., and T. Luckmann. 1967. *The Social Construction of Reality.* New York: Anchor Books.

Brooks, C. 1989. *Hare Krishnas in India.* Princeton,N.J.: Princeton University Press.

Burke, P., and D. Reitzes. 1991. "An Identity Theory Approach to Commitment." *Social Psychology Quarterly* 54: 239–251.

Carden, M. 1969. *Oneida: Utopian Community to Modern Corporation.* Baltimore, Md.: Johns Hopkins University Press.

Dasa, M. 1994. "All Dressed Up with No Place to Go." Paper presented at ISKCON's North American Board of Education Conference, Alachua, Fla., October.

Devi Dasi, M. 1994. "Why I Wear a Sari." *Back to Godhead* (November-December): 40–41.

Foster, L. 1991. *Women, Family, and Utopia.* Syracuse, N.Y.: Syracuse University Press.

Friedman, D., and D. McAdam. 1992. "Collective Identity and Activism: Networks, Choices, and the Life of a Social Movement." Pp. 156–173 in A. Morris and C. Mueller, eds., *Frontiers in Social Movement Theory.* New Haven, Conn.: Yale University Press.

Garfinkel, H. 1967. *Studies in Ethnomethodology.* Englewood Cliffs, N.J.: Prentice-Hall.

Goffman, E. 1963. *Stigma: Notes on the Management of a Spoiled Identity.* Englewood Cliffs, N.J.: Prentice-Hall.

Goswami, J. 1984. *Srila Prabhupada on Guru-kula.* Los Angeles: Bhaktivedanta Book Trust.

Holland, D., and M. Eisenhart. 1990. *Educated in Romance: Women, Achievement, and College Culture.* Chicago: University of Chicago Press.

Jacobs, J. 1987. "Deconversion from Religious Movements: An Analysis of Charismatic Bonding and Spiritual Commitment." *Journal for the Scientific Study of Religion* 26: 294–308.

Judah, S. 1974. *Hare Krishna and the Counterculture.* New York: Wiley.

Kraybill, D. 1977. *Ethnic Education: The Impact of Mennonite Schooling.* San Francisco: R and E Research Associates.

———. 1989. *The Riddle of Amish Culture.* Baltimore, Md.: Johns Hopkins University Press.

Lofland, J., and R. Stark. 1965. "Becoming a World-Saver: A Theory of Conversion to a Deviant Perspective." *American Sociological Review* 30: 862–874.

Mandelker, I. 1984. *Religion, Society, and Utopia in Nineteenth-Century America.* Amherst: University of Massachusetts Press.

Muuss, R. 1988. *Theories of Adolescence.* New York: McGraw-Hill.

Niebuhr. H. R. 1929. *The Social Sources of Denominationalism.* New York: Meridian.

Rochford, E. B. Jr. 1985. *Hare Krishna in America.* New Brunswick, N.J.: Rutgers University Press.

———. 1989. "Factionalism, Group Defection, and Schism in the Hare Krishna Movement." *Journal for the Scientific Study of Religion* 28: 162–179.

———. 1992. "Changing Patterns of Socialization with Hare Krishna: Education, Economics, and Transformation." Paper presented at the meetings of the American Sociological Association, Pittsburgh, Penn., August.

———. 1995a. "Family Structure, Commitment, and Involvement in the Hare Krishna movement." *Sociology of Religion* 56(2): 153–175.

———. 1995b. "Hare Krishna in America: Growth, Decline, and Accommodation." Pp. 215–221 in T. Miller, ed., *America's Alternative Religions.* Albany: State University of New York Press.

———. 1997. "Family Formation, Culture, and Change in the Hare Krishna Movement." *ISKCON Communication Journal* 5(2): 61–82.

———. 1998a. "Reactions of Hare Krishna Devotees to Scandals of Leaders' Misconduct." Pp. 101–117 in A. Shupe, ed., *Wolves Within the Fold: Religious Leadership and Abuses of Power.* New Brunswick, N.J.: Rutgers University Press.

———. 1998b. "Child Abuse in the Hare Krishna Movement: 1971–1986." *ISKCON Communication Journal* 6(1): 43–69.

Schneider J., and P. Conrad. 1993. "In the Closet with Illness: Epilepsy, Stigma Potential, and Information Control." Pp. 205–221 in D. Kelly, ed., *Deviant Behavior.* New York: St. Martin's Press.

Silver, I. 1996. "Role Transitions, Objects, and Identity." *Symbolic Interaction* 19(1): 1–20.

Snow, D., and R. Machalek. 1982. "On the Presumed Fragility of Unconventional Beliefs." *Journal for the Scientific Study of Religion* 21: 15–26.

Snow, D., and C. Phillips. 1980. "The Lofland-Stark Conversion Model: A Critical Reassessment." *Social Problems* 27: 430–447.

Stark, R. 1987. "How New Religions Succeed: A Theoretical Model." Pp. 11–29 in D. Bromley and P. Hammond, eds., *The Future of New Religious Movements.* Macon, Ga.: Mercer University Press.

Stone, G. 1981. "Appearance and the Self: A Slightly Revised Version." Pp. 187–202 in G. Stone and H. Farberman, eds., *Social Psychology Through Symbolic Interaction.* New York: Wiley.

Wilson, B. 1987. "Factors in the Failure of the New Religious Movements." Pp. 30–45 in D. Bromley and P. Hammond, eds., *The Future of New Religious Movements.* Macon, Ga.: Mercer University Press.

———. 1991. *The Social Dimensions of Sectarianism.* Oxford, U.K.: Clarendon Press.

CHAPTER 3

In Whose Interest?

SEPARATING CHILDREN FROM MOTHERS IN THE SULLIVAN INSTITUTE/FOURTH WALL COMMUNITY

AMY SISKIND

This chapter describes a unique "ideology of the family" and its impact on childrearing practices in a utopian psychotherapeutic community that existed for thirty years on the Upper West Side of Manhattan in New York City. The community was founded in 1957, originally as a psychoanalytic institute, based on the ideas of Harry Stack Sullivan. Its members lived communally and founded a leftist political theater company. The "Sullivanians" were both a product of, and a response to, the social and political ferment taking place in American society during the postwar period.[1] Although the Sullivan Institute never claimed more than four hundred members at one time, it was in many ways a microcosm of the sociocultural upheavals of that period, beginning in the late 1950s. The membership of the community consisted mostly of middle to upper-class intellectuals, artists, and professionals, reflecting the demographics of the Upper West Side at that time. For this reason, the history of the community's rise and fall is of greater social significance than the actual percentage of any population that was directly affected. The Sullivan Institute/Fourth Wall (SI/FW) community claimed for itself a role as the spearhead of the psychoanalytic, political, and cultural avant-garde in New York City.[2]

The 1960s and 1970s were a period of experimentation for many members of the baby-boom generation, which enjoyed a much longer phase of youth relatively free from responsibilities than had prior generations. Many of the people who joined the Sullivan Institute/Fourth Wall were young adults "in between" college and graduate school, uncertain about career decisions, and ambivalent toward marriage. The community provided a context within which they could explore various career possibilities (at least in the 1960s and 1970s), experiment with sexual relationships, and have a strong support system for their endeavors.

The delayed age of marriage for certain segments of the baby-boom generation (predominantly the educated middle class) was the result of many factors, among them the women's movement, the "sexual revolution," the integration of women into the workforce, the rising cost of living after 1976, and an ethic of "expressive" individualism. The SI/FW community evolved to address the changing needs of this population.

As Steven Tipton (1982) argues, the demise of the New Left and the rise of the counterculture at approximately the same time (early 1970s) left many young adults floundering with respect to the moral rules governing their lives. Many middle-class youths of the 1960s could not accept their parents' answers to the existential questions of life. The SI/FW community attempted to resolve conflicts between the "new" answers and the old social structures. Although the community may have started out as an attempt to provide a progressive alternative to the rather rigid family structure of the 1950s, this alternative was no less restrictive and in many cases produced more social dislocation and personal pain than its predecessor.

I am writing from the dual perspective of a sociologist-researcher and a former member who spent her childhood in this group. My experience as a participant-observer was gained (at the time, unwittingly) during my involvement in the community between the ages of five and sixteen and again between twenty and thirty-one. Through my husband, I have gained total access to documents and other secondary data, such as court records and ex-members' published accounts.[3] My purpose in embarking on this study is to describe, analyze, and criticize this community's unique attempt to subvert mainstream cultural practices and family values.

The History and Ideology

This community was initially founded as a psychoanalytic institute in New York City in 1957. The founders viewed this enterprise as an attempt to build on the theories and clinical work of Harry Stack Sullivan. Sullivan (1892–1949) was a well-known American psychiatrist and psychoanalytic theorist and one of the founders of the William Alanson White Institute in New York City and the Washington School of Psychiatry in Washington, D.C. One of his former students, Jane Pearce, M.D., cofounded the Sullivan Institute with her husband, Saul Newton. Not a psychotherapist by training, Newton held an administrative position at the William Alanson White Institute. Newton had been an active member of the Communist Party of the United States and had fought in the Spanish Civil War with the Abraham Lincoln Brigade. Pearce and Newton attempted to integrate Marxist and psychoanalytic theories with regard to developmental psychology and psychoanalytic theory.

For Pearce and Newton, the traditional white middle-class nuclear family of the postwar period was the cornerstone of the capitalist society they were determined to eliminate. They viewed the relationship of mothers to their children not only as the cause of almost all psychopathology but also as the source of all individual limitations. The mother was the first agent of repression in the individual's life. Only those needs of the infant that she met would become conscious; all others would be repressed by the child. In this view, the mother-child relationship was a microcosm of the injustice built into the capitalist system; the relationships between capitalist and worker, property owner and serf, master and slave, were thus recapitulated within the nuclear family of the 1940s and 1950s. For children to become healthy and politically radical adults, according to Pearce and Newton, changes in the structure of the family and in childrearing practices were necessary.

Social Organization

The patients of Sullivan Institute therapists, after a brief period in therapy, would be invited to become members. If they accepted, they were directed to break off contact with their families of origin and move into communal, same-sex apartments. The mainstream (white) nuclear family of 1950s America was the "straw man" against which the leaders and therapists of the Sullivan Institute leveled their critiques and sought alternatives to "traditional" family life.

In the formative years of the group, childbearing was limited to therapists and favored patients because the ideology of the leaders held that only the most "mature" individuals should have children. *Maturity* was a relative term, and its definition rested solely in the hands of the leadership. In later years more patient-members were allowed to have children, but the leadership exercised strict control over their choice of partners and their living situations.

Children born within the group were raised by full-time caregivers, who received directives not only from parents but also from the leadership and therapists. Many were sent to outside boarding schools; others lived within the community but spent very little time with their parents.

Psychoanalytical Theory and Restructuring of the Family

The "demonization" of mothers by these therapists was linked to a variety of cultural trends of the 1950s. One of these was certainly a popularization of Freudian theory. Writers for women's magazines and childrearing "experts" placed a great deal of the responsibility and the "blame" for childrearing on mothers during this period. In the formative years of the community (1957–1970), "the creation of hitherto unconceived social forms" (Pearce and Newton 1963:7) was undertaken via therapists who advised their patients to formally break off contact with their families of origin, by prohibiting childless patients from having children, and by requiring members who were already parents to either send their children out of the community to boarding schools or to hire full-time child care workers and housekeepers.

The first step in the creation of the therapeutic community involved a social and emotional restructuring of the adult membership. This involved two primary interventions on the part of the therapists, and these took place more or less simultaneously during the early years of "Sullivanian" psychoanalysis. One was to persuade patients to cut off contact with their parents, siblings, and other members of their families of origin. The other was to encourage the formation of primary groups through group living situations.

Whereas Freudian theory places a great deal of emphasis on the innate libidinous drives of the human species, arguing that every human must internalize his or her culture through the relationship to a libidinal object (i.e., a parent), Pearce and Newton maintained that individuals are merely *products* of the families and societies they grow up in. Newton and Pearce did not believe that infants are born with inherited personality traits or with innate characteristics and motivations in the Freudian sense. Thus, the traumas and pain that a child encounters are caused by parental hatred or envy of the child.

Therapists used various techniques to convince their patients of the truth of this assertion. For example, if a patient brought in a photograph showing her parent(s) holding her, the therapist would interpret the expression on the parent's face as indicating anger or discomfort, thereby demonstrating that the parent had not been "happy" about caring for the patient as a child. Naturally, in the course of life within the community, many parents of community members died. These deaths were often interpreted by Sullivan Institute therapists as "suicidal" in nature. That is, a parent's death was interpreted to be the result of self-destructive and/or self-neglectful behavior. Such interpretations were used to reinforce the overall picture of the parent as a destructive force in the patient's life. Therapists interpreted most memories and dreams as referring back to the parents; almost all menacing figures in dreams were deemed images of the patient's father or mother (usually the mother), and in memories any negative experiences were attributed to some action or inaction by the parent. In the case of married patients, aspects of the patient's relationship with the parent that were found to be destructive were often identified within the patient's relationship with his/her spouse. In other words, patients had transposed the unhealthy dynamics that had existed in their relationships with their parents into their marital relationships. Many patients were encouraged to have affairs while they were married and even to end their marriages. Several married couples joined the community, but none remained married if they continued to be members.

As the patient-therapist relationship became much stronger over the years, the patients gradually accepted this notion of their parents as the primary repressive force in their lives and in most cases told their parents that they would no longer have any contact with them.[4] The emotional impact of this decision was extremely powerful. The community began to see itself as the "rational" substitute for the family, and the therapist played the role of house parent in absentia or counselor.

In concert with this attempt to destroy the traditional nuclear family, Jane Pearce and Saul Newton incorporated the concept of a Leninist political vanguard into the hierarchy of leadership in the Sullivanian community. They—and later, other training analysts, Joan Harvey, Ralph Klein, and Helen Moses—were considered to be the most emotionally mature and therefore the political and interpersonal "vanguard" of the community.

Group living situations were held by the therapist/leaders to be the environments most conducive to the healthy growth of the patient. Nuclear family attachments were replaced by intense relationships among peers, and these were guided by the norms and values set forth in the therapeutic relationship. The development of nonerotic same-sex relationships was touted by the Sullivanian therapists as one of the most important components of "growing up." Almost all patients who became members of the community lived in apartments (usually group apartments) with other members of the same sex. At the same time, the practice of what could be called "casual sex" was encouraged; members were urged to seek out other members they wanted to have sex with but discouraged from forming any exclusive and/or romantic attachment with them. One informant, M. Z., describes the process of learning the community "rules," which included breaking with his family:

> And then I started learning the rules, which I was given the reasons for them, but I wasn't really sure. Some of the rules were that you shouldn't have a girlfriend because it's bad for you. You shouldn't have anything to do with your family, and you should trust the people who were in the group. I remember S. R. [M. Z.'s therapist] said one time, "It's like being in a large boat with other people having paddles, and it's much easier to paddle upstream with people who are going the same way." And then there was the stuff about dating, and for some reason it would be terrible to sleep alone. It just was the worst, so every night that you didn't have a date with a woman, you had to sleep with someone else. And there would be telephone calls that came into the house: "This is Mary Jones or Tom Smith; anyone in your house that doesn't have a date?"

This encouragement of promiscuous behavior resonated with the "sexual revolution" occurring in the larger society between the late 1950s "Beat" generation and the 1960s–1970s "hippie" counterculture.

Group living provided a substitute for family living. The role of "roommate" consisted of providing emotional, physical, and sometimes financial support for others. This expectation could be clearly seen in the context of the practice of "house meetings," which each group apartment held on a weekly basis. The meetings were primarily concerned with administering and maintaining the apartments, but they were also arenas for social control. Individuals would be asked to speak about their family histories or about their relationships with other roommates or possibly with other patient/members. Individuals who were becoming romantically involved with another person were targeted because it was felt by the therapist/leaders that this impoverished the individuals' other relationships—specifically, those with roommates. If a roommate was doing something considered to be wrong by the leadership, he or she could expect to be "confronted" about it. If a roommate expressed attitudes in a house meeting that seemed problematic, the members would discuss this with their therapists. The therapists might then consult with the leadership about the person's attitudes, and finally the therapist of the "offending" roommate would be contacted. Members would be instructed to confront the roommate in a house meeting, and they would often be told exactly what to say.

In sum, adult members of the SI/FW community were required in almost all cases to cut off or severely curtail their relationships with families of origin and discouraged from forming strong dyadic attachments. They were strongly advised to live in same-sex group apartments that functioned both as substitute for the family and surveillance of the individual, whose progress or "resistance" would be reported by roommates to their therapists and by their therapists to the other therapists.

Childbearing

Since parents, especially mothers, were held responsible for almost all psychological (and even physical or social) difficulties their children might experience in later life, parenting took on enormous valence in this community. To become eligible to have children, the members had to consult with their psychotherapists. Some members were not approved on the basis of their supposedly inadequate emotional and psychological development, and those who were approved were judged by the leadership as sufficiently "mature." It was reported that Helen Moses and Saul Newton believed that couples who had children within the community would become accustomed to "communal" childrearing and consequently would be unable to leave the community. In other words, the children would provide a kind of "glue" that would attach members to the group.

Between 1957 and 1960, no children were born. In 1960, Joan Harvey, the current wife of Saul Newton, had her first child. After this time, certain therapists who worked within the institute were "approved" to bear children. Until the early 1970s, however, there were very few births. Then, in 1974, Helen Moses and a few other female patients had children.[5] The "new generation" of patients who were entering the community at that time were quite young (early to midtwenties) and lacked significant financial means, were finishing their education, or were trying to establish their careers. Thus, childbearing was not an important issue until the early 1980s when some younger patients (who had initially entered the community as low-cost patients of the "trainee" group) began to express the desire to become parents. Those individuals who were "approved" were then required to consult their therapists in choosing a father or mother for the child.

Prospective parents might choose to go solo or find a partner. In the 1960s, two male therapists chose to have children without partners and adopted babies from South America. Three other therapist couples had children in partnership during the 1960s. In the early 1970s, three female patients became single parents and bore children who had no acknowledged fathers.

Another important procedure in the late 1970s and early 1980s was the custom of using a "sperm pool" for the Sullivanian women who wanted to conceive. This custom had reportedly been started by Helen Moses, who while married to Saul Newton found it difficult to become pregnant. She was said to have sought out "eligible" males at that time to impregnate her. However, there was at least one other member at that time who used this method. Later, the process became institutionalized. Several women who decided to become pregnant were assisted by their therapists in choosing four to five discreet male members to "help" them conceive. The "help" did not involve any emotional commitment beyond the initial assistance with conception. The rough outline of this custom was that when the woman was ovulating, she would contact this group of men and then schedule sexual intercourse with them all during her ovulation period. This practice maximized her chances of getting pregnant in any one month. Several women used this method and were successful in achieving rapid conception.

Although the children were very much identified with their parents, the fact that the parents had not chosen each other, but had been chosen by the leadership, weakened their ties to each other and consequently strengthened their ties to the community. Children who were born via the "sperm pool" method were in some sense children of the whole community. The men who had participated in the sperm pools could look at various children in the community and wonder whether they might be the biological father of some of these children. By breaking the usual social link between fatherhood as a social role and biological parenting, the community challenged yet another aspect of the "traditional" family, and the bonds between group members were strengthened.[6]

This practice appears to have been initiated by the female leadership, and it might be argued that it served to strengthen the position of women in the community as the recognizable biological parents. But because large numbers of children were adopted, the practice actually served to reinforce the authority of the leadership over their patients even more. The leaders felt they were in the vanguard of the feminist movement because they encouraged women to renounce the role of mother and housewife and the community was "ahead of its time" in allowing mothers to fully devote themselves to their careers, which was unusual for middle-class women between 1962 and 1973. But in effect children were hostages who could be taken away if their mothers did not behave, which enhanced the leadership's control over female community members.

The relationship between parents, who had been approved in many cases *because* their relationship was not romantic, was often strained. Even though the chosen father participated in the sperm pool as one of several "helpers," his biological paternity was not assured. Parents maintained separate residences and were seldom emotionally intimate. The community placed considerable financial strain on parents, and this often caused friction. All these factors contributed to the sense that the individual's primary tie was to the community and not to a spouse or child.

Childrearing

In the mid-1970s, Saul Newton legally married Helen Moses, his sixth wife, and Joan Harvey, who had been Newton's fifth wife, married Ralph Klein. The two couples bought a building together where they lived on separate floors as couples but with separate rooms. They were the only couples in the community that lived together. Although the leaders were the only married couples in the community who practiced cohabitation, these were not monogamous marriages; both spouses were free to have sexual relationships with other members and did so.[7] The rest of the therapists were considered to be directly below the leadership and the patients below the therapists regarding their level of interpersonal growth. These assumptions resulted in an elaborate and rigid hierarchy of political, social, and sexual power within the community.

The children usually lived with their mothers on a regular basis and spent one or two nights a week with their fathers. Neither parent was expected to spend what would conventionally be considered an optimal amount of time with their children (see Pearce 1963). Full-time child care was contracted on the basis of the beliefs that, first, no parent should have to take care of a child full-time, and, second, mothers usually behave in an envious and hateful manner toward their children. Sullivan first articulated the possibility of psychoses and neuroses arising out of specifically pathological mother-child relationships. Also, books such as Dr. Benjamin Spock's *Baby and Child Care* that were published after World War II promulgated the notion that the child's problems are caused by the parents. Since the mother was the primary caregiver, it was assumed, by Spock and other experts of the time, that whatever emotional difficulties the child had, she was responsible for them. Pearce and Newton expanded these assumptions to almost all aspect of mother-child relations.

After 1976, children born to members of the Sullivan Institute/Fourth Wall community were cared for by full-time baby-sitters. There were two types of baby-sitters in the community: full-time paid workers and voluntary workers. "Full-time" usually meant that baby sitters were "on duty" twelve to fifteen hours a day. These individuals were often community members, but in the early years and in the later years outsiders were hired as well. Community members also "volunteered" their time to do child care. It was part of the ideology that spending time with children could help the individual gain insight into his or her own personality and thereby lead to personal growth. Members who were interested in becoming parents were encouraged to offer their services as baby sitters as a form of "apprenticeship" for parenting. If a member was asked to baby-sit for a child, this was a sign that he or she was thought well of by the leadership, because all decisions regarding child care had to go through the therapists. Therefore, members who were baby sitters for the leadership gained a great deal of status in being selected for these positions. However, the full-time baby-sitters received low wages compared with the costs of living in this community or with the "going rate" for full-time child care in New York City.

Boarding Schools

Around 1970, nonleadership parents were instructed to send their children to boarding schools. For some children, this began as early as three years of age, the rationale being the less exposure there was to parents, the better the child's mental health would be. Conversely, parents were urged to "get on with their lives," meaning that they would be psychologically more fit if they developed interests and activities apart from their children. Pearce and Newton believed that one of the primary causes of maternal envy, and of neurosis in general, is a dearth of mothers' activities and interests that would stimulate their creativity as their children grew less dependent on them and finally left home. Therefore, as long as a parent provided his or her children with good child care, education, clothing, and money, it was preferable that they spend as little time together as possible. Judy Collins (1987:171), a well-known singer and a patient of two Sullivanian therapists between 1963 and 1973, describes the intrusion of therapy into her relationship with her son:

> Through Clark's therapist, the core of the Sullivanian principles began to emerge: they truly believed children and parents do not belong together. I have often puzzled over the strong relationship I had with these doctors. . . . The Sullivanian doctrine, I was to learn through Clark's and my experience, is separation, so that the neurosis caused by the family doesn't grow. I was Clark's mother; I had to be the problem.
>
> "Clark is in a total rage at you!" said Saul. I was frightened by his strong language. Saul was always extreme in his diagnoses. He told my therapist, Julie, and Clark's therapist, Mildred, that Clark must get away from me immediately and go to boarding school. I moved as though I had touched a hot stove. Saul Newton's words sent a spasm of panic through me. I didn't want to be the cause of Clark's troubles.

In 1976, one of the patients who had sent her son to boarding school was sued for custody by her ex-husband (the father of the child), who was not a member of the community. He claimed that D. A. was an unfit mother because she had sent her son away to summer camp at age three and to boarding school at age five. D. A.'s therapist was called to testify in the case, and he affirmed that she was not fit to raise the child and that she had been advised to send her son away "for his own good." On the basis of this testimony, the judge (predictably and understandably) awarded custody of the child to the father. A section of the court's judgment reads:

> Concededly, because of her heavy work and school schedules and psychiatric analysis plaintiff did not visit [her son] very often. In fact rarely. When [he] visited her in New York City, he was usually left in the care of baby-sitters, due to plaintiff's busy schedule. . . . The court must conclude that plaintiff is unable to accept the role of a mother and duties of motherhood. She continually defers parental responsibilities to others through schools and camps. . . . Plaintiff is still more concerned with herself, her school and her career. Undoubtedly plaintiff loves her son but spends more time with her therapist than she does with her son. She has been in therapy since 1971. ("*Bolinger* v. *Bollinger*" 1976)

This decision effectively ended the practice of sending children away to school, but it did not prevent several situations in which children suffered the emotional pangs of early and lengthy separation from their parents. Some of these children experienced debilitating psychological problems in later life. One eventually committed suicide, one attempted suicide, several became heavy drug users or alcoholics, and one became a repeat felon. This emotional anguish is expressed in this excerpt written by the stepmother, Alice, of a child named Katherine:

> Nine years ago, Virginia [Katherine's birth mother] sabotaged our plan to have Katherine live with Steven and me. Katherine was fourteen, and it had been more than ten years since she had lived in a family. I expected some passive disapproval from Virginia and the commune, little else. Our plan, after all, demanded almost nothing from Virginia, who knew that Katherine was unhappy to be so far away in New Mexico where the commune always sent their children to school. I thought, with Steven and I taking care of Katherine's day-to-day needs, Virginia might play the part traditionally reserved for divorced fathers. She could visit with her daughter now and then, and reap the benefits of having a teenage daughter who was eager to admire her mother's accomplishments.
>
> "She cries and says that she's miserable," Steven explained. "She wants to live with us. That's all she keeps saying."
>
> The headmaster told Steven that Katherine was rebellious and refusing authority. Our home represented far more than escape from school, he reassured us. It was a chance to live with a parent, a chance for Katherine to make a long-held fantasy a reality.
>
> "It would be very good for her," he said.
>
> Legally, Virginia was the custodial parent, and Steven also feared reprisals from the commune, but the headmaster was willing to take the risk of releasing Katherine in our custody.
>
> "What did Virginia say?" we asked Katherine as soon as she hung up the phone that first day home.
>
> "She didn't say much of anything," Katherine said. As the day un-

> folded, I grew confident that Virginia would do little to interfere with her daughter's new life. We relaxed. I helped Katherine unpack, and we discussed how we'd make small alterations in her bedroom. . . .
>
> Suddenly, the dog scrambled to his feet and barked angrily; the brass door knocker resounded throughout the house.
>
> "Who the hell is that?" Steven said loudly, and then, without opening the front door: "Who is it?"
>
> "Katherine! Katherine!" A shrill female voice: "Give me Katherine! I want my baby. My Baby!"
>
> "Oh my god, it's Mom," Katherine said. From the kitchen I saw the beams of flashlights. There were two people at the front door alone with Virginia. A third beam of light moved from the driveway toward the porch.
>
> "She's not alone," I said.
>
> "This is a commune scare tactic," Steven said. "Lock the kitchen door and the porch door. Hurry."
>
> . . . "Come back in the morning, Virginia." Steven opened the door a crack, positioning his weight behind it, so that he could shut it quickly again if he needed to.
>
> . . . Two weeks went by with no word from Virginia. Katherine broke the silence to telephone her mother and announce that she'd begun to menstruate: "So what do you want me to do about it?" Virginia responded. Katherine lay crying on my bed: "A girl wants her mother at a time like this."
>
> . . . For most of Katherine's life, Virginia had been a mother by long distance. Twice a year she saw Katherine for one day when she bought Katherine clothes and took her to the dentist and doctor for checkups. Katherine blamed the commune for coming between them. . . .
>
> After the third week, Virginia telephoned: "You have two weeks to return to boarding school. If you don't, I will wash my hands of you entirely. I will never speak to you again or have anything to do with you."
>
> . . . "If you ignore the threat, Virginia will give in," we told Katherine, but she was not prepared to take the risk. We did not blame her. (quoted in Neufeld 1989:80–81)

The tactics employed by Virginia were commonly used by community members to deal with threatening outsiders. They were almost always masterminded by Saul Newton and carried out by trusted members. Virginia was accompanied by two other group members in order to intimidate Steven, Alice, and Katherine. In most of these cases the dialogue was scripted by Newton and the individual's therapist, and Virginia would have been following specific orders regarding both her statements and her actions.

The Economics of Childrearing

In the 1969–1978 period, with the inception of the training program, the cost of therapy with a trainee was quite low relative to the amount charged by most psychotherapists at that time. Trainees began working for as little as $5.00 an hour, which made it possible for college students and other young people to afford therapy. Group living was also cheap, since the average apartment had approximately five members who split the rent of a relatively inexpensive (at that time) apartment on the Upper West Side.

The amount of money required for membership rose continually from 1970 on. Whereas in the 1960s students, artists, and freelance workers of various types could live without working full-time, in the 1970s the cost of therapy and of group living went up each year. The combination of these factors with the overall economic decline in the United States in the late 1970s resulted in the defection of many members.[8] Others took full-time jobs as typesetters (a high-paid skill that had recently been deunionized) or as waiters or waitresses, taxi drivers, or any other work that could provide enough money to pay for therapy and apartment expenses. Graduate students used government loans to pay their living expenses, thereby accruing large debts. Other members went to their families for money to pay for their therapy.

Many members who were also parents and therefore had even greater demands placed on them worked double shifts or held down two jobs. Although parents in most cultures have added expenses, it was much more expensive to have children in the Sullivan Institute community because the definition of a decent life for a child included full-time (and more) child care, private school, sleep-away camp, and, often, therapy. Many members were heavily in debt. Some borrowed from richer members, others refused to pay taxes, and still others declared bankruptcy. These situations were addressed in therapy—in fact some patients spent most of their therapy sessions discussing their financial problems. However, each patient was responsible for earning whatever it cost to live within the community; it never occurred to the leadership that the cost of therapy and all the attendant expenses might be more than some individuals could manage. In a group that professed to have a communal orientation, each individual was held responsible for raising the funds necessary to pay the expenses of life inside the community.

Custody Issues, Media Exposure, and the Decline of the Sullivan Institute

There are five known cases in which children were "given up" by their mothers to other group members on the advice of the leadership. In summer of 1974, H. S. gave birth to a son. Soon after the leadership decided that she was experiencing postpartum depression. Saul Newton and Joan Harvey (who had displaced Jane Pearce as leader by this time) then decided that H. S. was "too angry" to be a parent, and the baby was adopted by another woman in the community who was in favor with the leadership at the time. Over the period of 1974 to 1984, three other children were either formally or informally removed from their mothers' custody. Several other mothers, and one or two fathers, were also ordered by the leadership to have either minimal contact or no contact with their children. For those members who had children, the possibility of losing custody was a constant threat held over them by the leadership—until one mother rebelled.

In 1985, Marice Pappo, who had been a member of the community for fifteen years, was ordered by her therapist, Ralph Klein, to cease having any contact with her infant daughter, who was around two months old at that time. The father of the child, Christopher Hoy, upheld Klein's orders. Pappo had been very close to one of two therapists who had recently left the community and called on him to help her defect from the community with her child.[9] The act of contacting an ex-member in this way was totally forbidden and indicated that Pappo was ready to defy the leadership. With the assistance of her ex-therapist friend and an outside attorney, she hired two private detectives to help her physically seize the child, and she went into hiding (on her lawyer's advice). As part of her lawyer's strategy to help her maintain custody of her daughter, he contacted the press. A front-page article appeared in the *Village Voice* (Conason and McGarrahan 1986), and both television and print media coverage of the story resulted. This was the first time that either a member or an ex-member of this community had been willing to speak to the press,[10] and many individuals were contacted by journalists and recounted their versions of life within the community. The impact of this event on the members and on the future of the Sullivan Institute/Fourth Wall Community was overwhelming.

> *Hoy* v. *Pappo* . . . has blown open the closed world of the Sullivanians and the Fourth Wall. All the lawyers for Hoy, two of whom have either quit or been dismissed, have been infuriated by the judge's ruling that the lifestyle and philosophy of Hoy and his associates are relevant to . . . [the baby's] safety. Judge Shackman may have been influenced by the Sullivanians' eerie behavior on the first day of the hearing. It had hardly begun when Judge Shackman was informed by court officers that some members were circling the courthouse in cars and communicating by walkie-talkie (Conason and McGarrahan 1986:57)

Hoy v. *Pappo* was settled out of court in Pappo's favor, after several ex-members testified concerning the Sullivanian community's practice of divesting patient-members of their parental rights. "Miss J." testified that she had not spent more than three days with her oldest daughter, who was ten years old when she was sent to boarding school, from 1976 to 1985. She had stopped allowing her daughter to come home for vacations at the behest of her therapist, Marc Rice. In a February 11, 1986, deposition, A. W. described the relationship of parents and children within the community as follows:

> The relationship that parents had with their children was intensely scrutinized. I was very involved with several children as a baby-sitter and on many occasions sat with parents as they talked to either Helen Moses or Saul Newton who dictated the day to day care of their children. One child that I loved very much, D. M. was the child of J. M. and T. P. J. M. stopped seeing Danny when he was less than one year old and had no relationship with him at all until he was four. He then was allowed by his analyst to see D. M., though only for an hour or two a week. When Danny was four and a half years old he became intensely afraid of Saul Newton and Helen Moses, who were the parents of his friend M. Everyone else in the Fourth Wall was also scared of these two individuals and D.'s reaction seemed to me to be an honest mimicry of the adults around him. However it was promulgated that T. P. (the mother) was the cause of D.'s fear of Saul. For an entire summer D. was segregated from all other children in the Fourth Wall's country residence, and consequently had no children to play with. He was told that he had to stop being afraid before he could play with his friends again. In the middle of the summer D. was taken away from his mother and given to his father, who had little to do with him for three and a half years.

This testimony, combined with the strange behavior of members in and out of the courtroom, led to Hoy's decision to cede custody to Pappo. Within two years of the settlement, Hoy defected from the community and rejoined Pappo. They left New York City with their daughter soon afterward.

The *Pappo* case and the departure of two high-ranking therapists the same year had a devastating effect on the community. The *Village Voice* article, the television coverage, and news reports placed the community under intense public scrutiny for the first time in its thirty-year history. Reporters with television cameras appeared at community residences videotaping members as they entered and left. The impact of this sudden notoriety was experienced differently by various members.

At roughly the same time as the custody case was launched, other ex-members began to bring legal proceedings against the leadership and management of the building that had been ostensibly purchased in their names. These ex-members were requesting that they receive compensation for their investments in the building after they had been expelled or moved out. The case was settled in the plaintiffs' favor. The leadership interpreted the defeat in the *Pappo* case and the loss of the civil case as a declaration of war by ex-members against the community. Soon after this, two other ex-members, Paul Sprecher and Michael Bray, initiated custody proceedings against their ex-wives, Julia Agee and Alice Dobash, respectively, in order to remove their children from the community.

The majority of members were shielded by the leaders from any knowledge of these events, with the exception of the press coverage. Once the *Village Voice* article was published, a flurry of media activity ensued. Members could not help but be affected by the public reaction to the article. Some members were asked at their jobs if they were involved with the "Sullivanians," and some children of members were taunted at school by other children whose parents had read the article.

The media exposure affected the membership in several ways. It resulted in the leadership creating an ever-more insular, separate, and paranoid community. It raised secret doubts in the minds of members, who could not help but recognize some of the claims made in the article as accurate. It also prompted the leadership to solicit even greater sums of money from members in order to finance the ongoing court cases. Nevertheless, the media exposure forced the leadership to mitigate some of its most restrictive practices, such as prohibiting individuals from bearing children and removing children from their parents' care.

The custody cases were viewed by the leadership and by many of the members, as a battle between the forces of good and evil. In the *Pappo* case, trusted members had been assigned to follow some ex-members who were believed to know the whereabouts of the mother and child who had "escaped." In the Sprecher/Agee and Bray/Dobash cases (the two fathers who were suing together), group members were asked to form a "dirt squad" assigned to dig up incriminating information about the plaintiffs' characters and the characters of their witnesses. Several members cooperated in a plan to intimidate both of the defector therapists (one of whom was Bray) through violence. The first therapist was accosted on a subway platform by two men in hooded sweatshirts and threatened with further violence if he continued to assist Pappo with her custody case. Bray was assaulted in the vestibule of his apartment building by two men who beat him and broke his glasses. He recognized their voices as two members of the community's "security squad."

Both Paul Sprecher and Mike Bray initially sought joint custody of their children when they left the community but were denied access by their ex-wives, who were very close to the leaders. Agee (Sprecher's wife) was Newton's lover and one of his favorites; Dobash was a therapist who lived with the leadership. In the Bray/Dobosh case, the couple had been married but decided to divorce for financial reasons. Sprecher was married to Agee when he left the community, so his case included a petition for divorce, as well as for custody of their child. Sprecher and Agee had chosen each other; they had had a romantic relationship. This was not the case with Bray and Dobosh; they had been only friendly acquaintances before Dobosh asked Bray to father her children.

The two cases were to be tried together, but Sprecher's went to trial first. The arguments that were made by Sprecher and Bray in their cases were based on the allegation that Agee and Dobosh had ceded their parental decision-making responsibilities to the leadership. In other words, the fathers argued that the mothers were not fulfilling the role of parents in the sense that they were not making the types of decisions that parents are expected to make on a day-to-day basis. These decisions included weaning, administration of medicines, discipline, organization of "play-dates," school selection, caregiver selection, and decisions about how much time to spend with their children. To prove these allegations, both fathers had to provide evidence that the Sullivan Institute/Fourth Wall community was an authoritarian group that exercised extraordinary power over the lives of its members.

In the wake of the *Pappo* case, the newspapers and talk shows were eager to cover these trials as well. Sprecher's case was finally settled out of court when, after two weeks of testimony by Agee's ex-therapist (who testified for Sprecher), she agreed to leave the SI/FW community. Bray's case was also settled, after approximately four years of litigation, when his ex-wife agreed to a joint custody arrangement and they agreed to move to the same community, so that the children could go back and forth with relative ease.

The impact of the custody cases on the Sullivan Institute/Fourth Wall community was manifold. On the one hand, the publicity and the large sums of money required from the membership for the court cases brought the community closer together in an "us-against-them" bunker mentality. On the other hand, the onus was on the leadership to disprove some of the allegations to the members in order to maintain their allegiance. Regulations governing childbearing and mate selection within the community were suddenly relaxed. There was a large cohort of women at this time who wanted to have children and who were nearing their last years of fertility. Several of these women became pregnant, and some of them decided to live with the fathers of their children. This would not have been permitted in an earlier phase. It is safe to conclude that the pressure of the cases and the earlier "defections" forced the leadership to loosen their control over the remaining members of the community.

The Pappo/Hoy trial occurred in 1986. By 1992, the community had dissolved. Saul Newton died in 1992, and his wife and ex-wife fought over the leadership of the group. During this period, it became obvious to most of the remaining members that not much was left of the community that was desirable. Most left the group at this time, causing the gradual dissolution of the entire group. What remains now are twenty to thirty individuals who are still patients and "friends" of Joan Harvey and Ralph Klein, even though both of them surrendered their licenses to the Office of Professional Discipline after being charged by ex-members and found guilty of several breaches of professional conduct. Helen Moses recently had her license revoked and a $10,000 fine imposed as a result of charges leveled against her by ex-patients and supervisees.

Conclusion

Rosabeth Moss Kanter (1972:236) views utopian communities as "important not only as social ventures in and of themselves, but also as challenges to the assumptions on which current institutions are organized." In this context, the Sullivan Institute/Fourth Wall community represents an interesting social arrangement and a challenge to the social institutions of marriage and the family. The control that Sullivan Institute/Fourth Wall leaders exercised over the lives of the membership was extensive. On the basis of my observations, I could argue that some individuals seem to prefer not to have "too much" freedom regarding their life choices—perhaps more so during young adulthood than later in their lives. Erich Fromm (1941) contends that the development of the self does not take place simultaneously with the process of individuation. In other words, human beings develop the abilities necessary to survive and function independently of their parents (or caregivers) before they develop the inner mechanisms that make this independence emotionally viable. Thus, young adults may feel a greater need for guidance than they would be likely to accept from their parents and may therefore be inclined to choose charismatic individuals to guide their decisions, often in the context of high control communities.

A combination of the "generation gap" between the late 1940s and 1950s, the social upheavals of the 1950s and 1960s, and the sophisticated "technologies of the self" was responsible for the existence of this community. Traditional family values were in question; alternative social forms had not yet developed. The changing economy effected corresponding changes in family structure. By now, a pluralistic range of familial arrangements has become accepted in the more tolerant parts of the United States. The family of the 1940s and 1950s that the Sullivan Institute/Fourth Wall community was designed to counteract had all but faded out of existence by the time the group disbanded in the early 1990s.

Notes

1. I put Sullivanians in quotes because it is a word used by outsiders. Community members referred to themselves as "the group."
2. The *fourth wall* is a common theatrical term used to describe the invisible wall between the proscenium stage and the audience.
3. My husband, Michael Cohen, was a longtime (thirteen years) Sullivan Institute therapist.
4. Those patients who could not accept the interpretation and its attendant action usually left therapy and the community in a relatively short time.
5. Helen Moses was initially a patient of Jane Pearce before becoming a training analyst and one of the four leaders of the institute and the community.
6. This practice was quite different from the separation of biological parents in the context of adoption, where the biological parents give up their rights and usually do not have contact with the child until adulthood, if then. The intention here is to strengthen the bonds between the adoptive parents and the child.
7. The leaders' marriages were similar in some ways to the "open marriage" concept advocated in a book by O'Neill and O'Neill (1972). This book was referred to by Pearce and Newton.
8. To give an example, one individual who was studying dance left the community because he would not have been able to afford the pursuit of his career if he had stayed.
9. In March and December 1985, two high-level therapists left the group, causing a great deal of upheaval.
10. A 1975 *New York Magazine* article (Black 1975) was written by an outsider whose

only access to the community was several weeks of therapy with a Sullivan Institute psychotherapist. No additional television or print coverage ensued.

References

Black, D. 1975. "Totalitarian Therapy on the Upper West Side." *New York Magazine,* January 23, 12–13, 67–69.

"Bollinger v. Bollinger." 1976. *Law Journal* (May 4): 6–7.

Collins, J. 1987. *Trust Your Heart.* Boston: Houghton Mifflin.

Conason, J., and E. McCarrahan. 1986. "Escape from Utopia." *Village Voice,* April 22, 1, 17–19..

Fromm, E. 1941. *Escape from Freedom.* New York: Avon Books.

Kanter, R. M. 1972. *Commitment and Community: Communes and Utopias in Sociological Perspective.* Cambridge, Mass.: Harvard University Press.

Neufeld, A. 1989. "One Step Away from Mother: A Stepmother's Story." Pp. 77–92 in N. B. Maglin and N. Schniedewind, eds., *Stepfamilies: Voices of Love and Anger.* Philadelphia: Temple University Press.

O'Neill, N., and G. O'Neill. 1972. *Open Marriage: A New Lifestyle for Couples.* New York: Evans.

Pearce, J. 1963. *The Conditions of Human Growth.* New York: Citadel Press.

Tipton, S. M. 1982. *Getting Saved from the Sixties: Moral Meaning in Conversion and Cultural Change.* Berkeley and Los Angeles: University of California Press.

Part II

How Movements Mold Their Children

Chapter 4

God's Children

Physical and Spiritual Growth Among Evangelical Christians

Simon Coleman

Pray for the land of Sweden! Pray for the Swedish people to be saved. Pray for the Prime Minister. . . .

It's war! We have to pray. We're the ones who have to reach out with the Gospel. It won't happen by itself. We shouldn't just sit around gorging on God's Word. We've also got to reach out. There's little time. There's much to do. What are you waiting for? You shouldn't sit around waiting for God to talk to you. . . . Read Mark 16:15–20.

If you're wondering where to get teaching, I recommend the Word of Life in Uppsala. God bless you.—Jonathan Westergård (Nyhetsbrev n.d.)

These words, by a Swedish preacher named Jonathan Westergård, contain many of the sentiments and phrases commonly invoked by other participants in the Protestant Evangelical organization he mentions, Livets Ord (Word of Life) of Uppsala, Sweden. Westergård assumes that his urgent mission, and that of similar Christians, is not to set up a sectarian enclave but to assume responsibility for the spiritual state of the nation and its leaders. Prayer is the chief weapon available to all those engaged in the war he describes, and such urgent activity is justified by a characteristically literal reading of the Bible—the "Go ye into all the world, and preach the gospel" of Mark's sixteenth chapter. Finally, he reveals that his sermon is also a form of self-promotion: for those who have not already heard the good news, a fine new Bible school is available to cater for the whole of Scandinavia and beyond.

Westergård's words are initially significant not because they display any originality, but because they encapsulate so skillfully and concisely much that is said—and constantly repeated—at the Word of Life. Yet there is another reason, closely related to the subject of this book, that they are worth quoting:

Westergård, at the time of writing, while sounding like many of his older counterparts, was probably no more than ten years old. The implied authority contained in his message was derived not from a long lifetime's experience of meditation on the Gospel, but from his ability to deploy an Evangelical rhetoric based on a display of spiritual anointing rather than the fruits of biological or social maturity.

In this chapter, I discuss the roles played by younger children and youth within the Word of Life, a group within which I have worked as a participant-observer since 1986. It was started in 1983 by Ulf Ekman, a former student-priest within the Swedish Lutheran Church who was heavily influenced by a year's training at Kenneth Hagin's Bible Center in Tulsa, Oklahoma. Hagin is well known in the United States as an important figure in the increasingly international Faith Movement of charismatic, Evangelical congregations and Bible schools. The apologists for the movement argue that it combines a strong adherence to biblical principles with a charismatic desire to cultivate a living relationship with God.

The Word of Life Foundation in Uppsala is, like Westergård's sermon, a recognizable product of wider, powerful influences—a replication and further example of the broad Evangelical Protestant revival that has occurred in the United States and beyond since the 1970s (cf. Cox 1984). Like the sermon, the Word of Life derives at least some of its interest from its particular location: the group is remarkable not so much because, like many other contemporary Evangelical organizations, it combines a congregation with a Bible school, media business, and burgeoning sense of a mission to convert the world, but because it is culturally incongruous in a country renowned for its apparent secularity (Coleman 1989, 1991; Martin 1978). Such incongruity has been pointed out by the group's many critics, religious and secular. In common with many new religious movements in the West, the Word of Life has been treated in Sweden as an embodiment of much that is deviant and feared within society (Beckford 1985). It has been seen as a foreign (U.S.–inspired) import proposing politically conservative notions under the guise of religiosity. It has also been accused of recommending a health-and-wealth gospel, offering prosperity to both the bodies and the bank accounts of followers and therefore encouraging trust in the healing powers of prayer as opposed to the methods of medical doctors. Most significantly for present purposes, the group has been accused of brainwashing vulnerable members, not least by setting up and inculcating a notion of the person that is fundamentally opposed to more conventional ideals of the autonomous, freethinking individual.

I do not examine externally derived representations of Word of Life beliefs relating to the person in any great depth in this chapter. I do, however, want to argue that an appreciation of Evangelical Christian notions of personhood is key to an understanding of believers' attitudes toward children. My claim is that two, to some extent contradictory, views of childhood and maturity are evident among these Christians. On the one hand, believers maintain and even elaborate on widely shared (at least in the West) distinctions among children, youths, and adults in their attitudes and conduct. Each of these age groups, and further subdivisions among them, often have separate activities assigned to them within the broader rubric of the Word of Life program of action. Generational divisions are therefore defined and reinforced, to some degree, by functional and spatial distinctions, and in this sense it becomes important to examine the extent to which each division partakes of and creates a separate Evangelical world—even culture—of its own.

On the other hand, I want to argue that such tendencies are significantly undermined by other aspects of belief and practice. In common with many other Evangelical, charismatic Christians, Word of Life members divide the person up into body, mind, and spirit. The former two elements of the person are "of the flesh"—necessary to the state of being human but also fallible and corruptible. The spirit, however, is key to Christian identity and practice: when it is renewed within a person who is born again the Christian both sloughs off the old sinful nature and gains access to divine power. Not only can the Christian take the words of the Bible in new and more personal ways and gain access to the gifts of the spirit (tongues, perhaps prophecy, etc.), but she or he can also use prayer as a means to alter immediate circumstances. I say more about such beliefs later. The important point for the moment is that they set up a fundamental distinction between the biological and the spiritual ("the natural" and "the supernatural" in Word of Life argot). The biological nature of humans is seen as subordinate and subject to the controlling powers of the spirit, and to be born again is to replace an original, physical birth with a supernatural, self-empowering one.

One implication of these beliefs is that conventionally demarcated boundaries between childhood and adulthood can be made ambiguous in ideological terms, not least because two models of childhood can be employed. The *physical* stage of the person may not give any firm indication of *spiritual* maturity or immaturity, just as knowledge gained through study or logic cannot compare with the revelation knowledge granted to the Christian by God. An adult of highly advanced years can still be an Evangelical newborn, requiring instruction in order to achieve biblically prescribed growth, while a person young in years (such as Westergård) can legitimately reveal all the signs of spiritual precocity.

There is, I think, a powerful symbolic logic underlying this Evangelical tendency to stress the relevance of spiritual, rather than biological, criteria in assessing the nature and worth of the person. Word of Life Christians, who are distinguished by a literalist desire to see the Bible as a blueprint for existence as well as a charismatic tendency to seek authentic experience, emphasize above all the reliability and universal applicability of the rules of their faith. In common with Christians of a more conventional fundamentalist persuasion, they argue that the principles of faith are essentially valid for all people, in all cultures, at all times, and indeed that their beliefs can be adumbrated as spiritual laws expressed as rationally organized glosses from the Bible. Here, for instance, is an extract from a handbook (*Sharing Jesus Effectively*) produced by an American faith preacher known well to Word of Life adherents:

> I don't like to do anything without getting results. . . . If you will take the principles outlined in this study and apply them to your witnessing, you will have success with every person with whom you have the opportunity to share.
>
> Now, you may think, *Yes, but everyone may not accept Jesus immediately.* That doesn't make any difference. As long as you plant the seed, God's Word will not return void (Is. 55.11). . . . If you will do the planting, that makes you a winner because it is God Who gives the increase. (Savelle 1982:7–8)

The important point about such beliefs for present purposes is that they explicitly require the maintenance of internal *consistency* in the use of symbols and practices. A sermon that holds good in Russia or Bangladesh should also hold good in Sweden, just as the techniques of spiritual empowerment relevant to an eight-year old should also be usable by an eighty-year-old. To emphasize that age is to some extent irrelevant in the assimilation and employment of principles of religious faith is therefore also to argue for the unity and universal applicability of the symbolic system.

A further aspect of Word of Life beliefs emphasizes this sense that overt consistency in the presentation and deployment of the Word is a principle of faith. Personal spiritual development tends to be conceptualized in terms of quantity—in terms of assimilating more of the same faith—rather than in the sense of fundamental beliefs evolving in their essential character as a person gains in spiritual maturity or life experience. As the jacket notes of Ekman's early (1985) book *Faith Which Conquers the World* put it: "Every believer *has* a measure of faith. . . . In this book, the author discusses how faith emerges, how it functions and how it can grow. If you want to become a Christian or function better as a Christian, this is the book for you." We see here the idea that faith is a tangible thing to be appropriated by the person; that the ownership of such objectified faith empowers the person to take control of circumstances—indeed, "conquer the world"; that it can be cultivated and measured as it grows in a *spiritual* form of development and increase.

Childhood as Social Construction: The View from Anthropology

The logic and implications of these notions of the Christian person and ideas of maturity/immaturity can be examined in the light of anthropological writings on childhood and the life course. Not surprisingly, such work has emphasized that the notion of childhood is socially constructed, raising the question of the extent to which biological growth correlates with culturally specific ideas concerning maturity and roles. As Allison James and Alan Prout (1990:3) put the matter: "It is biological immaturity rather than childhood which is a universal and natural feature of human groups."

Despite the emphasis placed on cultural specificity, recent research has also opposed simple socialization theories according to which children can be regarded as mere passive receptacles of adult teaching. This research argues that these latter theories turn children into muted groups (Hardman 1973) or nonpersons (Hockey and James 1993), presocial fields of difference to be inculcated with adult norms. Instead, children should be regarded as active social beings, people to be studied in their own right (James and Prout 1990:8–10) and therefore shown to be makers of meanings independent of, and even resistant to, the adult world (cf. Hardman 1973; Toren 1993).

This chapter approaches the passive socialization versus active makers of meaning debate from a closely defined perspective. I aim to show how an important aspect of Word of Life ideology entails a partial denial of, or at least failure, to recognize the autonomous symbolic worlds of both younger children and youths. To acknowledge the autonomy of different generations as makers of meanings would be to compromise the apparent internal consistency of Evangelical beliefs and practices. After all, if biblical principles are applicable across cultures, then they should also be applicable across generations.

I also wish to argue, however, that these views on the universal applicability of spiritual power and its availability for widespread appropriation serve on a different level to give even the young a legitimate, if strictly controlled, voice. By being muted in one respect—in that the differences between the cognitive and symbolic worlds of the child and the adult are partially denied—children are empowered in another. Under some circumstances they may have almost as much authority as adults in the expression of spiritually anointed ideas, even if they have to adopt dominant modes of discourse to be heard. Furthermore, forms of resistance to the flattened-out, one-dimensional notion of the Evangelical person do exist, so that it becomes possible to see how, in practice, the symbols of faith are differentially appropriated by people of different ages. Finally, and more speculatively, I want to argue that the ritual and verbal forms through which these Christians express their faith are well adapted to such intergenerational appropriation. In certain respects, they not only allow children to behave as spiritually empowered adults but also encourage adults to behave as children.

Constructions of Childhood in Conservative Protestantism

The place of children in conservative Protestant churches is interestingly ambiguous. As infants they are too young to have undergone adult baptism or, if they are charismatics, baptism in the spirit (even if these landmarks can be achieved in the teen or sometimes even preteen years); yet they are usually regarded as legitimate Christians. Unlike people of mature years who choose to enter the church—and for whom the experience of being born again ideally involves a stripping away of an old, unredeemed identity—the children of members do not usually have to define themselves in schizophrenic terms, despite the common conservative Protestant notion that human nature is inherently sinful. They will probably have been dedicated to the church or congregation as babies and are expected to acknowledge commitment to the faith through baptism in their teens.

In her ethnography of North American fundamentalists, Nancy Ammerman (1987:160) notes that for younger children being brought up within an orthodox family, fundamentalism is the only plausible view of the world they know: "Children learn the Fundamentalist way of thinking, along with everything else, so that it becomes second nature." The congregation itself can act as a kind of extended spiritual family for the child, helping to create a world where biblical knowledge pervades perception: "By the time they are six or seven, they are as likely to have a favorite Bible verse as to have a favorite color, to be able to tell a Bible story as to be able to recite a nursery rhyme, to be able to sing a hymn as any other song" (Ammerman 1987:168).

As Ammerman's words imply, socialization of children within the conservative Protestant worldview is seen as vital. In a political sense, the exercise of the ability to bring up children according to biblically prescribed principles may be seen as a key factor in expressing autonomy from an overarching state, as well as secular society. As the child grows older, the risk increases that she or he might be exposed to, and therefore generate, potentially dissonant views and behaviors. Teenage children are often all too aware of alternative lifestyles, and the vigorous youth programs arranged by Evangelical congregations are frequently designed specifically to parallel and thereby counter such influences.

Parents must also decide whether to risk sending their offspring to a conventional school, exposing them both to secular systems of thought and non-Christian peers. James Davison Hunter (1987:6) notes that the present revival of Evangelicalism in the United States was bolstered between 1971 and 1978 by an increase of 47 percent in the number of private Evangelical primary and secondary schools. In the same vein, R. Stephen Warner's (1990:216) monograph on an Evangelical church in California quotes the pastor of the church complaining at the "garbage" picked up by children at public schools. To avoid such risks, the church assisted in the opening of the Good Shepherd School, neatly capturing in its title the idea of socialization as a process of leading an infant flock.

Children are valued not least because they are seen as providing some of the main building blocks for the construction of nuclear families. The latter have become symbols of social stability and traditional moral virtue for such Christians. Given this emphasis, it is hardly surprising that 10 percent of all mass market and trade books published in 1982 by Evangelical publishing houses in the United States dealt with aspects of the family and childrearing (Hunter 1987:77). In a recent analysis of such material, John Bartkowski and Christopher Ellison (1995:22) have contrasted models of childrearing provided in popular manuals by conservative Protestants and by secular experts. Bartkowski and Ellison argue that these Christians have consciously promoted "traditional" parenting techniques in opposition to those of the mainstream.[1] Literalist views of the Bible as providing fail-safe, sufficient truths to guide the conduct of all affairs, including childrearing, are generally maintained. Also evident are beliefs in the sinfulness of human nature, leading to concerns with punishment and salvation. Overall, an elective affinity seems to exist between literalism and authority-mindedness in the texts they examine, and this has an impact on childrearing. Writers imply that to succeed in adult roles, children must embrace principles of parental authority and family hierarchy. Virtually all of the Christian parenting specialists reviewed claim that children derive their initial image of God from the behavior of parents, so the cultivation of a correct image of parent as divinity must be maintained.

Such views, to the extent that they stress the importance of authority, generally fit in with conventional depictions of conservative Protestant families as idealizing a family form that involves rigid role demarcation according to gender and age: the father acting as spiritual head of the family and chief provider in an economic sense, the mother providing a stable home base for their offspring, and the children learning obediently to adopt roles as mirror images of their parents. Bartkowski and Ellison's work also has a number of resonances with the arguments presented here, such as the emphasis on biblical principles as a guide for all conduct and the notion of humans acting as mediators for the divine.

However, I wish to argue that their work cannot provide a full picture of childrearing and the parent-child relationship in two important ways. First (inevitably, given their material), they look more to ideal models than to practice. In fact, as Hunter (1987:111–112) has pointed out, since the 1970s many Evangelical families seem to have been affected by wider social trends involving the growing participation of women in the workforce and the increasing acceptance of androgynous role definitions among the Evangelical young—at least in the sense that women can take on more of the functions of men. Second, and more relevantly for this chapter, the emphasis on human nature as inherently sinful, while common among conservatives, is complicated in Faith theology (cf. Hambre et al. 1983) by a tendency to combine positive thinking and Pentecostal theology in interpretations of the Bible. The power of the spirit to control the rest of the born-again person is stressed, as is the importance of concentrating on possibility and self-empowerment rather than—or at least as much as—an ascetic requirement to keep sinful desires under check. This consciously cultivated, positive view of the self can in practice be extended to the children of Word of Lifers, who, like their parents, have a duty to be an example to others and mediators of divine power to the world. As Ekman (1985:79) puts it: "God created humanity in His image (Gen. 1:26). . . . Humanity should be like God, think like God, act like God and speak like God." Like their parents, children can be smaller versions of divinity itself as they appropriate sacred power to themselves and cultivate personal relations with Jesus. Again, we see how particular notions of the person shape the role and authority of children.

Training for Life: Constructing the Life Course

Word of Lifers reflect in their attitudes and behavior many of the features of conservative Protestantism mentioned in the previous section. The family is indeed widely regarded as a building block of society, not least as it defines an area of influence divorced as much as possible from state intervention (an important symbolic statement in a country regarded by such Christians as overburdened by centralized, secular bureaucracy). Most strikingly, the group is subdivided into a number of sections, each devoted to catering for the needs of—and therefore in some ways constructing—different age groups. Apart from the head pastor (Ekman) and other associate pastors who deal with adults, the group also maintains both a children's and a youth pastor. During main services and at other times, a kindergarten called "The Promised Land" is provided; for older children up to their late teens, youth groups with names such as Jesus Patrol and Jesus Generation combine Bible teaching and a range of activities (engaging in sports, learning survival techniques, watching videos, and even witnessing to the unconverted). Every Saturday night, the youth meeting at the church attracts hundreds of teenagers to a service incorporating songs, a sermon, and healing. A summer Bible school is held every year, headed by the youth pastor, that combines preaching and discussions of the Bible in the mornings with conventional leisure activities in the afternoons. Each winter, a youth conference is arranged, providing a counterpart to the group's summer Europe conference.

One of the reasons that so many activities can be oriented to young people is that the Word of Life is made up of a relatively youthful body of Christians. No reliable statistics are currently available, but the Bible school does appear to attract many believers in their twenties to forties, and at least according to Ekman (1988), the group has tended to attract a higher than average proportion of young couples (a constituency that can be contrasted to the generally aging populations of more established free churches in Sweden [cf. Gustafsson 1991:70]).

Implicit in many of the activities arranged for the young is the intention of giving worldly activities a spiritual gloss: sport becomes a means to achieve fellowship and learn discipline when juxtaposed with a morning of Bible study; Saturday nights can involve meeting other teenagers and dancing to modern music, but at a service of worship rather than at a disco. At the New Year youth conference for 1993–1994, participants were given the following message by Ekman: "The economy, religion, media, culture, music, leisure, education, politics . . . are created by God and . . . in reality belong to Him."[2] Such a statement includes many of the activities likely to tempt younger people into secular ways of life, and Ekman's point here is that all of these can be catered to within the group itself. He is therefore illustrating what I call the "assimilationist tendency of modern Evangelicalism" (Harding 1987): rather than setting up sectarian boundaries against the ways of the world, Christians should, in this view, have the confidence to extend their spheres of influence across secular boundaries, thus claiming the world for God. Youth culture itself can therefore be reformulated in Evangelical terms, just as the Word of Life can also, for instance, provide biblically prescribed versions of how to use the media or manage finances.

One of the issues Ekman raises in his New Year's message is that of education, and this, above all, has proved to be a defining activity of the group. From the very beginning, the Word of Life was conceived as both a congregation and an educational center for Christians, and indeed it now claims to be the largest Bible school in the whole of Europe, training some two to three thousand students at any given time both in Evangelical theology and in practical techniques such as missionary work, evangelism, music, and media work. The further growth of the group itself has been constituted to a large extent by the expansion of educational activities, and these have in effect served to plot a life course for the individual believer as he or she moves from infancy to adulthood. The group cannot create a "total" institution, controlling and surveying every aspect of the lives of adherents who are highly mobile. However, the provision of schooling alongside leisure and worship facilities comes as close as possible to potentially providing for the person's every need beyond that of the nuclear family.

In 1987, after a long struggle with local authorities who were concerned at the extent to which education would be dominated by a congregation depicted in the press as brainwashing its members, a school for young children in their first three years of education was approved. This development allowed Bible school students to place their children under Christian care during the day. In 1990, a school for older children was added, and by 1994 the Word of Life was running Sweden's biggest Christian free school, with 502 pupils. (By 1991, around twenty exclusively Christian schools existed in Sweden, of which over half had started in the 1980s.)

These activities—in the areas of both leisure and education—may seem consciously to be catering for the needs of different ages. However, many common ritual and symbolic threads run through them. All combine activities unremarkable in the secular world with the inculcation of Christian knowledge, so that the sacred and secular engage in dialogue, the former coming to seem a natural part of the latter. All the forms of education, running from the kindergarten to the university, involve the adoption of a rationalized approach to the Bible, seeing it as containing a set of principles applicable to everyday life. No matter what age, Christian are encouraged to think of themselves as having certain responsibilities, as well as certain powers. Here are the words of a woman who works in the Sunday school for younger children ranging from nine months old to twelve years:

> Our aim is that the children should get to learn the basic principles of God's Word, for example the importance of being born again, of winning others for Jesus, baptism in the Holy Spirit and tongues.

These skills are seen as a form of "evangelical tool kit" that runs through all aspects of life, and indeed these basic elements are used in virtually all activities put on by the group.[3]

Such symbolic replication across the generations is evident in other ways also: a monthly cassette club, run by the group and designed to provide adults with a regular dose of sermons, has its counterpart in a children's cassette club. As an advertisement in the group's newsletter says: "Give your children the best—God's Word!"[4] Admittedly, such cassettes contain a wider range of activities than those for adults, as they include teaching, songs, and drama, but these aspects of worship and education are not so far from those on offer at ordinary services in the group: both are supposed to contain sacred language to be assimilated by the individual person. Again, a report in a newspaper edited by a member of the group describing the Word of Life 1994 summer conference notes that the children "had their own conference"—separate from, but replicating the activities of, the adults.[5]

At the school for younger, pre–secondary school children, a similar process of assimilation occurs, designed to make Christian teachings and practices as natural as learning how to read or ride a bicycle. Each week, lessons on traffic, the clouds, the seasons, and so on are juxtaposed with others on Creation, the Holy Spirit, and healing. A fresh verse from the Bible is put up in the classroom each week and is to be learned by heart. Services are regularly held as assemblies, at which pupils learn the appropriate behavior for adult services: listening to sermons, body movements such as swaying in time with music, prayers for particular ends, and possession of a Bible at all times. According to a congregation newsletter, there has been at least one occasion when a visiting evangelist from the United States took the time to come into the school, preach to the children, and lay hands on each of them.[6] At the school for older children, the gymnasium, normal teaching taken from the national curriculum, including religious studies, is complemented by a specific concentration on Bible knowledge, taking the Bible itself to be a course book. Each morning gymnasium pupils and teachers sing, praise God, and pray together.

Metaphors of Growth and the Exercise of Authority

The quotations that follow reflect sentiments designed for three different generations of Word of Lifer: young children, youths, and adults. Each comes from slightly different contexts: the words of a songbook, a sermon preached at a youth meeting, and a formal ceremony attended by thousands of people at which the group celebrated the opening of its vast new premises on the outskirts of Uppsala:

> Read your Bible, pray each day, pray each day, pray each day. Read your Bible, pray each day, if you want to grow, if you want to grow, if you want to grow. Read your Bible, pray each day, if you want to grow.[7]

> Jesus said "Our daily bread" and he meant it physically. . . . You can't desist from spiritual breakfast for a single day. . . . You'll come in to heaven like a spiritual bodybuilder. . . . God wants to give you spiritual nourishment, and when you're newly born you get milk. . . . When you grow you get a little bread. . . . But then when you've eaten for a sufficiently long time when God knows that you can eat. . . . He gives you a real ox, you know. . . . You go around like a giant . . . like a Sumo wrestler. You become the biggest when you eat God's Word.[8]

> Our God is a big God![9]

Despite the differences of context and audience, however, a central metaphor runs through all the extracts: that of size, particularly the notion of growth. Indeed, this metaphor illustrates an aspect of the symbolic consistency evident in the various contexts of Word of Life practice: growth is a concept and an ideal that can be applied to many different occasions and describes a process of increase, so that future expansion is made possible. Furthermore, the assimilation and use of the power provided by God's Word are believed to have predictable, visible results. Thus, God is said to be "big" in a context where the new building of the group demonstrates its apparent success both in attracting adherents and in building up a variety of missionary activities. Growth can also be applied to the person, however, and we see how the youth pastor's words and those of the children's song both combine notions of *spiritual* growth—reading, assimilating the words of the Bible, or even "gorging" on it, to use the image deployed by Westergård at the beginning of this chapter—in contexts where the *physical* growth of the person will also take place. The children's song is most explicit in this sense: physical and spiritual maturation should naturally occur together, and if the spiritual side of growth (reading the Bible) is not attended to properly, correct physical increase will not occur.

The assimilation of the Word in this way may help children mature, but it is also an activity necessary to the self-development of adults: all Christians are seen as needing to ingest large quantities of God's message to stimulate their faith to grow. Even though adults will have had more opportunity than children to read the Bible, both age groups are engaged in essentially the same project. At the center of Word of Life notions of empowerment through faith is the idea that words are very similar to things—they are like objects that give the person spiritual nourishment and that can be taken into the person (or sown in the world) without problems of interpretation or contested meaning (Coleman 1996). If the Word is sown correctly or read correctly, it will have predictable results—as implied in the earlier extract from *Sharing Jesus Effectively.* We come back again to issues of authority, especially how much children can be said to be empowered by this system of assimilating power through language. The following extracts from the yearbook produced for the Bible school students of 1984–1985 illustrate children displaying spiritual maturity that is often greater than that of adults:

> A harassed mother to her four-year-old son: "Soon I'm going to lose my patience!" "No, Mamma, it's down there in your stomach. You get it from God's Word."
>
> Mamma is playing and mucking around with the children, falls over for the second time and says: "If I carry on like this I'll get lots of cuts." At which one of the children replies: "If you say you'll get them, you will get them."
>
> Conversation between one of our kindergarten children, four-year-old Maria, and a friend, overheard by Mum:
>
> "Do you have Jesus in your heart? . . . If you want to let Him in you have to pray."
>
> So they prayed: "Jesus come into my heart."
>
> Maria continued: "You must recognize Him as your Savior and Lord as well." So they prayed together again and then began to laugh. Maria ran to her mother and said: "How happy he was when Jesus came into his heart!"[10]

These extracts reveal the Evangelical tendency to collect narratives that can be repeated to others to indicate the power of divine influence. Each of them also consists of dialogue itself—dialogue about language and its power to create reality in a world of Pentecostal-style positive thinking. A striking aspect of the first two extracts is that they actually show children lecturing adults as to the principles of Word of Life ideology. Despite the implicit hierarchy of age and experience evident in any child-adult context, the person who is depicted as taking control of the encounter is the person best able to generate and verbally articulate an interpretation in line with Evangelical thinking. In theory, a four-year-old is far too young to be born again (even if baptism in the spirit can occur as early as eight or perhaps even younger), but this technical detail does not prevent the depiction of such a child as an appropriate vehicle of the truth and generator of anointed language. The final incident, that of the child as evangelist helping to convert another infant, again implies that a child can be sufficiently empowered to spread the Word and that the equally young recipient is a legitimate person to take Jesus "into his heart."

That these representations of children blur the boundaries between adulthood and childhood in terms of spiritual empowerment can, of course, be interpreted in more than one way. These children appear far from muted, and it is significant that adults not only seem eager to record narratives of children acting in spiritually precocious ways but also perceive no great sense of incongruity in such incidents. Yet we must remember that these are *representations* of children, incidents plucked from a host of other activities that more closely reflect conventional adult-child relations. In addition, these children appear to be empowered only because they are adopting and reflecting back adult conceptions of language and behavior appropriate to a good Christian. In this sense, they demonstrate merely that the child speakers have been efficiently socialized into the adult world—and that an excellent way to self-socialize into a belief system is to attempt to convert another to it, as the little girl does in the third incident. More generally, it is notable that youths (as well as Bible students) in particular are encouraged to witness to others, in schools and beyond, and such a process may help to inculcate a sense of internal discipline through external action.

Ammerman (1987) notes how children in the church she studied not only come to accept the faith at an early age but also realize that witnessing to others is a central act of their faith and therefore start to practice very early. She (1987:173) records the words of a mother describing her young child, who is in the first grade: "She got the three kids to say the prayer after her. . . . She was real excited, and she said, 'I think I'm a missionary, Mom!'" Such activity seems similar to young children playing at adopting adult roles, as in doctors and nurses. Yet as these quotations indicate, there is also a definite sense that children can produce statements that make a real difference to the world: they can be empowered by the possession of faith and indeed are sometimes referred to in literature as "God's Soldiers," participating in a broader image constructed by Word of Life adherents (and also evident in Westergård's sermon) that Christians are at war with the forces of secularity and darkness.

Not only does Word of Life practice indicate how boundaries between an apparently childish *playing* at the role of being an effective Christian and actually *being* one are broken down; it also positively values aspects of being physically young. Children, of course, represent the future—as the American preacher Bob Wiener put it at the youth conference of 1993: "Revival in Scandinavia will come from you taking the Gospel to your town, school or workplace yourself. It's the young generation who will carry the revival. 51 percent of the world's population are under twenty-five."[11] A similar sentiment is expressed in the notes of a worker in the Sunday school that she sent out to other helpers: "You invest in God's kingdom through sowing into Sweden's future—children!" In a single sentence, she manages to encapsulate much of the message preached by the group: the economic metaphor of work as investment, with apparent altruism also a form of self-interest; the notion that sowing will reap an inevitable harvest; and the sense that what takes place in a relatively small organization has significance for the nation as a whole.

More broadly, in a group that chooses to represent the forces of revival rather than tradition (of developing a dynamic "spiritual career," as some adherents put it), notions of process, growth, and coming to maturity are valued more than the fixed state of having reached maturity. Even the emphasis on health and the cultivation of the body as temple favors the positive evaluation of youthful energy. Interestingly, the youth conference actually has an upper age limit as high as thirty-five, perhaps partly to attract a large audience, but also to enable an older worshiper to see him- or herself as still developing at a comparatively mature age.[12]

The valuing of youth is reinforced by a slightly different perspective that pervades the Evangelical discourse of preachers and ordinary participants. Adults are encouraged to see themselves as God's children, in a relation of dependency to God as a child is to a parent. "Pappa" God is a source not only of potential sanctions but also of protection and rewards—the prosperity that people seek. In addition, children are sometimes represented as actually being better than adults at accepting faith and therefore as valuable role models. They are depicted as being more efficient at memorizing verses from the Bible and as having fewer barriers in the unproblematic reception of faith. Thus, an article in a Word of Life publication breaks down the boundary between adult and child in this way: "God wants you to accept that you are His child. That in fact you are completely helpless and need His help. . . . Children have no pride. They ask for help with everything. . . . The other side of childhood is that in fact you have a pappa. God is your father. Small children often believe that pappa can do everything."[13] We have the sense here of the invocation of childhood as a rhetorical device: childhood is clearly a position of dependency, but it is also the ideal state in which to receive divine blessings, since it allows the believer to bypass human vanity. Those who are biologically adult, and possibly parents themselves in a physical sense, should therefore attempt to become infants on a spiritual level.

Admittedly, some of the literature for children (educational or otherwise) claims to devise particular, generation-specific activities. In the 1980s, for instance, the group started to promote the use of texts by North American pastor Willy George. These encourage children to think about spiritual or theological issues in concrete terms: in times of sickness, children are urged, for instance, to call on God's name and declare that they are healthy; the texts also suggest that the names of illnesses be written on pieces of paper and then burned as a way of ridding the body of these illnesses. An exercise (highlighted in the press) suggests that children draw a picture of the devil in the classroom, blindfold themselves, and then throw darts at the image, gaining points for the number of hits they achieve.

However, Word of Life modes of worship might also bring adults closer to children in certain respects. If the activities mentioned previously seem to involve some basic elements of children's play, with magic and metonymy employed both to enchant the external world and make it manipulable by the person, they also have very direct parallels with forms of adult worship and prayer. The notion of positive confession among faith Christians, based as it is on the idea that words have direct physical effects on the world, teaches the person to claim prosperity by uttering it in words and correspondingly to avoid talking negatively lest unfortunate consequences befall the speaker. Services also frequently involve forms of healing through collective uttering of anointed words (often tongues) over sheaves of paper containing prayer requests from Christians who are sick or in need of some other form of help.

Conclusion

I have emphasized the ways in which the Evangelical culture of the Word of Life recognizes the need to create separate spheres of activity for different generations but also partially neutralizes such apparent generational differences by constructing a consistent symbolic world of faith in which all people, of whatever age, can participate. Of course, this argument should not be overemphasized. Infants and younger children often do not perceive or interact with the group in ways that entirely mirror their parents. Not all infants in the kindergarten are fully aware of the meanings of the words and actions surrounding them. Teenagers, in particular, articulate with secular forms of youth culture in their expressions of worship, wearing fashionable clothes and buying forms of Christian hard rock whose Manichean imagery is not always very different from its secular manifestations. On a more covert level, I have also seen teenagers from the group (as well as those attending Faith conferences in Uppsala) experiment with smoking—presumably a double thrill as it represents an illegitimate activity for younger teenagers in both the secular and Evangelical worlds. The youth pastor, meanwhile, shows his awareness of the particular needs of younger people at Saturday night services, where, although the basic pattern of all Word of Life services is evident, incorporating songs of praise, a sermon, and healing, some concessions to the concerns of his audience are made. A special youth choir replaces that of the adults, and sermons sometimes focus on issues of most relevance to the teenage generation: how to cultivate the discipline required to get up in the mornings, how to avoid records or videos that are too worldly, how to avoid the "compromise" of watching television on a Saturday night when a service is available at the group, or how to realize that it is not a sin to buy new clothes, such as jeans.

Nevertheless, Word of Life ideology often acts to incorporate and therefore defuse aspects of youth culture, bringing it into the safe orbit of Evangelical activity. During the 1980s, a Christian rock group called "Jerusalem" was closely associated with the Word of Life, and at one concert put on by this group in the hall of the new building the lead singer moved easily from singing to preaching, ultimately calling troubled young people to come to the front for the laying on of hands. In March 1987, American preacher Greg Glassford gave some lectures at the group called "Can God Use Christian Rock?" where he argued that such music could be used in congregations provided it was sufficiently anointed: dedicated to God rather than to pure self-indulgence. In the 1990s, sermons started to deny the necessity for rock music, however, and thereby removed even this particular form of expression from disturbing the consistency of group worship.

We have therefore seen how the Word of Life links the cultivation of a rationalized, apparently universally applicable form of faith to the empowerment of the Christian person. My point has been to show how such ideology has had an important impact on representations and activities of the children of members. On the one hand, Word of Lifers consider it important to socialize the young into a worldview that permits relatively limited overt opportunities to create radically experimental or autonomous symbolic worlds. On the other hand, young people gain a legitimate voice *within* Evangelical discourse to the extent that they can articulate appropriate, seemingly spiritually anointed language. For both children and adults, the rhetoric of Evangelicalism gives the impression of empowering the self even as it provides a means to view the world through strictly limited lenses of perception.

Notes

1. Bartkowski and Ellison (1995:25–26) expand on this contrast by arguing that mainstream writers focus on how to help children develop such characteristics as self-esteem, self-confidence, and creativity; without necessarily opposing these traits, conservative Protestants place more emphasis on cultivating the ability to submit selfish desires to the divine authority of God.
2. "Nyårsprofetian: Vägskäl I Skandinavien," *Magazinet* (February 1994): 20.
3. In a Word of Life newsletter from January 1986.
4. *Livets Ord Nyhetsbrev* (May 1991): 19.
5. Krister Holmström, "Ny Tro för Väckelse," *Trons Värld,* August 19, 1994, 12.
6. *Församlingsbrev* (Autumn 1985).
7. These words are taken from a songbook, *När Vi Barn Prisar Gud* (Uppsala, Sweden: Livets Ord, n.d.), designed for infants. The song quoted here is not exclusive to the Word of Life but is used in wider Evangelical circles.
8. Sermon no. LO S10, by Word of Life youth pastor.
9. North American preacher, recorded at opening ceremony of Word of Life new premises, summer 1987.
10. From "Collected Sayings," in *Livets Ord Bibelcenter Årsbok* (1985).
11. This sermon was delivered December 29, 1993, and was published as "Undervisningen från Nyårskonferensen," *Magazinet* (February 1994): 20.
12. The age limit was in place at least on those occasions I attended.
13. Ulf Ekman, "Fördömelse och Egenrättfärdighet—Hinder för att Höra Guds Röst," *Magazinet* (February 1994): 19.

References

Ammerman, N. 1987. *Bible Believers: Fundamentalists in the Modern World.* New Brunswick, N.J.: Rutgers University Press.

Bartkowski, J. P., and C. G. Ellison. 1995. "Divergent Models of Childrearing in Popular Manuals: Conservative Protestants vs. the Mainstream Experts." *Sociology of Religion* 56: 21–34.

Beckford, J. 1985. *Cult Controversies: The Societal Response to the New Religious Movements.* London: Tavistock.

Coleman, S. 1989. "Controversy and the Social Order: Responses to a Religious Group in Sweden." Ph.D. diss., Cambridge University.

———. 1991. "'Faith Which Conquers the World': Swedish Fundamentalism and the Globalization of Culture." *Ethnos* 56: 6–18.

———. 1996. "Words as Things: Language, Aesthetics, and the Objectification of Protestant Evangelicalism." *Journal of Material Culture* 1: 107–128.

Cox, H. 1984. *Religion in the Secular City: Toward a Postmodern Theology.* New York: Simon and Schuster.

Ekman, U. 1985. *Tro Som Övervinner Världen.* Uppsala, Sweden: Livets Ords Förlag.

Gustafsson, G. 1991. *Tro Samfund och Samhälle: Sociologiska Perspektiv.* Örebro, Sweden: Libris.

Hambre, C., M. Hammar, L. Hiding, M. Lindh, I. Moritz, S. Olsson, C. J. Rudman, and T. Strand. 1983. *Framgångsteologi: En Analys och Prövning.* Stockholm: EFS-Förlaget.

Harding, S. 1987. "Convicted by the Holy Spirit: The Rhetoric of Fundamental Baptist Conversion." *American Ethnologist* 14: 167–181.

Hardman, C. 1973. "Can There Be an Anthropology of Children?" *Journal of the Anthropological Society of Oxford* 4(11): 85–99.

Hockey, J., and A. James. 1993. *Growing Up and Growing Old: Ageing and Dependency in the Life Course.* London: Sage.

Hunter, J. D. 1987. *Evangelicalism: The Coming Generation.* Chicago: University of Chicago Press.

James, A., and A. Prout, eds. 1990. *Constructing and Reconstructing Childhood.* London: Falmer Press.

Martin, D. 1978. *A General Theory of Secularization.* Oxford, U.K.: Blackwell.

Savelle, J. 1982. *Sharing Jesus Effectively: A Handbook on Successful Soul-Winning.* Tulsa, Okla.: Harrison House.

Toren, C. 1993. "Making History: The Significance of Childhood Cognition for a Comparative Anthropology of Mind." *Man* (NS) 28: 461–478.

Warner, R. S. 1990. *New Wine in Old Wineskins: Evangelicals and Liberals in a Small Town Church.* Berkeley and Los Angeles: University of California Press.

Chapter 5

Osho Ko Hsuan School

Educating the "New Child"

Elizabeth Puttick

The Osho movement was the best known and most fashionable new religious movement (NRM) of the 1970s. Osho (formerly known as Bhagwan Shree Rajneesh) began his career as a professor of philosophy at Jabalpur University, India, and later set up an ashram in Poona. There he initiated disciples, or *sannyasins,* into a path of life-affirmative spirituality drawn from Eastern and Western philosophies. Osho moved to America in 1981 but was deported four years later amid various allegations of crimes and misdemeanors. He died in Poona in 1990, but the movement continues to attract members worldwide to its headquarters. Much of its popularity derived from its praxis, an innovative program of psychospiritual development based on a combination of Osho's own meditations and techniques from the human potential movement. Personal development has always been integral to *sannyas* (the movement's own informal name for itself), and education is seen as an important basis necessary to its successful implementation.

Osho Ko Hsuan School (named after the Chinese Daoist sage) is the only school of the Osho movement, catering to the children (and a few grandchildren) of sannyasins from all over the world. They are a cosmopolitan community, in exotic contrast to the conservative rural society of Devon, England, where the school is located. It has now been in existence since 1986 and is gaining a high degree of acceptance among its neighbors—in contrast to previous sannyasin communities, which provoked strong hostile reactions, particularly in India and America.

The English educational system provides universal state-funded schooling while allowing a wide range of independent schools, from the famous (so-called) public schools to some highly experimental and avant-garde "alternative" schools. Religious schools come under this sector, mostly under the aegis of the world religions, but also set up by the new religious movements. Osho Ko Hsuan is formally in this category, but it has more in common with the English secular tradition of independent "free" schools, such as Summerhill or the Steiner and Montessori schools, than with more typical religious schools.

The very existence of Osho Ko Hsuan is a paradox in the light of the Osho movement's ideology. Osho's teaching is based on a vision of personal, social, and religious freedom that challenges and deconstructs all forms of authority. His three worst hates, often declaimed, were priests, pundits, and politicians, whom he held responsible for much of the neurosis, misery, and exploitation suffered by humanity. These antiauthoritarian views made it hard for sannyasins to set up or endorse any institutions, however radically alternative. Such problems are inherent in any libertarian movement that outgrows the size and informality of its charismatic origins, but they become especially sensitive when the issues of children's vulnerability and the shaping of their future arise. How can a school equip children to live in a complex technological society without overloading their brains at the expense of their hearts and souls? What structures will support their growth without suppressing their natural intelligence and instincts? And how can ethical and spiritual values be inculcated without indoctrination?

Since we are dealing here with an NRM, the educational and organizational issues are largely subsumed in the larger religious question of whether Ko Hsuan may be termed a *religious* school. As the official school of a new religious movement, inspired by the spiritual vision and practical guidance of a guru, the answer may seem self-evident. However, one of the most strongly held beliefs and oft-repeated statements at Ko Hsuan is that "this is not a religious school." The lack of formal teaching, compulsory ritual, and other forms of "indoctrination" supports this claim, raising questions about our definitions of religious schools and religious education in schools. The school is conducting a radical and timely experiment in basing education on spiritual/ethical values without formal religious indoctrination and in imparting skills that will enable students to survive and prosper in society without sacrificing their individuality. These aims are paradoxical, but the school has achieved some creative and successful resolutions.

Osho's Teaching: The New Child

The Osho movement's renown in the 1970s grew partly out of its large, innovative program of psychospiritual development and partly out of Osho's controversial teachings. The movement's appeal was particularly strong in the counterculture, and at this time thousands of well-educated (mostly) young people flocked to the ashram in Poona, India, to "take *sannyas*" (become disciples of Osho). The movement came to world attention after establishing its headquarters at Rajneeshpuram, Oregon, in 1981. It flourished in this Oregon valley ranch for four years, attempting to realize a grand vision of an ecological "New City for the New Man." The community collapsed in 1985 after the U.S. government charged it with, among other things, tax evasion, wiretapping, attempted murder, and illegal immigration. Three of the community's leaders were imprisoned, and Osho was deported. This appeared to signify the demise of the movement, but a year later Osho moved back to Poona, where the movement has quietly flourished ever since.

Part of Osho's appeal to his disciples, in contrast to most other spiritual teachers and gurus of the time, was his critique of society, including religion, gender, sexuality, the family, community, and childrearing. Part of his "work" was an attempt to replace what he saw as an outdated, ineffective, damaging system with a new vision of self-realization and social salvation that could be achieved through a combination of consciousness and technique. To this end, he set up communities offering programs of therapies and meditations based on an integration of Western psychology with Eastern meditation.

Ko Hsuan School is best understood in the context of Osho's theories on the family and how these were expressed in earlier sannyasin communities and schools. Many of the countercultural seekers who formed the majority of the original membership were in rebellion against mainstream society and its institutions, which they saw as agents of socialization, imposing a false persona on the pure energy and innocence of the child. The main target of this critique was the nuclear family, and a cornerstone of Osho's teaching was his denunciation of the family, in the language of the radical psychology of R. D. Laing (1971:102): "Families, schools, churches are the slaughterhouses of our children." Osho (1987:165) claimed: "With all good intentions, all parents are murderers of their own children. You see all over the earth only dead people walking, who have lost their souls even before they had any notion of what it is." He (1984:505) further maintained: "The most outdated thing is the family. It has done its work, it is no more needed. In fact, now it is the most hindering phenomenon for human progress. . . . The family is the root cause of all our neurosis." In another lecture Osho (1991:68) admitted that there were "beneficial" families, nonauthoritarian and nonpossessive, but these accounted for "not more than one per cent." This statistic may be compared with that advanced by the influential recovery movement in the United States, whose practitioners claim that between 90 and 99 percent of all families are "dysfunctional." Osho (1984:508) quite explicitly proposed the spiritual commune as an alternative to the nuclear family: "The real family is not your father, your mother, your brothers, your sisters, your wife, your husband, your children; they are just accidental. Your real family is the family of a Buddha. If you are fortunate to feel joyful in the company of a Buddha, then dissolve into that company—you have found your family."

In the early stages when the movement was smaller, the emphasis was on each individual's personal growth. As Osho's following grew, he developed the concept of a community of seekers, a modern equivalent to the Buddhist *sangha*

(Ling 1973:124). This "new commune" was to be "a great experiment in Buddhahood," part of a grand millenarian vision of human enlightenment and social transformation. Osho believed that most adults, even sannyasins, were too "conditioned" to achieve this exalted state, but enlightened childrearing practices could help children attain their full potential. He subscribed to Jean-Jacques Rousseau's theory of children as innately good and innocent but corrupted by society. It was therefore better to let them run wild than to socialize them, as they would find their own path to virtue. His theories on childhood, parenting and education are compiled in *The New Child* (Osho 1991: 52, 62):

> The first expression of love towards the child is to leave his first seven years absolutely innocent, unconditioned, to leave him for seven years completely wild, a pagan. . . .
>
> It needs guts and it needs immense love in a father, in a mother, to tell the children, "You need to be free of us. Don't obey us, depend on your own intelligence. Even if you go astray it is far better to commit mistakes on your own and learn from them, rather than follow somebody else and not commit mistakes."

Early Experiments in Child Care and Education

Sannyasin communities so far have been predominantly monastic in the sense of being set up for adults for the purpose of spiritual development. Dyadic relationships have been permitted, even encouraged, so long as they do not interfere with the primary commitment to the master and the work.[1] Childbearing and childrearing were not encouraged in Poona (the first Poona ashram) or in Rajneeshpuram. In Osho's (1987b:18) view, this situation was beneficial and liberating, particularly for women: "A woman is not only capable of giving birth to children, she is also capable of giving birth to herself, as a seeker of truth. But that side of woman has not been explored at all."

Despite the discouragement of childbirth, a number of women had children. Parenting in India presented problems regarding health and nutrition and a general lack of facilities, partly compensated by cheap local child care. Almost all the families were single parent, usually single mother. However, the problem of the absent father was perceived to be largely offset by one of the main benefits of communal life: the availability of a wide variety of adults as caregivers, friends, and alternative role models. Although some parents felt that more stability would have been beneficial, most people echoed Osho's teaching on the damage done to children by their looking later in life for a partner modeled solely on their opposite-sex parent (Osho 1984:188). The communal model was lifted up: "Probably the best thing we could do was be there, because [my daughter] did have father figures, good men friends who reached out to her, loved her, took an interest in her, and she still has those connections. And she now has good, balanced relationships with men, no problems with boyfriends."[2]

The weight of responsibility was eased by the widespread belief that Osho had taken on personal responsibility for the children. One of my respondents quoted him as saying, "Don't worry about your kids, I'm taking care of them." In addition to his own "godfather" role, Osho (1978:305) taught that the commune itself should take precedence over the biological parents: "Kids should belong to the commune, and the commune should take care of the kids. The mother should be known, who the mother is, but the father should not be known—there is no need. That was the original state of humanity: matriarchal. Then society became patriarchal: father became important. And with the father came a thousand and one illnesses."

As a result of this libertarian ideology, children enjoyed great freedom, which at the time was seen as an advantage, though with hindsight some parents express doubts. Little provision was made for their education, which was not considered a high priority. There was a rudimentary ashram school, in practice little more than a play school, where attendance was voluntary and usually sporadic. This approach was in line with the libertarian 3D "deschooling" philosophy of education fashionable at the time.

When the movement left India, children found themselves labeled retarded when they went on to state schools. One girl had not learned to read, but the shock of finding herself (aged nine) in the five-year-old class proved salutary; she caught up very quickly and eventually got into art school. At this time, proper schools were opened at Rajneeshpuram and Medina (the main British commune) and available for government inspection. To some extent, this change represented a "routinization" of Osho's pure, unfettered vision of childhood, but he personally authorized it as giving children a beneficial, supportive structure and preparing them for Western life. This ideological shift was also in line with the mainstream educational move away from 1960s liberalism and toward more formal teaching methods.

The Medina school, from which Osho Ko Hsuan emerged, was a primary school with around thirty pupils and four qualified teachers. The curriculum was based on Osho's rather vague guidelines, concentrating on core subjects and a range of sport and leisure activities. The emphasis was on such values as freedom, joy, and creativity, often at the expense of the academic side—artistic and expressive subjects, as well as practical and social skills, were taught. Some parents felt that this experiment had not worked: that the children were perceived by other sannyasin workers as nuisances and distractions and that the parents worked too hard to give them enough attention. But even the most critical mother I interviewed admitted that her son had enjoyed the school, was now doing well at his state school, and had probably been better off in a commune than a single-parent family. The "kids' house" was a separate building, but the children were allowed to see their parents whenever they wanted (Mullan 1983). At both Medina and Rajneeshpuram, they spent part of each day working with the adults at a variety of jobs, which integrated them into the community. Observers agree that the children at both schools seemed "normal," if anything confident and mature for their age (Mullan 1983; Thompson and Heelas 1986; Gordon 1987; Carter 1990).

History and Development of the School

In 1985, the premises of Medina were sold, so the school was closed and the children sent back to their parents. Osho Ko Hsuan was opened a year later in response to a group of children, parents, and former teachers who wanted a sannyasin school to continue. The new school began with the former headmaster and five teachers from Medina and nineteen pupils aged between seven and fifteen. It has since expanded considerably in size and facilities and in 1994 had seventy pupils between the ages of nine and sixteen and sixteen teachers (a ratio of almost 1:4, which is far beyond that of all state and most private schools). The fees are £1,725 ($2,000) a term, which is comparable to other independent schools. In 1994–1995, the sexes were evenly balanced (thirty-nine girls, thirty-one boys) and came from all over the world, reflecting the cosmopolitan membership of the movement. All but a couple of the children come from split families. This is a startling statistic, even in the context of the national increase in single-parent families, but reflects the sannyasin tendency toward serial monogamy (Puttick 1997). This finding may also account for the sannyasin tendency to send the children to boarding school at such young ages, some as young as seven, although at the moment the minimum age is nine. All the teachers are sannyasins, and almost all the children are sannyasins or from sannyasin families.

In 1994–1995, the children came mainly from Europe (39 percent Germans, 10 percent British, 10 percent Italians, 9 percent Spanish). The next largest group was Japanese (7 percent). The rest were mainly from the United States, Australia, and India, with a few from countries such as Mexico and Chile. Again reflecting a general sannyasin tendency, many of the students were of mixed nationality and not strongly identified, such as a half-English, half-German boy who lived in Spain and did not think of himself as any particular nationality. In the past there have been a few nonsannyasin children at the school, usually those seeking an alternative education. However, although they are welcome, no efforts are made to reach them, and in practice there are few applications.

Sannyasins are mainly accepted in the neighborhood as harmless, if exotic, incomers with their "Bedouin names"—particularly in Chulmleigh, the more distant of the two villages, where most of the traders are located. The teachers' social contact with the locals is limited, as is the children's. This separation appears to be maintained as much by the village as the school. The local primary school is a great contrast with its traditional curriculum and entirely local intake of interrelated families. One teacher explained that they could not possibly allow their children to mix with "that kind of thing," meaning the "lovey-dovey" behavior and the "hyperventilation" of the meditations, as viewed on a television program. However, the sannyasin children are said to be mainly well behaved when they do visit the village. Local teenagers are more friendly, sometimes attending the school disco and even occasionally taking sannyas.

Ko Hsuan is less "world rejecting" in its stance than the sannyasin communities of the 1980s were, although some friction is probably inevitable given the contrasts with the local community and the greater conservatism and uniformity of rural life. The school's AIDS policy tends to create misunderstandings, with its insistence that all residents over the age of fourteen take six-monthly HIV tests. At the request of Social Services, they have now produced a leaflet explaining their policy in the light of Osho's teachings. Osho announced that AIDS had the potential to become an epidemic that would destroy two-thirds of the world's population and insisted that all his meditation centers be "AIDS-free zones." Visitors to all centers, including Ko Hsuan, are required to produce a recent HIV-negative certificate. Otherwise, they are required to use separate bathrooms and separate crockery that must be washed separately—precautions that exacerbate a sense of segregation. Otherwise, the school is quite relaxed and open to visitors, who are welcome at the annual fund-raising event and open day, the Ko Hsuan Summer Event.

Visits from government inspectors, Her Majesty's Inspectors (HMI), and Social Services were initially regarded with some trepidation but are now welcomed, following their very positive and constructive feedback. Researchers, both journalists and academics, are still regarded with some suspicion, partly on account of past negative publicity. My own application to do research was initially rejected, partly on account of its religious context. However, the initial rejection also reflected a division between the more orthodox, inward-looking members of the camp who did not want any research even if it provided positive publicity and a more world-accepting group that favored disseminating information to the wider public. This division reflects a current debate in the wider sannyasin community regarding the degree of openness to the outside world; this debate is also taking place in other NRMs. Once accepted, I did receive full cooperation, including access to government reports and a warm welcome from the guest coordinator, the other teachers, and the pupils.

The school brochure describes four stages in its short history, the first being "survival." This was followed by "learning the art of living together authentically and harmoniously." At this time, lessons did take place, but within a loose curriculum that was superseded by psychosocial and spiritual aims. The third stage introduced a more structured academic syllabus, largely in response to the children's demands, at a time when increased size, funding, facilities, and stability allowed this development. The fourth and current stage is described as allowing "the dimension of meditation [to] take root and flourish," although there is some disagreement as to its successful realization.

The brochure also contains the school's manifesto, which lays out a strongly child-centered philosophy. The main values are humanistic: freedom, self-responsibility, authenticity, uniqueness, harmony, sensitivity, and inner consciousness. In an interesting contrast to mainstream liberal thought, equality is "not an aim": "We recognize that we are not all equal and that we have different roles to fulfill." Democracy is rejected in favor of "mutual agreement": decision-making through "trying to find a synthesis of the general wisdom of all rather than by polarizing different viewpoints and having to choose between them." The manifesto also attempts to reconcile the educational "guidelines given by the Department of Education and Science (DES) and Osho"—a synthesis not always easy to achieve.

Social Organization

Osho was antiauthoritarian almost to the point of anarchy. Although this ideology did not translate into the social organization of the movement, it still provides a framework for its thinking on community, as well as education. This paradox confronts all libertarian founders of schools and sometimes hastens their demise, as happened with Bertrand Russell's experimental school in the 1920s. Successful democracy depends on a balance between responsible pupil power and sensitive teacher participation if the school is not going to slide into chaos or revert to authoritarianism.

There is little in the way of an authority structure at Ko Hsuan. The title of "head teacher" is a formality, in compliance with DES requirements, and the post is currently held by the only teacher with formal qualifications and experience. The teachers all have equal status and rotate roles and responsibilities. The authority relationship between staff and pupils is not specified. In practice the structures and rules are created and maintained by staff, but often in response to the children's requests and requirements, as one teacher explained:

> The rules have evolved over the years from a mixture of inspiration from Osho and pragmatism. They are open to being changed by kids as well as adults, but we are unlikely to keep changing rules at whim. A certain amount of order is needed in any commune and if something works, there is not so much need to keep tinkering with it. We are more concerned with the "spirit" of the school and the promotion of joy, individuality, responsibility, freedom—and the rules should enhance and not inhibit these qualities.

The most important quality of the teacher-pupil relationship is friendship, and both teachers and pupils affirm the reality of this ideal. As one teacher expressed it:

> We are more like friends to the kids, but we have very different functions. We do play roles, and I may be like a sergeant major sometimes, but I'll drop that role very quickly when I'm not trying to achieve that objective, like when we're sitting having dinner. There's a mutual respect that the kids are kids, but they're as intelligent natively as we are only they haven't had the same life experience in order to know how things work or what needs to be done. Their status is the same as ours, but we have different functions.

Both the school inspectors and Social Services reports noted the positive relationships in the school. Out of the five areas of good practice highlighted in the 1993 Inspection Report by the Social Services, the first three were "(i) The high level of commitment from all staff; (ii) The warm, supportive, caring and happy atmosphere fostered and maintained by the staff; (iii) The quality of relationships between staff and pupils."

Discipline is not a high priority at Ko Hsuan, and one of the few criticisms in the 1992 Social Services report was the lack of a written sanctions/rewards policy. The manifesto claims that there are no punishments, but the report highlighted the use of "loss of privilege" as a possible sanction noted on end-of-term reports, but not in the context of any systematic monitoring of individual behavior. The report also pointed out that the school relied on "real responses" from others as a sanction, and that negative feedback could be punishing in itself. The school itself regards this process as educative in terms of learning to live with others. The report raised some concern regarding the health and safety aspects of organization, such as keeping track of children leaving the grounds, points that have now been dealt with by the school. With this proviso, the report concluded that "relationships and disciplinary measures within the school are satisfactory and conducive to safeguarding and promoting the children's welfare." I was told that the HMI had also commented that discipline was better than at a nearby public school.

The school has now agreed with the Department of Social Security to a form of progressive sanctions: a formal warning, followed by one month's trial, followed by expulsion, either for a term or for an indefinite period. This procedure was invoked at the end of the last academic year when two students were asked to leave, two others asked to take a term off, and two more who had planned to leave and then asked to stay were refused. These were all aged fourteen and fifteen, and their dismissal was the result of a combination of poor attendance, lack of effort, and undermining of school rules.

The emphasis generally is less on discipline than on cooperation. Nevertheless, an appreciation of the benefits of order and stability has grown out of the earlier more experimental approach—partly a response to size, which has given rise to the present system of rotating chores. There was a consensus that people wanted a reasonably clean environment and meals on time. There is no outside help with these functions, but staff and pupils operate a weekly rota, which functions well. Every Monday morning the whole school participates in a "deep clean," and every day there are cleaning before lessons, lunch and dinner preparation, and clearing. It was impressive to see the pupils, including teenage boys, industriously vacuuming and chopping carrots. Indeed, I was informed that one of the changes most enthusiastically commented on by parents was their offspring's increased self-reliance and helpfulness during the holidays. What was particularly impressive was that this condition appeared to have been achieved not through indoctrination or (usually fruitless) coercion by parents and teachers, but through the children's own sense of identity with their school as a home and their desire for its effective functioning. Of course, not all the children cleaned their room with equal enthusiasm, but one teacher explained that the policy was to "nag but not force," which usually achieved the desired results. As one teacher expressed it: "Most rules are practical, there to help the school run, not to tell kids how they should feel or be—just telling kids how not to harm other people; live their life, do what they want to do, but be part of the commune. The manifesto quotes Osho on freedom and responsibility going together. The kids have to do their jobs, though we'll help them, remind them."

As stated in the manifesto, agreement is the desired outcome and the basis of organizational structures. The children must accept some basic agreements in order to come to the school.[3] On the whole these work, since they are subject to review. For example, the teachers agreed to leave the storeroom unlocked at the children's request—a policy that did not work not because the children ate all the food, but because they left the room in a mess. So it was closed again between meals. The 1992 Social Services report concluded that "the overall impression gained during visits was one of a well-ordered environment; management by mutual agreement seems to be working at Ko Hsuan."

One teacher, however, suggested that in some ways the word *agreement* glossed over the underlying power structure:

> They could be seen more like rules. Kids have to agree to them in order to come here, but they are agreeing them in order to come here. So it's not something their energy's totally behind necessarily. They may not want to keep their room clean, but if they keep insisting not, we might ask them to leave. So it's a little unclear what to call these things really. The power does shift, and on the whole the adults have a way of how we see Ko Hsuan, and what the kids see may be totally different. We may want a group of twelve-year-old boys to not have their laundry lying all over the floor and empty Coke cans lying around, and they haven't even noticed!

Thus, teachers and students tend to be quite open about the lack of consensus on key issues but feel that the minimal structure is flexible enough to accommodate these differences. There are weekly Sunday meetings attended by the staff, which are partly an opportunity to meet as a group and share or clear any issues and partly a practical occasion to discuss any problems with the children or organization.[4] Monday meetings are attended by the whole school, one of which I attended. I found it relaxed, but orderly, a mixture of announcements, requests, and complaints. People sat on the floor and stairs and spoke one at a time without an agenda or prearranged order. Staff and children had an equal voice, though some spoke louder than others—as in any group. They were listened to mostly in silence, though with occasional restlessness—the speaker being responsible to restore order, since there was no chairperson. Their comments sometimes led to an agreed course of action. The main message that came through—sometimes gently, sometimes quite aggressively—was, "This is our place; let's all take care of it and of each other."

I found the meeting an impressive demonstration of pupil participation in management, a process that is now beginning to be encouraged in state schools. It reflected a successful resolution of the authority issue through giving both power and responsibility to the students while still ensuring staff intervention where necessary to prevent bullying and to maintain order.

Environmental issues are greatly emphasized, and students are involved in intensive recycling projects. Race appears to be a nonissue, since the school is very international, and there are no signs of racism. As for class consciousness, the children are predominantly middle class, but not all the parents are well off, and some work as cleaners to pay the fees, but there appears to be no class prejudice. Attitudes to gender reflect contemporary Western society. Boys and girls all cook and clean, do math, woodwork, and art. Teachers assist the teenagers as much as possible through the uncertainties of adolescence, which they claim the girls handle better than the boys—enjoying dressing up, flirting, and being "girly." One teacher shared his observations of gender roles in the school as follows:

> They all do the same classes. I would hesitate to generalize regarding academic competence, but the girls are equally as good as the boys in all subjects, left- and right-brained. There are some very hot maths and science students among the girls. The boys are very good on the dinner prep team, but I don't notice the difference so much there. I do notice boys are noisier, more aggressive, running around, and the girls are quieter, more in touch with themselves.

Living and Learning at Ko Hsuan

Osho continually denounced the pundit as a symbol of the domination of mind (specifically intellect) over heart and spirit. He believed that this imbalance lay at the root of humanity's ignorance, neurosis, and misery. In his teaching, the mind almost becomes the devil barring us from enlightenment. A notice at the entrance to the ashram's meditation hall exhorted meditators to leave their minds with their shoes—shoes in India symbolizing the lowest state of untouchability. This was a radical reversal of traditional belief, since in the Hindu caste system pundits were the scholars of the highest Brahman caste, whereas the Untouchables were outside the caste system altogether. In contrast, the heart was perceived as a higher state of being and the route to spiritual progress. In regard to the mind, sannyasin attitudes have changed since Osho's death toward a more flexible balance between head and heart.

Ko Hsuan has since developed in a way that would have been unthinkable in its early years, with the introduction of the national curriculum and the General Certificate of Secondary Education (GCSE) examinations. This change occurred at the children's request and increased the need for structure. Whereas class attendance had once been optional, it now became compulsory (although it may not be closely monitored, since there is no register and there are pupils wandering around during class time seemingly unoccupied). The staff has taken on board the HMI suggestion that unless the children experience a subject, they have no grounds to reject it. The introduction of these new syllabi caused some upheaval and trauma, particularly among the staff, whose philosophy of education was radically challenged.

On one afternoon of my visit, there were no lessons taking place, apart from an unscheduled aikido session. It was an exceptionally hot day toward the end of term, and after exams, so swimming and cream teas were arguably more appropriate activities.

Previously, the curriculum at Ko Hsuan, as well as at the Medina and Rajneeshpuram schools, had been based on Osho's highly original vision of "five-dimensional education" (5D). This condemned examinations, competitions, and even teachers, whose function should be reduced to simple guidance. On the positive side, education should consist of five dimensions: (1) informative subjects, such as history, geography, and language, which can be learned through television and computer; (2) science—a more complicated subject that can be covered technologically with the help of a teacher; (3) the art of living, including humor and reverence for life; (4) art and creativity; 5) the art of dying, including meditation and martial arts (Osho 1991). This model, outlined in inspirational but sketchy terms, had been the basis of a creative and flexible educational approach, continually adapting to the requests of the children and the expertise of the available staff.

With the introduction of GCSEs came a switch of emphasis from the five dimensions to the five core subjects of math, English, art, science, and a foreign language. The overall approach remained "multidimensional," but all pupils staying on for the final two years (ages fourteen to sixteen) have to participate in the examination program. Despite the angst of the transition, the results have been successful, mostly passes, with about one-third *A* and *B* grades and a particularly success in art (eight *A*'s and two *B*'s out of fourteen). These results are in line with the national average. As a result, a wider range of subjects is now available. There is a regular timetable of classes, four in the morning, two in the afternoon.

Teaching styles have not yet fully adapted to the curricular changes. There is a reluctance to mark and grade, both of which activities teachers see as encouraging competition and loss of self-esteem. The lessons usually have specific objectives, sometimes following a course book, but the few I attended were unstructured, sometimes to the point of anarchy. This was probably a partial result of a libertarian philosophy and a lack of training. Of the fifteen teachers, some had degrees, but only one had both training and teaching experience; one had trained but was in her first job; and the sports teacher had done outward bound training but was unqualified in math, which he also taught.[5]

The staff makes up for lack of training in enthusiasm and commitment and often finds ingenious and creative ways of teaching. One teacher explained the rationale behind an apparently chaotic lesson that ended in a competition among the brightest boys in throwing Coke cans into wastepaper baskets.[6] He explained that he let them go at their own pace, and rather than giving them the official ten-minute break between two lessons that lasted nearly two hours (which tended to extend to half an hour, after which it was hard to reestablish concentration), he started slowly, warming up through conversation, and building to a period of hard work and concentration, then winding down again, letting them leave early. This approach succeeded in keeping the more restless, disruptive children at their desks (if not quiet), but at the expense of the quieter ones, who received almost no attention. But he felt that it was counterproductive to push the rebellious children, since they would only resist harder. If trusted, they would get through the work in their own time.

The pupils themselves were, on the whole, very positive about the teaching. They expressed a preference for the more creative and expressive subjects, art, drama, and English. Some worked hard, despite distractions and disruptions; on my first visit I found a group of girls doing their homework indoors on a sunny Saturday afternoon. Some of the foreign children were clearly experiencing language difficulties, though they did receive remedial help and learned quickly from the other children. They all seemed to appreciate the kindness and freedom of this child-centered approach, although some of the teenage boys exhibited the "cool" indifference of their age group. A few of the brighter children got bored and frustrated, which may account for some of the disruptive behavior and may also lead to underachievement. Mixed-ability classes exacerbated this problem, although the high ration of teachers to pupils compensated.

Ko Hsuan lacks many of the resources of state-funded schools. It has made great strides over the last few years in building extensions, including a large hall for sports and theater and an arts and crafts room. Photography is popular, and the darkroom is well used. There are a science room but very little equipment, only two computers, and a severe shortage of books apart from basic course books, and a minimal library. The musical instruments consist of one piano, four guitars, and some drums, although the children do make enthusiastic use of these.[7] The prospectus claims the school offers a wide range of sports, but there is little evidence of these, although during my visit a visiting aikido teacher was the main attraction. Otherwise, there is a small football pitch, but "sports" may consist simply of a walk by the river or even shopping. The grounds themselves are very beautiful and spacious, including gardens, meadows, and woodlands for the children to play in, which is clearly a great benefit.

A Religious School?

The main question here is whether, or in what sense, Ko Hsuan may be considered a religious school and whether there is any religious indoctrination.

Both staff and students insisted, "This is not a religious school." Indeed, this was the main reason for their initial refusal of my research application: they did not want to be involved in a comparative project with other religious schools or defined as a religion.

There was always a tradition of antipathy toward organized religion, particularly Christianity, in the old Rajneesh movement. Osho's most trenchant criticisms were reserved for priests as the agents of religious socialization, which he considered spiritual enslavement. According to his Marxist analysis, priests exploited the mass's fear by creating concepts of sin, guilt, and punishment—establishing a rift between humanity and God that only priests could bridge. He believed that their main method/weapon was indoctrination.[8] This critique of institutionalized religion presents a challenge to a school set up to present and preserve his vision without carving it in stone.

Anti-Christianity was a striking element in the children's subculture, expressed as an insult in slanging matches ("I bet you're a Christian, too!"). I noticed a pervasive hostility toward Christianity among the teenage boys, who had reacted negatively toward a perceived indoctrination into Christianity at their former schools: "Praying to God, reading the Bible, singing hymns—it's all ridiculous! Disgusting!" The sign of the cross was used as an insulting gesture to each other and strangers. One girl was wearing a cross around her neck, but she described it as "an ancient symbol of eternal life—not a cross!" The teachers were not aware of encouraging these feelings, since many of them shared them. When questioned, they admitted that this anti-Christianity probably originated with them and the children's parents.

The Osho movement does not recruit children, but most parents give sannyas to their children, sometimes while they are still babies. This is an initiation ceremony in which Osho's disciples are given their sannyasin names. Some children may take sannyas voluntarily at a later stage. Parents who give sannyas to their children do not feel they are imposing a religion on their children; rather, it is the best gift they can give them and one that the children are free to reject at any time. One mother explained: "My experience of sannyas is not as a religion. It's an invitation to live life as honestly, as creatively, as spontaneously, as caringly, as totally in the moment as possible. To me it's the opposite of giving [my son] a fixed religion. It's inviting him to see what his reality is, and how he experiences life, rather than giving him a list of set rules." Her view is in line with Osho's (1984:185) teaching: "When I give sannyas to a child, it is not that you have to impose an ideology on him. You have just to persuade him towards meditativeness. . . . One day he will be grateful for it—that you helped him." In a formal sense, Ko Hsuan does not fit the category of a religious school. Both Robert Mullan at Medina (1983) and Shirley Harrison at Ko Hsuan (1990) found that there was no formal religious education. This is still the case, although 5D resembles both personal and social education and religious education.

In most religious schools, and even in purportedly secular state schools, a daily assembly containing a religious component (Christian in state schools) is compulsory. However, at Ko Hsuan there is no religious morning assembly. There is a preclass meeting for practical issues, sometimes followed by an optional meditation: a version of Osho's Mystic Rose meditation shortened and adapted for children. However, only about four adults and twelve children participated in 1994. All have tried the meditations, but it is not a popular pursuit, except among some of the teenage girls, who enjoy it as an emotional outlet. The teachers' explanation for this low interest was that the children were rebelling against their sannyasin upbringing.[9] The teachers expressed mixed feelings about the lack of participation in meditation:

> I feel it would help us reach agreements easier in the business meetings, and I think that was one reason why Osho was insisting that happens at least for the people running Poona. I wouldn't want to insist, I just feel it's important for me. I wanted it to happen for the whole school, but now I feel it's my life and me I need to take care of first and then see if others want to come. But at least people support the space of meditation.

There appear to be no attempts at coercion: "We don't shove it down their throats." This is in accord with Osho's (1991:99) belief that meditation is not socialization: "If you teach a child meditation you are not indoctrinating him. You don't say he has to believe anything, you simply invite him to an experiment in no-thought. No-thought is not a doctrine, it is an experience."

The master-disciple relationship, that profound experience that fueled the Rajneesh/Osho movement, appears to have diminished in intensity now that it has reached the second generation. Although dead almost a decade, Osho is still experienced by most adults as their master. Sannyasin children have always tended to accept Osho as their master, but in a more relaxed, less devotional way than the adults, and they seem to regard him less as an authority figure. Mullan (1983) quotes several of the Medina children's descriptions of Osho, which convey a feeling of fatherly love and, in one case only, a wise teacher (see also Thompson and Heelas 1986; Gordon 1987). One young sannyasin who had grown up in Poona and Rajneeshpuram described Osho as someone who had "opened my eyes a lot" but not as someone who could lead her to enlightenment, which she felt she could do only on her own. She also disliked sannyasins using Osho's words as an authority, since "he's always contradicting himself, so you can't take him seriously. You have to laugh, but some people take him totally seriously!" Her sister, however, felt a connection even though she never went to his discourses: "He was a kind of grand-dad to the kids, like 'Look what I got!' when we got presents from him. He was definitely a big figure, though not necessarily spiritual growth—I don't think kids are interested in that."

Most of the children had visited Poona, but only two of those I spoke to at Ko Hsuan had met Osho, and they could not remember him. A typical response was, "It's my life; I've grown up with it." Osho elicited positive comments, although more about his general philosophy than about him as a spiritual teacher: "It's just a different way of life which I've really enjoyed. I chose it and I really like it, the things he says, the way of living, the freedom."

There was a consensus that insofar as the master-disciple relationship still exists, it is not about reverence but "about being who you are and doing what you want to do." This is a change of emphasis from the old days, when love for the master and the desire to "do his work" were predominant. But paradoxically, the one child who said categorically that Osho was not her master described the relationship more intimately than anyone else: "I don't pray to him. I just think of him as a friend who wanted to guide me in some sort of direction—the right direction." This perhaps provides the model for the ideal teacher-pupil relationship at Ko Hsuan.

Whatever the students' feelings are about him, Osho's presence is certainly pervasive throughout Ko Hsuan, which has the status of an Osho meditation center and is thereby entitled to hold initiation ceremonies. Some adults and children wear *malas* (necklaces of wooden beads with a locket containing Osho's photograph), but this is not compulsory. Osho's photos are everywhere, his words quoted on some classroom walls and on everything printed by the school, from prospectuses to playbills. Although the effect of Osho's pervasive presence is undoubtedly a subtle socialization, his books are not used for teaching purposes. He never intended for his ideas to be compiled into a formal doctrine, and this has not happened.

Susan Rose (1990:115) makes the important point that, although in Christian schools values are communicated to the children, "it is done more through subtle forms of socialization than through explicit teachings in the schools." Inevitably, the sannyasin children are experiencing this process. The point is that it occurs in a less overt, programmed, and intensive manner than in a typical British public school, let alone an evangelical school. It is a case not of indoctrination, but of shared values.

Conclusion

One of the most important criteria for assessing educational success is what happens to children after they leave school. It is normally measured by the kind of employment (if any) they find, although a comprehensive profile would include subjective and qualitative factors such as personal development. Records of this kind are now kept at Ko Hsuan, although the school has not been in existence long enough to provide long-term data.

As sannyasin children grow up, they diverge in many directions. Some have "dropped sannyas" (left the movement) and merged into mainstream society. Some are full-time sannyasins, spending most of their time in Poona, while others stick together in groups traveling around the world. Maintaining a group identity is typical of children who have grown up in a close community segregated from the rest of society, such as the ex-pupils of Summerhill—or, indeed, any boarding school. Of the children I spoke to in Ko Hsuan, none had long-term plans, which was unsurprising at that age, but the teachers believed that most of them managed to find work. Some were working, mostly in creative areas such as photography; others were drifting, partying, and working part-time in bars and discos. Not one had gone to work at a multinational corporation. Despite their national-average GCSE performance, a below-average percentage went on to further education: only five out of the last group of fifteen "leavers," although four more intended to after a break.

This low academic achievement might reflect an inherent conflict between the five-dimensional and five core subject approach and is perhaps a side effect of the residual anti-intellectualism in the movement's ideology. We can reasonably assume that this low achievement results from the lack of resources and of training in the teachers.

Academically gifted pupils may therefore be deprived of their opportunity to fulfill their potential. This seems to be the most problematic area that the school needs to address, although it has already made impressive progress in raising academic standards. The children clearly enjoy their school and receive an excellent affect-oriented education. At a time when emotional intelligence is beginning to be recognized as perhaps the most important determinant of achievement in work, as well as relationships, this success (acknowledged by government inspectors) needs to be valued. It is also good preparation for a learning society that encourages continuing education and training.

For the most part, the children receive an adequate academic education in spite of the lack of resources and a narrower range of subjects than the average state or independent school. In compensation, the school offers a rich, supportive social and emotional environment beyond the scope of most schools in either sector. Daniel Goleman (1966) in his book *Emotional Intelligence* argues that our idea of intelligence should change from a narrowly intellectual concept of intelligence to a more holistic understanding that includes such skills as knowing and managing emotions, empathy, flow, self-awareness, intuition, and the ability to handle relationships. He presents an impressive weight of evidence indicating that proficiency in these areas is a better indicator of future achievement than high IQ scores. The enormous success of his book (and its imitators and successors) on both sides of the Atlantic demonstrates an extensive shift in values toward an acceptance of these ideas not only in education, but also in other areas of public life, including business. Osho Ko Hsuan is working along these lines with considerable success.

In terms of ethos and values, Ko Hsuan is closer to the English liberal/radical tradition of free schools, such as Summerhill, than to Christian Evangelical religious schools. Its values are primarily humanistic: concerned with freedom, creativity, and naturalness rather than with inculcation of a specific religious worldview and conditioning. As in free schools, the children appear eminently "normal," but there is a preponderance of bright, yet difficult pupils.

This raises the question of how to balance ideological versus the organizational requirements: rebellion is encouraged as a positive quality, and yet the school has to function. Ko Hsuan's largely successful resolution of this paradox owes much to the shared values of staff and students. The creation of shared values is a key component of social thinking around community, as well as education, so in this respect Ko Hsuan is a highly relevant social experiment.

The key difference between Ko Hsuan and a typical "free school" is the inclusion of the transpersonal dimension. The praxis of the Osho movement is a synthesis of humanistic psychology and meditation. Its educational philosophy attempts to integrate humanistic and metaphysical values. One teacher commented that the school was similar to Summerhill except "there's nothing like a master behind Summerhill, though Neill himself [the founder] was a great guy." This teacher was unable to pinpoint specific differences, but he felt that the fact of everyone being sannyasins affected the "energy" and that people "experienced Osho's presence or meditation in the way they feel it in an Osho meditation center".

Whether Ko Hsuan may therefore be termed a *religious school* depends on our concepts and definitions. I argue that a distinction needs to be made between orthodox and fundamentalist religious schools that practice systematic indoctrination and schools influenced by more liberal ideologies such as the human potential movement and holistic spirituality. Osho himself was against religion in its organized, ritualistic, and doctrinal aspects but promoted in its place an authentic search for self-knowledge, truth, and freedom as the basis of personal development. Nowadays, a distinction is often made between "religion" in the former sense and "spirituality." The latter is becoming the preferred term for a holistic, life-affirmative worldview that embraces the body, nature, and sexuality, as well as the transcendental. I (Puttick 1997) argue for this definition as a major distinction between conservative, traditionalist old and new religions and those based on a more liberal, experimental ethos of meditation and personal growth. Accordingly, I endorse the refusal of Osho Ko Hsuan to be defined as a religious school, proposing that it should instead be termed a *spiritual free school.*

This distinction is important at a time when all schools are grappling with the paradoxes of education in a pluralist, multifaith society. Our democratic ideal of tolerance requires freedom of worship rather than the imposition of the dominant religion on other faiths. But ethical and spiritual concerns are a crucial agenda, requiring a nonsectarian, noncoercive response and input. Historically, most avant-garde educational experiments have failed, but Osho Ko Hsuan has so far been an impressive success story. Educationally and socially, it offers valuable lessons and an original, holistic, and challenging model to the wider society.

Notes

1. Traditionally, seekers have been required to sacrifice everything, including family life for this goal. Barker (1989:87) cites scriptural references to Jesus' and Buddha's exhortation to their disciples to renounce their families for the spiritual path. Tipton

(1982:148) finds that in American monasteries "the monastic role takes precedence over marital and parental roles." Kanter (1972) notes the hostility of nineteenth-century communes toward couples and families, and Boucher (1985) writes on the challenge for Buddhist women who are mothers of integrating motherhood with spiritual practice in Buddhist communities.

2. This and all subsequent unattributed quotations are taken from my 1990–1994 fieldwork on sannyasin women and children.
3. This is the only entrance requirement, preceded by the child's choice. Children are not accepted if placed by their parents unless they themselves are in agreement.
4. Previously, some pupil representatives had attended, but the 1994 senior pupils were uninterested in attending.
5. Within the English independent school sector, unlike the state system, no formal qualification are legally required of teachers.
6. I was informed that this incidence was not typical of classroom disciplines but reflected postexam relaxation. The exam results do demonstrate that the children are capable of hard work and focused concentration.
7. I was informed that visitors had commented that the resources were "quite good" for a small private school.
8. A common charge against NRMs is the indoctrination of the children. Rudin (1984) even accuses "cults" of actively recruiting children. It is ironic that many of the accusers are conservative Christians in the countercult movement who might be considered by some as "indoctrinated."
9. Meditation is played down in some respects. The meditation room is called the adults' sitting room, although it is empty apart from Osho's robe and photograph, a video recorder, and some cushions.

References

Barker, E. 1989. *New Religious Movements: A Practical Introduction.* London: Her Majesty's Stationery Office.

Boucher, S. 1985. *Turning the Wheel: American Women Creating the New Buddhism.* San Francisco: Harper and Row.

Carter, L. F. 1990. *Charisma and Control in Rajneeshpuram: The Role of Shared Values in the Creation of a Community.* Cambridge, U.K.: Cambridge University Press.

Goleman, D. 1996. *Emotional Intelligence: Why It Can Matter More than IQ.* London: Bloomsbury.

Gordon, J. S. 1987. *The Golden Guru: The Strange Journey of Bhagwan Shree Rajneesh.* Lexington, Mass.: Stephen Greene Press.

Harrison, S. 1990. *"Cults": The Battle for God.* London: Christopher Helm.

Kanter, R. M. 1972. *Commitment and Community: Communes and Utopias in Sociological Perspective.* Cambridge, Mass.: Harvard University Press.

Laing, R. D. 1971. *The Politics of the Family.* London: Tavistock.

Ling, T. 1973. *The Buddha: Buddhist Civilization in India and Ceylon.* London: Temple Smith.

Mullan, R. 1983. *Life as Laughter: Following Bhagwan Shree Rajneesh.* London: Routledge.

———. 1987a. *The Messiah.* Cologne: Rebel Press.

———. 1987b. *A New Vision of Women's Liberation.* Cologne, Germany: Rebel Press.

———. 1991. *The New Child.* Amsterdam: Osho Publikaties Nederland.

Puttick, E. 1997. *Women in New Religions.* London: Macmillan.

Rajneesh, S. 1984. *The Book: An Introduction to the Teachings of Bhagwan Shree Rajneesh.* Antelope, Ore.: Rajneesh Foundation International.

Rose, S. D. 1990. "Gender, Education, and the New Christian Right." Pp. 99–118 in T. Robbins and D. Anthony, eds., *In Gods We Trust.* 2d ed. New Brunswick, N.J.: Transaction.

Rudin, M. 1984. "Women, Elderly, and Children in Religious Cults." *Cultic Studies Journal* 1(1): 8–26.

Thompson, J., and P. Heelas. 1986. *The Way of the Heart: The Rajneesh Movement.* Wellingborough, England: Aquarian.

Tipton, S. M. 1982. *Getting Saved from the Sixties: Moral Meaning in Conversion and Cultural Change.* Berkeley and Los Angeles: University of California Press.

Chapter 6

Growing Up As Mother's Children

Socializing a Second Generation in Sahaja Yoga

Judith Coney

Like many new religious movements, the small Hindu-based contemporary movement called "Sahaja Yoga" has a distinctive image and model of childhood.[1] Although this ideal model has certainly influenced the upbringing of Western children within the movement, it has had to compete with other models of children and childhood. This chapter addresses the issue of the translation of an ideal model of childhood into practical reality within a sectarian religious environment. Toward this end, I examine how the ideal model affects the children and how competing models gain influence. I suggest that where competing models exist, the influence of the ideal model is most evident in such areas of the children's lives as their understandings of the status of the founder of the religion and their ritual practice. In other words, the model's effects are largely, though not exclusively, confined to the spiritual domain. However, even when children are not obviously exposed to competing models of socialization, other factors can disrupt the imposition of an ideal model of childhood on their behavior.

Sahaja Yoga

The founder of Sahaja Yoga, Sri Mataji Nirmala Devi, was born on March 21, 1923, in Chindwara, India. The second of six children and the eldest daughter of a leading Indian barrister, Nirmala seems to have enjoyed an affluent childhood in a Protestant Christian household. However, the peacefulness of this childhood was shattered by the Indian struggle for political independence, in which her family was actively involved. After Independence, she was married to Chandika Prasad Srivastava, a successful diplomat, and they had two daughters. Subsequently she accompanied her husband to his new post in London of secretary general of the United Nations International Maritime Organization. Building on her own experience of self-realization and on an already established reputation as a healer, Sri Mataji founded Sahaja Yoga in the early 1970s. By 1979, while still in London, she had unequivocally declared her divinity to her followers:

> [Today] is the day 'I' declare that 'I' am the One who has to save the humanity. 'I' declare', 'I' am the one who is Adi Shakti, who is the Mother of all the mothers, who is the Primordial Mother, the Shakti, the purest desire of God, who has incarnated on this Earth to give meaning to itself, to this creation, to human beings; and 'I' am sure that through 'My' Love and patience and through 'My' powers 'I' am going to achieve it. (Sahaja Yoga 1988:8)

Her conviction is affirmed by devotees, who describe her as all powerful and believe her to be the Goddess of Indian mythology returned: "Oh supremest One! Thou art the Great Incarnation. Let it be announced. . . . Almighty Sacred Mother I prostrate myself at Thy Feet. From these Feet spread the cosmic rays that generated the whole universe. This is the greatest of all times because we can behold Thee in the human flesh" (Kalbermatten 1979:298). Supported by a pantheon of lesser, though still powerful, deities, she is seen to have provided the ark of Sahaja Yoga for all those who would climb aboard to escape the evils of the world and even, some believe, its destruction. In common with many other world-rejecting movements (Wallis 1984), boundaries between Sahaja Yoga and the rest of the world are typically high, and it maintains a low profile in its relations with outsiders (Kalbermatten 1979).

Sri Mataji teaches that each individual has seven chakras, or spiritual centers, located at specific points on the central nervous system (this teaching accords with traditional Tantric understandings of the body), and a spiritual energy, kundalini, that lies in a dormant state in the sacrum. Kundalini can be induced to rise through the chakras, by Sri Mataji or her followers, until it pierces the fontanel area at the top of the head. When this happens, participants feel a cool breeze, sometimes on the palms of their hands or above their heads and sometimes more generally. This process, called "self-realization," is said to produce a state of "thoughtless awareness," the first stage in a progression toward "God Realization" (Kalbermatten 1979). Members have stated that they become increasingly sensitive to positive and negative "vibrations" in their environment as a result of this process.

All committed Sahaja Yogis have a shrine in the home that is set aside for Sri Mataji; members meditate before it at least once daily. Benefits are said to include an increase in good health and relief from stress (Kakar 1984; Rai 1993; Sharma 1993; Spiro 1993). Purification is an important ritual theme within the group, and most members perform a number of other ritual activities relating to this theme regularly. These include soaking their feet in warm salted water each evening to rid themselves of accumulated negativity, performing daily rituals of protection to ward off impurity, and, on occasion, putting lemons and chilies under the bed for seven days at a time to exorcise negativity and spirits.

In common with other sects (Shupe and Bromley 1980; Bromley and Oliver 1982), members of this group embrace a fictive kinship system held to be of greater spiritual validity than their families of origin. Adults are encouraged to relate to each other as brothers and sisters, and Sri Mataji is called "Mother" by her devotees. Similarly, her followers are referred to as her "children." Reflecting this sense of belonging to a large family, some members live in collective households, or ashrams. The rest live with their own families, some within arranged marriages or, in a minority of cases, with nonmembers or alone. Even in the latter instance, however, they come together regularly at public meetings and Sahaja Yoga events, and the lifestyle of committed Sahaja Yogis is regulated by group activities and a preeminent obligation to the movement over and above other considerations and relationships.

Sahaja Yoga has a growing membership, and the group is engaged in international expansion (Coney 1995), so far claiming a presence in over twenty-five countries around the world.[2] It attracts a predominantly middle-class following in Britain, where it is also steadily expanding in numbers. As Table 6.1 shows, there were around three hundred fully committed British adult members in 1993, representing an increase of about 40 percent from the number in 1987.[3]

Table 6.1 also indicates that the numbers of children in the group rose during this period. Indeed, the growth rate outstripped that of adult members and increased at a rate of over 90 percent. This, in turn, affected the ratio of children to adults in the group. Having children is encouraged in Sahaja Yoga, abortion is not condoned, and the majority of female members are of childbearing age. Given these facts, it is easy to assume that most of these additional children were born into the group. However, although twenty-nine babies were added to "the English collective" over the period 1987–1993 by this route, their number was largely offset by the twenty-one children who left it, either because of schooling, their parents' relocating, or leaving Sahaja Yoga. By far the biggest group of new children, fifty-six in all, were those brought into Sahaja Yoga by one or both parents.

The Model of Childhood and Children in Sahaja Yoga

Sri Mataji, as the Divine Mother of all Sahaja Yogis, has put forward a model of childhood that is at least partially based on the understanding that children in Sahaja Yoga are different from ordinary children. Many children who

TABLE 6.1 *Children and Adults in Sahaja Yoga in Britain*

	Number of children	Number of adults	Ratio of adults to children
1987	68	222	3.26:1
1993	132	311	2.36:1
Growth rate	94.12%	40.09%	–27.6%

have been born in Sahaja Yoga, says Sri Mataji, are "realized" from birth, have chosen to be born under her tutelage, and are particularly sensitive to the vibrations of others. Those children "brought in" to Sahaja Yoga are, in practice, of equal sensitivity, having been given their realization by adults in the group during this lifetime. Thus, all children require an upbringing that Sri Mataji, as a result of her authority and divine wisdom, is most qualified to dictate. Indeed, Sri Mataji has stressed the primacy of her relationship with the children in Sahaja Yoga by saying to their parents:

> I would advise you: . . . don't get too involved with your children, that's a dangerous thing. . . . You have to just do the work like a trustee of the child, just a trustee of the child, but don't get involved with the child—that's my job. . . . The children are mine, not yours, so you just don't get involved with them, that's a temptation for you, too much involvement with the children, that's a sign of degradation. (Sahaja Yoga 1984:n.p.)

Thus, although parents, especially mothers, usually take on the responsibility for childrearing in the early years, Sri Mataji's advice on the subject of child care is seen as highly significant.[4] Her tips have covered the minutiae of infant care from breast-feeding to toilet training, and most of these tips accord with traditional Indian wisdom and common sense. Other advice has concerned such matters as the ways in which babies pick up negativity: "Sri Mataji has . . . explained that God can protect the children from most harmful vibrations, but cannot protect them from the vibrations of the parents. Therefore it is important that the parents cleanse themselves as much as possible. . . . Almost all vibrational problems that the babies and children have is that of the parents (Sahaja Yoga 1984:n.p.)."

Once the babies have become toddlers, Sri Mataji has said, an environment in which Sahaja Yoga norms prevail should ideally produce children who possess the qualities most extolled in the movement: innocence, sweetness, respectfulness, cleanliness, and obedience. Moreover, the period between two and six years is crucial, in her view, for the correct upbringing of children. It is at this stage that the young should begin to be formally socialized in the values of the movement and should learn the fundamental virtue of detachment. Thus, she (Sahaja Yoga 1986:n.p.) has counseled,

> the child should be allowed to be slept *[sic]* alone but in parents room till the age of 2 years. . . . But when they are grown up, say after 2 years or so, they can sleep in another room together in collectivity, all the children. . . . Keep their clothes together, put things together, then they should not belong to anyone personally. Let them be together away from the parents, that's important.

The children are to be encouraged to see all adult Sahaja Yogis as their "Aunties" or "Uncles" and to accept praise or reprimand from all alike. Natural ties are, to an extent, to be superseded by the primacy of the group, and the children are to be discouraged from relying too much on their parents.[5] They are expected to learn by modeling their behavior on the adult Sahaja Yogis, who must strive to be exemplary: "They will mature very sweetly if we manage to give a good example they can follow" (Sahaja Yoga 1994a:1).

To stimulate their self-reliance, Sri Mataji (Sahaja Yoga 1986:n.p.) advises that Sahaja Yoga children not be encouraged to adopt a questioning attitude during this period: "Then another thing is asking questions, by children, it should not be allowed, at all, till 6 years, they should not be allowed, so 'what is this, what is that' not to be allowed. . . . Don't ask them to trouble you so the habit will not develop." Instead, by being brought up in an environment that encourages "natural" qualities to emerge, the children are expected to learn to emulate values espoused by the group. In terms of gender, for instance, Sri Mataji (Sahaja Yoga 1994a:7) says that girls "can play such sweet games with the toys, for example giving nice names to the dolls, teaching them how to behave, to be quiet and polite with their elders, or how to put the dolls to sleep without making any disturbing noises. Motherhood develops from that age," whereas "cars and horses and things like that can be given" to the boys. To enforce the ideal model, she (Sahaja Yoga 1994a:8) has proposed: "If they answer back give them two slaps, that's allowed. . . . If you do not teach them they will be disrespectful to other people and other people will smack them, then you won't like it. But they have every right to smack if a child misbehaves, because children must know how to behave themselves."

Indeed, children, Sri Mataji has stated, are often wayward because of a lack of such discipline. Occasionally, however, she has attributed more sinister causes, such as possession or mental illness, to a refusal to conform. Thus, she (Sahaja Yoga 1986:n.p.) explained the behavior of a two-year-old child belonging to a devotee who would not say good morning to her in the following terms:

> I asked all of them, how is Sita, very sweet, very sweet. . . . Soon as I saw her I said "I'll go blind with this." Little thing like that, as if a big cunning woman had taken over her and so cunning her ways were, so cunning for a little girl of 2 years, none of us could manage her. . . . There was nothing natural in her. . . . Children can be very very cunning if they are [possessed] and extremely clever. . . . They'll end up with

cancers, I'll tell you, or with lunacy. This girl might become, she's already schizophrenic, already she is schizophrenic.

Before examining the impact on the children of Sri Mataji's prescriptions for childhood, I want to look at how the children themselves understand her role in their lives as a gauge of the importance attributed to her. In terms of contact with her, the children are usually taken to see Sri Mataji as babies or when their parents become committed followers, and many have photographs of themselves with Sri Mataji that help to cement this tie. More generally, they grow up surrounded by photographs of her and are regularly told stories of her miracles. Some are given Indian names by her, a few are allowed on her lap during festivals, and the children often put on performances, such as dances and plays for Sri Mataji at the end of festivals. All, then, know who she is, and not surprisingly, all of the children whom I asked about her status expressed an awareness that Sri Mataji was special. Those belonging to more committed parents were most likely to articulate the belief that she is divine, as in this extract from a television interview with infant Sahaja Yoga children in Australia:

Interviewer: Is [Sri Mataji] a good person?
First infant: Yes.
Interviewer: Why is she a good person?
First infant: Because she protects us from baddies.
Interviewer: Who do you think she is?
Second infant: The Goddess.[6]

Similarly, one seven-year-old from Britain explained: "Well, I think she is God . . . God and Jesus. Because she is sort of my Mother and God, I call her 'Godmother.' I feel nice about her. Sometimes I think her picture moves and that she is staring at me" (Interview January 13, 1995). The majority worldwide are likely, moreover, to echo the sentiments of one little girl who remarked to her natural mother, "You're not the best mother because Mother is." But, she continued, "you are definitely the second best!" (Interview September 13, 1994).

Practical Applications of the Model

What has been said so far might suggest that Sri Mataji's injunctions on the upbringing of children are followed to the letter and that all parents relinquish control over their children's development to her. This assumption, however, does not take into account factors such as the polyvocal nature of any community, even sectarian ones; differences in levels of commitment among members that allow competing models to be introduced; and differences in group pressure in different locations. All these variables tend to reduce, to differing extents, the impact of the ideal model of childhood Sri Mataji has proposed. Thus, despite the fact that Sri Mataji is an important presence in the lives of Sahaja Yoga children, and despite the importance she herself attaches to her advice to parents, there is variation in the degree to which children in the movement are brought up to emulate the ideal image of childhood that she has set out. Because of this variation in socialization, it would be misleading to present a "typical" picture that encompasses the lives of all the children in the movement. Instead, two examples from two opposite ends of the range of child socialization in Sahaja Yoga can inform us as to how and to what extent the model is translated into practice. Whereas the children in Britain are subject to a number of competing influences in their primary socialization, those in the Sahaja Yoga school in India are almost entirely isolated from socializing forces other than those in their immediate surroundings.

Sahaja Yoga Children in Britain

In family homes and ashrams across the United Kingdom, Sahaja Yoga children appear well cared for and as cherished and loved as any other normal set of youngsters. The picture in Britain is of a group of children who are exposed to a number of differing socializing influences and who generally appear to be happy and well adjusted. The girls tend to be dressed in pretty feminine clothes, and the boys are also well dressed, even when the parents have little money themselves. The children have toys, often chosen according to Sri Mataji's advice, and all the other normal accouterments of childhood in the United Kingdom. Their diet is usually nonvegetarian and varied, although it often includes more sugar than is common in the West. Childhood ailments are likely to be treated in the first instance with meditation and/or medications prescribed by Sri Mataji, but conventional medical advice is also sought when necessary.

In Britain, the children are expected to call adults "Auntie" or "Uncle" and relate to them as family members, deserving of affection and possessing some authority over them, although in practice their parents exercise the greater authority. Through these relationships, the children learn informally many of the beliefs of the movement, such as the status of Sri Mataji. More structured socialization into the values of the movement is derived from ritual and from the education provided in Sahaja Yoga.

The vast majority of the children, including babies, are integrally involved in the daily ritual practices of the group that take place in the home.[7] The children are expected to meditate every day and to foot-soak with the adults each evening; most of the adults I asked said they enjoyed the children's participation. They learn about ritual postures mostly from their parents, although at one festival I noticed a young child of no more than five years being instructed in how she should sit with arms outstretched to feel vibrations from Sri Mataji by another child of a similar age. The young are also told about kundalini, chakras, and vibrations from an early age.

More collectively, the British children I observed clearly enjoyed being involved in sessions of singing *bhajans* (devotional songs) extolling virtues of Sri Mataji. The children are involved in larger rituals as well. Indeed, in one, the *puja,* all Sahaja Yoga children are called on to play a key role.[8] During this ritual, at an early stage in the proceedings the children wash a photograph of Sri Mataji's feet, or her own feet if she is present. This practice is performed to release good vibrations for the rest of the puja, and the innocence of the children is understood to make them ideal agents for this task. Such rituals can last for a number of hours. However, the children are fed and given drinks during the proceedings and often slip out quietly to play after their participation in the ritual is over, rejoining the company in time for the sharing out of *prasad* at the end.[9]

The vast majority of Sahaja Yoga children in the United Kingdom do not have a full-time education in the movement, despite the tendency of members to feel apprehensive about the negativity in the outside world. Instead, most receive a state education, although a few are in the independent sector. Perhaps because "normalcy" is usually a prized commodity among children, and learned in the early stages of peer interaction at school, most appear to reveal little about Sahaja Yoga while at school, either to other children or to their teachers. Ben said, for instance: "Jennifer was my friend at school when I was really small and I . . . meditated on her and she didn't even know. She thought I was tickling her. I didn't do it again" (Interview, January 13, 1995). The children are not withdrawn from religious education lessons, since Sahaja Yoga says that it upholds the authentic spiritual teachings of major religious traditions. However, some parents have withdrawn their children from sex education sessions to protect their innocence.

Daily foot soaking, meditations, and other rituals of purification are usually practiced after school to rid the children of any negative vibrations they may have, often inadvertently, picked up during school hours. In the absence of socialization in Sahaja Yoga values during full-time education, some efforts are made to supplement the socialization gained from interaction with adults in the movement and from ritual practice. Thus, parents are encouraged to send their children to weekend or weekly camps that are arranged from time to time. A day at a weekend camp is summarized by one of the organizers:

> 6.00 A.M. . . . and the children were up and washed and dressed for meditation. . . . The children were very good, calm, quiet and serene. Once meditation was over they made their way to the breakfast room. The children were then split into three groups according to their ages and commenced various activities, including: making a card for Sri Mataji, learning about the subtle system and learning about integrating their Sahaja knowledge into their everyday school life. Later in the day they discussed and rehearsed a play. . . . After supper the children had a meditation and bhajan session, and then washed and went to bed. (Sahaja Yoga 1994b:3)[10]

Despite such efforts to augment the children's education, however, the children appear to be most influenced by their involvement with Sahaja Yoga in terms of their positive images of Sri Mataji, in their ritual lives, and in the feeling they have of belonging to an extended family. The children, especially through mainstream schooling, and through friends outside Sahaja Yoga and television, come into contact with other values. Thus, children over the age of ten in 1998 were as likely to have pictures of Leonardo Di Caprio or Kate Winslett on their bedroom walls as a photograph of Sri Mataji. In other respects, then, the Sahaja Yoga children do not appear very different to their contemporaries outside the movement.

Children in the Sahaja Yoga School

The Sahaja Yoga school, which provides full-time education for children in the movement, has accepted children from the age of four, and often very young children are separated from their natural parents. Moreover, this separation is for much longer than the separation more usually involved in the boarding school system (a month off at Christmas, Easter, and three months over the summer). The children stay in India for nine months, returning home for the other three months of the year. Thus, the school offers an opportunity for the children to develop almost entirely without access to competing systems of socialization, especially since their parents are likely to be the most devoted of Sri Mataji's followers and therefore most likely to follow her pronouncements at home.

Relatively few of the British children in Sahaja Yoga, no more than a few dozen, have so far undergone full-time education in this school, and apparently there is no pressure on U.K. parents to send them. However, the extent to which parents feel pressure, from either their peers or the leadership, to send their offspring to the Sahaja Yoga school in Rome or in India does vary markedly depending on the country of residence. In Switzerland, for example, where most Sahaja Yogis live in ashrams, the vast majority of children are educated in Sahaja Yoga schools. One ex-member commented, "They always said that people from other countries just made excuses for parents not to send their children" (Interview, June 20, 1995).

Those British Sahaja Yoga parents who do choose to send their children to school in India have given a number of reasons for their decision: a desire for their offspring to be brought up according to Sahaja Yoga principles; the small class sizes; a belief that, because India has the purest vibrations, it is the best environment for their children; and an assumption that in India the children are protected from the corrupting influence of the West (Sahaja Yoga 1992b). The aims of the school stated in its prospectus include the provision of "basic knowledge in all subjects in a happy, friendly, homely and stimulating environment." Each child is, moreover, said to be encouraged "to develop personality and individuality and yet retain the ability to relate, work, share and play harmoniously without evoking competition and enjoy the reality of collectivity."[11] A recent independent report on the Indian school done by the Austrian Embassy noted: "There are 10 classes for 196 pupils . . . of elementary school class. . . . Among the children there are some Australians, Italians as well as some Europeans, North Americans and Asians but very few Indians. . . . The main building of the school including the inner school yard, the classrooms, the dormitories, the canteen and offices are newly built and bright, the furniture simple."[12]

The day begins early, at 6:00 A.M. for the younger ones and 5:30 A.M. for the older children. The timetable is full, and the children retire to bed at 9:00 P.M., sleeping in dormitories of up to fifteen students. The curriculum includes English, math, science, social studies, art, craft, and dance, and English is the spoken language. One foreign language is compulsory, with German or Hindi being offered. The children adhere diligently to the rituals of Sahaja Yoga. Depending on the pupil's age, they meditate for up to an hour in the morning and evening, and the yearly reports on the children contain assessments of meditative concentration, collectivity (the ability to live harmoniously in a group), obedience, and self-esteem. The environment of the school appears to be is one in which the ideal model of childhood set out by Sri Mataji is being implemented.

It is clear, too, that in contrast to the British children of Sahaja Yogis living in the United Kingdom, those attending the India school have little access to outside influences. A statement made by Sahaja Yogis about the school in India says that "many women from the village come to see the children, bring presents for them and look after them. The whole village enjoys looking after these children" (Sahaja Yoga 1992b:3). But the Austrian report on the school in 1995 stated: "People dropping in at the door are—[in a] more or less unfriendly [manner]—refused. Because of that refusal of contact, the domestic and foreign population nearby does not know anything about the teachers, pupils and the daily routine at the school, which is—regarding the rustic surrounding—an astonishing fact."[13] The school takes no children other than those belonging to Sahaja Yoga. Access to television and radio is not allowed, and "the children seem to lack further information of or about their home countries."[14] Contact between the children and their parents has been limited. The children have been allowed to write home once a week and receive packages from home twice a year; parents may telephone from time to time.

However, to conclude that the children are therefore exclusively inculcated in the Sahaja Yoga model would be overly hasty. A number of parents have voiced concerns about the regime at the school. These concerns are worth exploring briefly, since they indicate that the socialization of the children does has not always corresponded to the ideal model. It may be that the application of the ideals has either run into practical problems or conflicted with other models.

There are some parents who say that their children are happy and well looked after there and that their vibrations are wonderful as a result of being in such an environment. They are perfectly satisfied with their children's development and eager for them to return to India. One mother typically reported in 1994 that she was able to talk to her daughter on the phone. These conversations and the regular letters that she received suggested that her daughter was fine and had settled in well. Such parents send their children to the schools secure in the belief that Sri Mataji is watching over the children and is the guiding hand. Illustrating this point, a group interview of British Sahaja Yogis with children in India was conducted in October 1992 by a representative from INFORM who asked, among other things, about the caregiver/child ratio at the school. One of the mothers commented afterward that this question had made her realize that she simply did not know the answer. She felt, however, that the interviewer was not asking the right questions because "Mother is looking after the children, so of course they are all right" (Interview, September 13, 1994).

Others, however, have privately expressed misgivings about the socialization of the children. Their concerns include the quality of supervision at the school, particularly that not all of the adult caregivers are long-standing Sahaja Yogis, although the parents have assumed that they were.[15] The parents were anxious, therefore, that the children are not having sufficient contact with group members. Another relevant complaint is that the children are inadequately supervised and left too much to fend for themselves. This practice may be in line with Sri Mataji's statement that children should spend time together and not continually look to adults for guidance, but it undercuts her suggestion that the children be encouraged to model the behavior of adults. There have also been instances of children having been beaten in previous years, and the headmaster was removed from his position as a result, although he has subsequently been reinstated. The reason given for the beatings were that these reflected "teething troubles." Some of the children were "running wild" and had to be disciplined. Again, although this kind of discipline may have been done to enforce the values espoused by Sri Mataji and appear to fit with her own views on corporal punishment, they run counter to the generally peaceable and gentle natures of most of her devotees.

Lastly, there are those parents who feel that the state of their children on return from the school is evidence that the care the children have been receiving is not sufficient and is at odds with the happy and loving environment they expected. In one extreme case, for example, a child arrived home from the school having lost more than fourteen pounds and was so changed in appearance that his mother failed to recognize him at the airport. The school, however, had consistently reported throughout the year that he was "doing fine." Thus, despite the isolation of the children from competing socialization practices, it cannot be assumed that the child development model espoused by Sahaja Yoga has so far been unproblematically translated into practice.

Conflicting Models of Childhood

Primary socialization in a sectarian context often leads to conflict, mainly as a result of friction with a competing mainstream model. Sahaja Yoga is no exception in this respect, and some outsiders have been concerned about the model of childhood favored by Sri Mataji. The views of grandparents are of special significance here because the movement claims that these will be taken into consideration in any decision to send offspring to the Sahaja Yoga school. A number of British grandparents who hold understandings of a "normal" childhood that do not fit with those of Sahaja Yoga have expressed concern over the socialization the children in the movement. The main area of disagreement for most is the spiritual development of their grandchildren and their acceptance of fictive kin relations with members. Grandparents naturally fear that the children are being estranged from blood relations and are being involved in alien beliefs and practices. A few have not been allowed any contact with their grandchildren.[16] Others feel considerable distress at the thought of a grandchild being separated from parents for nine months of the year. However, those who feel disquiet have so far opted for maintaining what ties they have and have not sought actively to take the children out of the group. The reasons they have given include being too frightened to contemplate legal action, in case contact is severed completely by the parents, and fear that such action would not be successful because the courts would uphold the religious freedom of the parents.

Nevertheless, the number of U.K. grandparents who have turned to official channels for information and help is relatively small in relation to their total size. Indeed, in a couple of instances school fees were paid for by grandparents. One probable reason for this is that most grandparents expect to leave the upbringing of children to their parents and are tolerant of differences between their views and those of their children. Significantly, too, Sahaja Yogis adopt a low profile in relation to outsiders, tending to be more secretive about things that might cause conflict than is usual. This may at least partially explain the apparent lack of conflict over children in the United Kingdom, along with the relatively low-key resistance of anticult organizations in Britain.

In Europe as a whole, however, the amount of concern voiced over children in the movement is significantly greater than in Britain. This is the case partly because more Sahaja Yoga children on the Continent either live in ashrams or attend the Sahaja Yoga school, where the influence of Sri Mataji's model of childhood is significantly greater, and partly because anticult organizations on the Continent have successfully drawn attention to the differences in the children's upbringing from most other children as a way of highlighting the alienness of the sect. Thus, media coverage of Sahaja Yoga on the Continent has particularly concerned the treatment of children in Sahaja Yoga, especially in France and Italy.[17] The focus of the attack has been on Sri Mataji's emphasis on detachment. Her model of childhood centers on detachment from parents and grandparents and isolation from the dangerous effects of contact with the outside world. In France, particularly, where a different model holds sway, legal action has been successfully taken by grandparents. At the Court of Appeal in Rennes, France, in 1991, for example, a Sahaja Yoga mother was allowed custody of her two children only if she let them live with her at home. This prevented her from sending one of them back to the school in India—as was the intention of the ruling. The reasons given by the court included the following: "that the child's schooling and professional future is completely uncertain that he would for a very long time be in a situation of geographical and psychological isolation, without any real contact with the outside world, and that because of his young age and the absence of other references, would be completely incapable of refuting this situation."[18] The court concluded, "His mental health is in danger and his conditions of education very severely compromised."[19]

Conclusion

This chapter has addressed the problems of the translation of an ideal of childhood into practical reality within Sahaja Yoga. It has explored where the ideal model most influences the children and in what ways it has led to clashes with other models of childhood. Conflicts surface either when the reality does not live up to the aspirations of the ideal for Sahaja Yoga parents or when the ideal model—held by a small and therefore relatively weak section of the population—has had to compete with dominant models held by those outside the movement. We have also seen that even when overt conflict is avoided, the ideal model can be undermined through access to other models, notably as a result of mainstream schooling.

The most significant influence of the model can be seen in the spiritual development of the children, in their ritual practice, and in their acceptance of the spiritual status claimed by Sri Mataji. Further evidence of the successful application of the model lies in their acceptance of a fictive kinship system. Application of the model is at its weakest in terms of the kind of detachment from parents and other blood family members favored by Sri Mataji. In some cases, parental doubts have been both shared and played on by concerned relatives vehemently opposed to sending children away for nine months at a time.

Other factors have also conspired to mitigate the implementation of the ideal, even within a sectarian setting. Isolation from competing influences does not guarantee that the children in Sahaja Yoga schools receive intensive socialization in the values of the group. If, as it has been alleged, the children are left largely unsupervised and spend the vast majority of time with their peers, the majority of the socialization they are receiving, outside their ritual practice, is not from adults in Sahaja Yoga. Furthermore, if at least a few of the adults with whom they have the greatest contact, their teachers, are not Sahaja Yogis, this also undermines exclusive contact with the ideal model.

This is not to say, however, that even if the ideal model of child development set out by Sri Mataji was followed minutely, the children would develop naturally as she intends. As Allison James and Alan Prout (1990:8) remind us, "Children are not just the passive recipients of social structures and processes." Thus, even if they were to receive socialization that accurately mirrors the model articulated by the guru in every respect, some divergence, even in an intensive environment, could be expected to occur. Additionally, such divergence is more likely in those families where other aspects of Sri Mataji's teachings on the family have not been applied successfully. For example, the family lives of at least a few of the children have at times been unstable. Divorce, for example, or the breakdown of relationships arranged by Sri Mataji, is officially unknown in Sahaja Yoga but unofficially fairly common. The guru has also been known to split partnerships up if she decides they are destructive. The anger that can be generated in children by such experiences is not conducive to a happy acceptance of group values and indeed can initiate rebellion against them.

Sri Mataji has expounded an ideal model of childhood in a sectarian environment where, because of the commitment of parents and the exclusion of other views, this model might be expected to reign unopposed. In practice, as we have seen, this is far from the case. Those aspects of the model involving the detachment of children from their parents and beliefs and practices that appear alien to outsiders have caused the most anguish for those holding competing models of socialization. Despite the secrecy of Sahaja Yoga, and the isolated setting of the Sahaja Yoga school itself, other models have not been kept at bay. The lasting impact of growing up as Mother's children—within a family, the extended family of an ashram, or even the institutionalized setting of a Sahaja Yoga school—may therefore not be quite as Sri Mataji herself has anticipated.

Notes

1. Sahaja means "spontaneous." The material on Sahaja Yoga presented in this chapter has been collected through participant observation, informal interviews in Britain and Russia with members of the movement from 1992 onward, group literature, and interviews with ex-members. Permission from the guru for formal interviews or the filling in of questionnaires by members has been applied for and denied. The children of ex-members who have been interviewed have had their need for privacy respected (see Melton 1992:75). Some declined to be interviewed, in which case attempts to elicit information were stopped. However, occasionally information has been volunteered by such children at their own volition at a later date. All names have been changed.
2. In 1994, Sahaja Yoga claimed a presence in Argentina, Australia, Austria, Belgium, Bulgaria, Canada, Colombia, the Czech Republic, Finland, France, Germany, Greece, Holland, Hong Kong, Hungary, India, Israel, Italy, Lithuania, New Zealand, Poland, Romania, Russia, South Africa, Spain, the United Kingdom, Ukraine, and the United States, and a membership of over one hundred thousand (in correspondence with INFORM, an organization, based at the London School of Economics, that provides impartial information on new religions).
3. These figures have been compiled from two "phone tree" lists of U.K. members circulated in Sahaja Yoga during 1987 and 1993. The lists are not exhaustive, and the figures should be seen as suggestive rather than as entirely accurate. In addition, there were perhaps as many people on the periphery of the group, who followed some of the practices but who rarely made contact with other Yogis and did not fully embrace the path.
4. The vibrations of a few parents in Sahaja Yoga, however, are considered by Sri Mataji so unhealthy for their babies that they must be separated from them, and this has

happened on occasion. According to Sri Mataji (Sahaja Yoga 1986:n.p.): "Now there are some children in Sahaja Yoga who are born all right but because of their mother or father being very overactive they develop a new disease called overactivity of the child. So such a child must be immediately removed from the parents, especially from the mother, because they get it from the mother, you can find out from the character of the mother, and should be sent to some other *ashram* to be looked after, so that the child doesn't get the influence of the thing."

5. Here are two examples of many comments made by Sri Mataji on this theme: "another type of Sahaja Yogi are *[sic]* very self-centered. . . . Some people came to Bombay with their children but didn't come for the [festival] in Delhi. They are more worried about their children than about Sahaja Yoga or their own emancipation. . . . They try to find excuses to get out of the collectivity. You are judged all the time and you judge yourself" (Sahaja Yoga 1992a). Furthermore, "sometimes people get too attached to their wives, their children or their family" (Sahaja Yoga 1993:n.p.).
6. Australian Broadcasting Association, *A Report on Sahaja Yoga* (1992).
7. Mothers are advised that "working on the babies with Sahaja Yoga techniques is an important practice. While the baby is being massaged with oil, a specific mantra can be used according to the vibratory problems. Sri Mataji has recommended that young children should meditate with us in the early morning from being young babies" (Sahaja Yoga 1994a:3).
8. Puja is defined by Werner (1994:125) as "ritual worship," in this case a worship of Sri Mataji and other deities that involves flowers, lights, incense, food, and other offerings.
9. Prasad has been described by Werner (1994:123) as "the portion of a consecrated offering returned to worshippers."
10. Sometimes, activities not specifically involving socialization into group values are also organized. In spring 1997, a camp activity available to older children was abseiling (jumping down a rockface while tied to a rope) in Austria.
11. Quotations are taken from the International Sahaja Public School Prospectus.
12. Republic of Austria, *Report on the Sahaja Yoga School* (Vienna: Ministry of Justice, May 1995), 3.
13. Ibid., 4.
14. Ibid.
15. In a translation of a legal deposition lodged in January 1992 by a German Sahaja Yogi outlining her reasons for sending her child to India she says, "I should mention that not all teachers in Dharamsala meditate in the Sahaja Yoga manner."
16. There have been encouraging signs in the United Kingdom since 1996 of members reestablishing links with estranged grandparents.
17. For example, there was negative press coverage in *Le Figaro,* May 16, 1991; *Paris Match,* January 30, 1991; *Noveau Detective,* June 6, 1991; *Marie France* (February 1992).
18. The Judgment of the Court of Appeal, Rennes, Y. Case, September 23 (1991) (trans.).
19. Ibid.

References

Bromley, D., and D. Oliver. 1982. "Perfect Families: Visions of the Future in a New Religious Movement." In F. Kaslow and M. B. Sussman, eds., *Cults and the Family.* New York: Haworth Press.

Coney, J. 1995. "Belonging to a Global Religion: The Sociological Dimensions of International Elements in Sahaja Yoga." *Journal of Contemporary Religion* 10(2): 109–120.

James, A., and A. Prout. 1990. "A New Paradigm for the Sociology of Childhood." Pp. 7–33 in A. James and A. Prout, eds., *Constructing and Reconstructing Childhood.* London: Falmer Press.

Kakar, S. 1984. *Shamans, Mystics, and Doctors: A Psychological Enquiry into India and Its Healing Traditions.* London: Unwin Paperbacks.

Kalbermatten, G. de. 1979. *The Advent.* Bombay: Life Eternal Trust.

Melton, G. 1992. "Respecting Boundaries: Minors, Privacy, and Behavioural Research." Pp. 31–62 in B. Stanley and J. E. Sieber, eds., *Social Research on Children and Adolescents.* Newbury Park, Calif.: Sage.

Rai, U. 1993. *Medical Science Enlightened.* Bombay: Life Eternal Trust.

Sahaja Yoga. 1984. Sahasrara Day Talk, Mesniere en Bray, France, May 5.

———. 1986. Shri Mataji's Talk on Child Care, Vienna, Austria, July 9.

———. 1988. *Guru: A Collection of Lectures, 1979–1987.* Andorra.

———. 1992a. Easter Puja, Rome, Italy, April 19.

———. 1992b. "Education in Sahaja Yoga: Why Do We Choose to Send Our Children to a Sahaj School in India?" United Kingdom: Sahaja Yoga. Unpublished internal document.

———. 1993. *The Divine Cool Breeze* (September-October).

———. 1994a. "Advice Given to Mothers by H. H. Shri Mataji Nirmala Devi." 2d ed. United Kingdom: Sahaja Yoga. Unpublished internal document.

———. 1994b. *Sahaja Newsletter* (London), no.7 (September).

Sharma, H. S. 1993. *Sahaja Yoga: The Divine Path for Physical, Mental, and Spiritual Evolution.* Delhi: Shanker Publishing.

Shupe, A. D., and D. Bromley. 1980. *The New Vigilantes: Deprogrammers, Anti-Cultists, and the New Religions.* Beverly Hills, Calif.: Sage.

Spiro, D. 1993. "A Pilot Questionnaire Survey into the Effects of Sahaja Yoga Meditation on Health." London: Sahaja Yoga. Unpublished ms.

Wallis, R. 1984. *The Elementary Forms of the New Religious Life.* London: Routledge Kegan Paul.

Werner, K. 1994. *A Popular Dictionary of Hinduism.* Richmond, U.K.: Curzon Press.

CHAPTER 7

The Children of ISOT

GRETCHEN SIEGLER

*I*n Search of Truth (ISOT) is a Christian-based communal new religion located in Canby, a small, rural town in northeastern California. It is particularly well-suited for a study of religiously based childrearing because it has created a special communal environment for children and families. Its members agree that God has "called" them to care for children. Although they believe it is essential to their unity to emphasize the whole group as a spiritual entity over separate families, they value highly the parent-child relationship. They have developed strategies to socialize their own youths, who number over fifty, in an effort to ensure that when these children reach adulthood, they do not become absorbed into the larger social fabric. But ISOT members also feel a calling to care for children sent to them from outside. For many years they ran a child care facility for the state of California. Other affiliated religious communities show a high regard for their reputation as child care specialists by sending them families who need special help with their children.

This chapter explores the conditions that contribute to the success of this intentional religious community by concentrating on their methods of socializing children. Rodney Stark (1987:25) asserts that to explain the success of some new religious movements, "much more needs to be known about socialization and its connections with effective mobilization [as they relate to] demands for sacrifices [that are] crucial to building and maintaining commitment." I address this issue by describing how the children of ISOT are educated into ISOT values, but I also explore it further. Socialization can be adequately understood only in relation to six other conditions, enumerated by Stark (1987:11–29), that affect the future success of new religions: "cultural continuity," "a medium level of tension," "a normal age and sex structure," "a favorable ecology," "dense internal network relations," and a resistance to "secularization." Thus, by identifying the presence of these conditions throughout the history of this community, I demonstrate that the ISOTs have always made efforts, through their childrearing, to enhance these other conditions, thereby ensuring their members' commitment.

Even though Stark's theoretical model is useful, his measurement of success is not applicable here. He (1987:12) weighs "the degree to which a religious movement is able to dominate one or more societies . . . [and] influence the behavior, culture, and public policy in a society." Rosabeth Kanter's (1972) classic measurement of success (as lasting twenty-five years or more) is more appropriate to ISOT because it takes into account those small groups whose members create a satisfactory lifestyle for themselves that they then are able to pass on to future generations. The ISOT community can be considered a success because it has maintained a small, but stable population of approximately two hundred members for over thirty years. Many of its original members remain, as well as most of those who as children were raised in the group. Although not financially independent from the wider community, ISOT adequately supports its members and continues to attract new converts.

My exposure to ISOT was initiated in 1981 when I drove through the area and saw women who wore handmade dresses to the ground and men with beards and overalls operating the only available store in town. I went into a nearby hotel filled with mill workers and ranchers and they informed me that their town had been taken over by a "cult." I then sought out members of the group who directed me to their two leaders: Joseph, a confident, articulate man in his late thirties, and his wife, Marie, who was in her early fifties and possessed clear, penetrating blue eyes. They introduced me to their community with warmth and pride and provided a tour of its facilities, most of which were trailers and small structures that, while simple, were well tended with fresh paint and flower gardens. Families lived together in six clusters of buildings, each consisting of a main house that served as a dining and living area and associated structures providing bedroom quarters. Nearby were a ranch, a park with a lake, and a large Quonset hut that housed work areas for auto mechanics, carpentry, maintenance, laundry, and storage. Trailers provided classrooms for the community school near a central "meeting house," where everyone assembled for social and religious activities and for at least one meal a day.

I returned to work with the group in the late 1980s and periodically returned for visits until 1994. Most of the information presented here is my perspective of their childrearing during the late 1980s and some of the changes I noted during my last visit in 1994.[1]

The Community

The members of ISOT consider themselves Christians and therefore exhibit Stark's (1987:13–15) condition of cultural continuity. Although they have developed an autonomous community, their roots are in an earlier charismatic, neopentecostal movement. This movement began in the late 1940s when evangelists spread a "Spirit-based" Christianity that differed from traditional Pentecostalism. In 1951, a meeting of the Full Gospel Business Men's International was held in California to provide outreach to non-Pentecostals searching for charismatic fellowship. By the mid-1950s, an umbrella organization called "Christian Growth Ministries" had formed in Fort Lauderdale, Florida. Through teaching conferences and then a traveling ministry, charismatic pastors were trained to be leaders. Some of these leaders demanded a commitment from participants that was expected to be stronger than that of regular church involvement (Burgess and McGee 1988:130–137). They formed a scattered network of communes and congregations loosely assembled in an organization that eventually became known as The Body. One of these communes is ISOT. Although many of the original groups affiliated with The Body no longer exist, the ISOTs claim that there are still over two hundred active communities in North America. Differences in beliefs caused them to stop interacting with The Body in 1974, but they had reinitiated contact by 1990.

The members of ISOT share the religious beliefs taught to them by Marie. Followers claim that she is a prophet with the ability to foretell events because of a direct connection with God. She tells them that we are approaching the final days of a one-thousand-year period preceding the end of the world as we know it. Unlike other millennialists, ISOTs place little emphasis on the notion of a catastrophe at some specific time; instead Marie points to major global events as indicators that it is already in the process of occurring. Unlike other Pentecostals, but like many Neopentecostals, Marie does not teach about a "rapture" when God's "chosen" will ascend to heaven. Instead, God is expected soon to call on a "Body" of people who "manifest Christ" to prepare others for the new world . . . a heaven on earth.

Marie's followers learn that they could be among those who have been chosen to fulfill this covenant, but they must prepare themselves. Their primary goal is therefore spiritual progress, demarcated by a series of revelatory experiences, both small and dramatic. Such progress can best be fostered, they believe, within a community that heightens social relations, so that religion becomes a part of everyday life. In this way, they are able to dedicate themselves to spiritually heal those around them. They hope that as they transform their individual "natures," they will become interdependent parts of a whole with others in the community. At some point a spiritual level will be attained when they will transcend themselves and become that Body of people who manifest Christ.[2]

The community originated in the mid-1960s on the central coast of California and in 1972 moved to its present location in the northeastern part of the state. Marie began the community by holding religious meetings in her home that attracted mostly young, troubled people from the streets. They enjoyed the familial atmosphere, Marie's clarity in her interpretation of the Bible, and her support of spontaneous religious experience. As members accumulated, they bought a hotel, began to live communally, and became licensed as a nonprofit religious organization. A core group worked in various low-income jobs to support the others who were either too young or unable to work. When ISOT relocated to the rural north, it had to support a burgeoning birthrate and a substantial number of foster children. Community gardens, labor to local ranchers and the Forest Service, and ventures in small businesses helped them succeed. In a short period of time, with help from members' inheritances and loans from their families, ISOT was able to purchase a large number of the buildings and most of the land within and surrounding Canby.

Stark (1987:19–22) might say that the ISOT community fits another condition for success because it has occupied a favorable ecology for new religious movements. Some conventional faiths responded to social disruption during the 1960s by moving toward secularization. This caused schisms within these churches which resulted in a proliferation of new religions in central California, a region with an unregulated religious economy. Spiritual leaders like Marie offered the transient youths of California new social and spiritual ties. But ISOT did not find such an accepting environment when the members of the group moved north. Their new neighbors viewed them as deviant. In response, the ISOTs intentionally developed boundary-maintaining behaviors, including the wearing of distinctive dress and the creation of a private school for their teenagers. These behaviors increased hostility from the members of the wider community who had few opportunities to come to know individuals in the commune. Many believed the group was trying to take over their town and subscribed to the cultural myths that were popular at the time about brainwashing by leaders of new religious movements. On occasion, a vocal minority would create problems for ISOT, calling the sheriff about petty incidences and in general attempting to sabotage the group's activities. Neighborhood children mimicked their parents' hostility toward ISOT children who attended the public grade school. Their principal at the time described them to me as "unmanageable," "undisciplined," and "culturally deprived." Eventually the ISOTs were forced to withdraw their children from this public school. In the late 1970s, a local minister picked up a foster child who had run away from the ISOT compound because she claimed she had been handcuffed to a bed. The incident led to public accusations of child abuse, but the group was never charged.

This withdrawal from the wider community created some problems for the group, but it also contributed toward later success. The ISOTs believed that assimilation would diminish their distinctive values and roles, and they therefore resisted secularization (Stark 1987:23–24). Membership continued to increase, so the tension experienced with neighbors, while disruptive, apparently allowed the ISOTs to feel different enough to enhance their internal network relations (Stark 1987:22–23). They partially isolated themselves completely from society but continually evaluated and adjusted their boundaries in an attempt to maintain their religious beliefs.

Child Care Business

By the 1980s, the members had come to believe that God wanted them to take care of troubled youths on a full-time basis. To accommodate this calling, the ISOTs had to reduce the ongoing tension with their neighbors by lowering their boundaries and opening themselves up for scrutiny. They began to provide lodging and counseling services for seventy-odd children, called "placements," who were wards of the state of California. These "group home" activities allowed the ISOTs previously unknown financial success but also created conditions that jeopardized previous successes. The state required that they separate the placements from all religious activities unless they specifically requested to attend religious meetings. Since these children lived in the clusters with ISOT families, religion could no longer be practiced or discussed in these homes. The ban on spontaneous everyday religious expression moved the ISOTs in a secular direction. Moreover, they lost access to new converts because a primary source, the children they cared for, were no longer included in their religious life.

The ISOT children were affected by the presence of placements. They had always slept and lived with their own age group, but their parents frequently resided with them. Now, many parents had to live in clusters with placements, which proved uncomfortable environments because these wards of the state often had severe social problems. ISOT children found that they had to compete with the placements for attention. Any hope that the commune would provide an environment offering their own children more attention was impeded.

The ISOTs responded by creating new organizational boundaries within the commune, so that the presence of nonbelievers would have minimal impact on them. Religious activities were formally held in separate places at specific times. Their children over the age of preschool were moved into a separate cluster designed especially for them. These children considered this move a privilege. It served to strengthen their identification with their peer group, and it allowed the adults to concentrate on particular aspects of their socialization that promoted the communal lifestyle. At around twelve years of age, children moved to a cluster on the outskirts of the community supervised by Marie and Joseph. The adults intentionally attempted to make this move meaningful because they wanted it to be considered part of a "rite of passage." In this separate environment, they were socialized to "exhibit and build commitment" (Stark 1987:24–25). Religious instruction and communication skills were emphasized, and confrontation (described later in the chapter) was intensified there, since the children had reached the age where they were expected to gain insight into themselves. This separate housing cluster also prevented their mingling with the Placements who already went to a separate, county-funded school. Contact was allowed only during group activities and under strict supervision.

Harsh accusations of child abuse forced the ISOTs to relinquish their control of the group home in the early 1990s. On this occasion, the formal charges included psychological, physical, and sexual abuse and were directed toward the well-established senior members of the group. The accusations came from children they had cared for in the past and a man hired by a state regulator to find evidence to close down most group homes in California.[3] But the most damaging and painful accusations were those that came from some disgruntled ex-members. They had left on bitter terms because they had forfeited the personal investment they had made in the community over the years. A few also happened to be closely related to central figures in the group, including Marie. Three choices were available to ISOT. A plea bargain would allow the group to retain the group home, but the accused would have to assume guilt and have no future contact with children. A lengthy trial would allow them to defend their reputations but would also force a public airing of family matters and ruin any possibility of a future reconciliation with their relatives. ISOT choose the third option: to close down the group home and start over.

This crisis may have saved the ISOT community. Despite efforts to reduce tension with neighbors, so that the ISOTs would be considered credible child care providers, the child care business served to focus regional attention on the commune and opened it up to criticism. ISOT lost some members because of this crisis, but social bonds among those who remained were strengthened. They also began to realize that, after almost twenty years of estrangement from the rest of the communities in The Body, they needed to make amends. By 1994, the community was supporting itself through a variety of other financial endeavors, such as building contracts with the federal government, and yet its members had not lost their interest in child care. The focus shifted to working with the families sent from other communities in The Body, who recognized ISOT's success in helping children. The communities that sent dysfunctional families expected that after a period of counseling, they would return home. Some did, but others stayed with ISOT. This recruitment of family units helped to normalize group demographics, another of Stark's conditions for success.

Once the group home no longer existed, children's living arrangements were once again based on their individual needs. Some continued to live in a children's unit, but many moved back into clusters with their parents. Elders and parents sometimes decided that a child would benefit from a separate residence because the child had problems with a parent or needed the influence of another adult; in some cases the adults listened to a child's request to live in a particular place. For example, teenagers often wanted to move in with Marie and Joseph and would put their names on a waiting list for this privilege. Although the Elders were fairly flexible in their decisions about who lived with whom, these considerations were made very carefully. Some young adults raised in the group hoped that in the future the children would once again have their own, separate household cluster. Most of them recalled their experiences in homes apart from their parents as rewarding.

Religious instruction was once again part of the children's everyday lives by 1994. Religious books appeared in every home, beliefs were discussed, and religious meetings were resumed. Children mimicked their parents in singing, clapping, and occasional dancing and were sometimes handed tambourines or rattles. Special peer group meetings were held that taught them how to apply religious tenets to daily life.

The Commune as an Extended Family

The members consider themselves part of the "ISOT family." They contend that a strong "extended family" unit is the best environment in which to raise children. It teaches them to trust the viewpoint of people who are not their parents. Children are involved in most adult activities and are expected to sit quietly in one spot for long periods of time learning from adult conversation. One woman spends time each week with a child whose parents have various difficulties. Another may tell a young adult with a newborn when she should feed her baby. This emphasis on the extended family is reinforced by the use of kinship terms. Children are taught to call adults in the group "Aunt" or "Uncle"; Joseph may be called "Papa," and Marie is called "Mom" or "Grandmother." As children reach their early teens, they make use of these fictive kinship terms in a more discriminatory fashion conditioned by both the situation and their personal relationship with the adult. One young adult says that she believes that her aunts and uncles belong to her as much as they belong to their children.

ISOT mobilizes its members effectively through a hierarchy of leadership (Stark 1987:16–17). Titles signify the order in a hierarchy composed of "Elders," "Timothys," "Members," and "Affiliates." Most of the Elders have been members for a few decades, including women. They offer spiritual guidance, supervise various aspects of community life, and have the final say on everyday affairs and childrearing. A new status, "Timothy," was created to provide training for future Elders. "Member" is the title given to most others not considered ready, or simply unwilling, to take on much responsibility. Affiliates are recent arrivals who must prove to the Elders that they are committed enough to become members. The community has created strong governance, and it expects strong commitment.

An emphasis on the extended family does not mean that the ISOTs deny the importance of the nuclear one. Like many in the charismatic movements described by Mary Jo Neitz (1987:133–134), they believe in "the primacy of the family as the fundamental social unit . . . but these are 'trying times' and marital and parental roles are seen as impossible to fulfill without the support of God and a Christian community." When the group home occupied much of the parents' time, free time with their families was often limited to a few evenings of the week. As a result, a few children appeared to have a problem identifying with their family unit. If a child had difficulties in this regard, the family would receive counseling from others in the group. Now, children see their parents much more frequently because they are more apt to live with them. They learn that the Bible also guides their position in this smaller family unit through a "divine order in which authority passes from Christ to the husband to the wife to the children" (Neitz 1987:137). The husband is considered "the law," the wife is expected to submit and implement that law, but the Elders make the final decision if the wife believes that her husband goes against God.[4]

The Development of Commitment

Stark (1987:24–25) emphasizes the important role commitment has in the success of a group. Members of the second generation tend to have different reasons for committing to a communal group than their parents did. Kanter (1972:69) outlines three different types of commitment in communal life—"instrumental," "affective," and "moral"—and she finds that "they have different consequences for the system." Certainly, children may find it easier to remain with family members who help them instrumentally and to whom they are affectively bonded. But these reasons alone do not bode well for the future success of the group. Members of the future generation must also be socialized to believe that they can only truly uphold their values, their self-identity, by living the life in which they were raised. According to Kanter (1972:73), "The person making a moral commitment to his community should see himself as carrying out the dictates of a higher system, which orders and gives meaning to his life."

Spiritual transformation is the primary concern of ISOT members. An environment has been created in which emotional and spiritual change is emphasized on a daily basis, with a focus on the importance of conformity, open communication, the development of social responsibility, confrontation, and transitory rituals.

Children are taught to surrender their individuality through conformity and a responsibility to others' needs. They are told that if they insist on worrying about their "self-image," they will be sacrificing community goals at everyone's expense. Therefore, any behavior that exhibits personal autonomy, such as reclusive behavior, is not only detrimental to self-transformation but also makes community goals, or God's purpose, secondary. A person who wants to be alone is believed to be avoiding "accountability" and avoiding the communal responsibility to develop a concern for the needs of those around them. If an argument with someone develops, the person is forced to interact within a support group and resolve the issue. She or he is also taught to make sure all members are included in activities, even if it means that the activity must be changed to accommodate them.

Part of social responsibility involves openly communicating with others, developing a vulnerable countenance, and being accountable for members of a peer group by denouncing them if they do something wrong. Children are told that personal secrets are unhealthy because if someone is not totally honest, "deluded thinking" may develop. They are rewarded for being completely open about their problems. They also are taught that they are unfair to others if they help them to keep things hidden. When I questioned some youths about this, they concurred that morally, if they believe in principles and then let their friends controvert them, they are hypocrites. Furthermore, it is their duty to make sure that those who commit themselves to God not be tempted to go against Him. A distinction is made between "tattling" and telling on others. The latter is a gesture of concern, or of being "held accountable," and helps the deviant person confront the problem. In contrast, tattling is done with a "mean spirit" and is an attempt by the tattler to improve his or her own self-image.

According to ISOT beliefs, transformation often takes effort and elicits pain and all members must allow themselves to experience it. Children learn that everyone moves at his or her own pace through the stages of spiritual development, but occasionally someone will become complacent and not progress. Adults will then attempt to cause the individual a certain amount of discomfort, so that he or she can move forward. It may be elicited through confrontation, such as a public, verbal attack by Elders directed at a number of children or an individual one. Confrontation corresponds to what Kanter (1972) calls "mortification." Indeed, charges by ex-members of the group of psychological abuse may have much to do with the confrontation they experienced while in the group. Members in ISOT admit that, whereas in the past they thought of themselves as a "confrontative community," they now are more apt to first consider gentler methods of promoting change.

Children are encouraged to have transformative experiences during rites of passage and when they receive prophecies from Marie. Around their eighth year, children are expected to ask the Elders to be baptized. The Elders decide which ones have reached the appropriate level of religious awareness, since baptism is supposed to coincide with the first level of spiritual progression. Children go through another meaningful ritual passage at puberty. Initiates receive symbols at that time that convey their responsibility for the community and remind them of their covenant with God as a chosen people. Many hope to receive the "gift of tongues" during one of these rites. They may also receive prophecies that warn the community about the child's upbringing and convey information about the child's talents, weaknesses, and responsibilities. Prophecies may also be given outside of the context of a ritual when a message is needed. Thus, everyone must learn how to make a distinction between insightful advice and prophecy (as when God speaks through Marie). Her son admitted that when he was young he was at times unsure whether he was arguing with his mother or with a prophet. He began to understand the difference by noting her "emotional emphasis." When she began to speak very fast and, unlike the prophet, her voice became emotional, high pitched, and demanding, he knew he was not arguing with his mother.

Learning to Live Communally

The foregoing socialization methods not only encourage moral commitment to a religion but also help the children adapt to a communal environment.

Adults in ISOT generally agree that, although they do not want the children to be totally insulated from the world, their exposure to it must be regulated. Children learn early to respect these boundaries. Life beyond is considered "dark" and disturbing; it is reflected in horror movies, certain books and magazines, and certain types of music deemed inappropriate. Children are not permitted to wander around by themselves unsupervised.

Activities are highly structured to enable regulation of the large number of youths. Beginning as toddlers, they are divided into peer groups, which then share all activities outside of the immediate family. All children experience a stringently scheduled day made up of school, called "experience time," during which they practice music and do special projects. Showers are timed, and a rotation system gives everyone an opportunity to take care of personal needs. Daily chores are posted on a bulletin board. Preschoolers are assigned small chores, which expand when they reach grade-school age.

Children have most of their needs taken care of in the community, but the community accords stipends to individuals based on their age. The stipend is regulated by the individual's parents, although the community specifies where the money should go. The ISOT children hold some things in common, but they do have their own toys and clothing. Simple gifts are given at peer birthdays celebrated every five years with the group and also when parents celebrate privately with their children each year and during Christmas. Children learn in preschool to share, for selfish behavior is punished. Clothing remains a constant source of contention among teenagers because of the community dress code. Males wear long pants but may swim in shorts. Females, unless they are exercising, must wear dresses to the knee, and their shoulders cannot be exposed. Anyone who breaks these rules is admonished by others because it is considered a rebellious attempt to separate themselves from the group.

Although the parents ostensibly have the final say in their child's discipline, they are expected to follow community rules because the goals of the community surpass that of the individual. The group shares a code of behavior, and any adult disciplinarian expects to be supported. But disagreements do occur, and then the Elders must work out a solution. The type of discipline a child receives depends on the "spirit" of the action. Unfortunately, this strategy leaves the doors open for a variety of disciplinary inconsistencies. To alleviate this ongoing problem, only one person is supposed to be responsible for a peer group at any given time. Yet in practice, children continue to be told what to do by a large number of people. On a more positive note, the children are exposed to people who have special skills with different age groups. One young adult said that because other adults disciplined her during her teenage years, she was able to maintain a friendlier relationship with her parents.

Social separation has always been the most common form of discipline, although in the past physical punishment did occur. In the 1980s, preschoolers who lied would have a string tied around their arm; at the end of the day the strings were counted to determine the amount of paddles they would receive from their fathers in front of the rest of the household. Children more often were removed from social contact and forced to stand in one spot. A four-year-old who was normally never left alone found it devastating when told to stand against a wall for over an hour at a time. Most adults now agree that physical punishment is ineffective and have changed their tactics in separating a child. Children are forced to sit and talk about their problem with an assigned adult. One child sat all afternoon with an adult when I arrived and still sat there when I left ten days later. Because his punishment was lengthy, a parent or older sibling was expected to be present.

Retaining the Young

The ISOTs deliberately socialize their children to make a moral commitment to the group by the time they are eighteen. Some groups, such as the Bruderhof (Zablocki 1980) and the kibbutzim (Shenker 1986), encourage their teenagers to learn about the outside world before they make this commitment. The ISOTs consider the desire to leave simply normal rebellious teenage behavior, but they also believe it is not possible to live in accordance with their religious beliefs outside of the context of the community. Adults encourage early marriage and procreation among the youths, who rarely discuss college because they understand that their parents would consider them insufficiently spiritually mature to combat the ill effects of secular education.

Romantic relationships are taken very seriously by the whole community. Those in the same peer group who were raised together do not desire to date, and there is little opportunity to meet others their age. Therefore, single newcomers to the community are very popular. A group of teenage girls became excited when Marie discussed her plans to take them on a trip to meet boys from another community that is part of The Body. They all knew that these boys would be considered appropriate partners, since they shared similar religious views. Two teenagers who wish to date each other must ask permission from the Elders, who then discuss their maturity and compatibility. If permission is granted, the two are strictly supervised until they go in front of the Elders and ask to become engaged. Girls may be considered ready for this serious step at seventeen and boys at nineteen. The period of engagement is expected to last at least a year or more and is called "walking it out." Elders watch the relationship, and any inkling that either the boy or girl is not committed to the community and may eventually leave will hold up the process. Premarital sex is not allowed, but marriages have occurred early because of pregnancy.

Although retention of the young is high in this new religious movement, most who were raised in the group admit that they thought of leaving at one time or another. In the late 1980s, life was particularly hard for the teenagers because they were forced to separate themselves from the placements of the opposite sex. The rural environment and the community's separation from everyone created a sense of isolation. One teenager declared that no one could imagine what it was like to graduate in a class of two, having no girls to date, no privacy, living in total isolation. Many of these teens left. Most who leave believe that it is only for a few years. Usually they enter the military or move in with relatives or ex-members of the group. Those who leave and return usually agreed that loneliness was a key problem but said they also felt guilty because they would not be available when God calls on them as a "Christly Body" to help others make the transition to the new world.

Those who were teenagers during my visit in 1994 exhibited far less dissatisfaction. Their parents' renewed relationship with The Body created a steady influx of newcomers and visitors. It not only increased the number of teenagers they came in contact with but also expanded their relationships with other adults who reinforced the beliefs of their parents. A young adult described the joy she felt when she found out after introductions to these other religious communities that the ISOT community was not alone.

Conclusion

The ISOTs have managed to retain their youth by encouraging a moral commitment to ISOT beliefs and way of life. They have maintained a normal demographic balance in their community, without relying on the conversion of nonbelievers, by attracting new families from affiliated religious communities. In fact, they now claim to turn some away. Joseph contends that he would like to increase their numbers to about five hundred, the maximum number that would be manageable in one community. But they must first ensure that they are able to support these numbers in their rural environment. Their exposure to the wider community through work hours outside ISOT to support themselves could threaten the group. Yet members explain that exposure to the outside world and time spent away from the community only reinforce their commitment to the lifestyle they have created at home.

Marie's vision has created this community of people who do not aspire to become a dominant religion and do not claim to know when they will be needed to fulfill their role as God's chosen people. Problems may arise when Marie is no longer able to direct the future of the group through her prophecies. Yet others who were raised in the group are also believed to have strong prophetic powers and have already been allowed to assert themselves in decision-making. Certainly, they have learned from Marie's lessons, which they now pass on to their own youths. These include maintaining an extended family environment in which everyone has responsibility for one another. The ISOTs take pride in the maintenance of very structured lives for their children that are enriched by the presence of many different people to whom they are strongly attached. ISOT members support the emphasis on behaviors, such as social responsibility, that force them to internalize their religious values and that determine the unity of the group. Most important, they expect a moral commitment from their cohorts to focus on their transformation, so that they are worthy to be called as God's chosen people. These are not abstract precepts; they are practiced every day. Life in this environment where members are taught that they are different from others, may sometimes be difficult for both children and adults. Yet it also has its rewards because the group has so far been successful in perpetuating community goals through the community's youth.

Notes

1. A number of people and organizations contributed to this study over the years. I especially want to thank the members of ISOT for all of the work they have done to help me understand their life in community. Robert Winzeler, professor at the University of Nevada in Reno, and a research grant from the National Science Foundation guided me through the study until 1992. At that time, I completed a dissertation on the topic (Siegler 1992). The Society for the Scientific Study of Religion and a Weyher Summer Grant from Westminster College of Salt Lake City provided support for subsequent visits and analysis.
2. More detailed information about these beliefs can be found in Marie's pamphlets, which are published by the community. See Tolbert (1970, 1974, 1976, 1979, 1982, 1988, 1990).
3. I was told by this state employee that a new government policy in California was to abolish group homes and send children directly to juvenile hall. The state regulator had hired this man, who had closed down other group homes, to investigate the commune covertly by expressing his intentions to join the community. I was researching ISOT at the time and, like the members of ISOT, did not suspect his intentions.
4. A number of scriptures describe this hierarchy, including Eph. 5:21–33 and 1 Cor. 11:3–10. Except when God speaks through Marie, she is expected to follow this order in the position of a woman.

References

Burgess, S. M., and G. B. McGee, eds. 1988. *Dictionary of Pentecostal and Charismatic Movements.* Grand Rapids, Mich.: Zondervan Publishing.

Kanter, R. M. 1972. *Commitment and Community: Communes and Utopias in Sociological Perspective.* Cambridge, Mass.: Harvard University Press.

Neitz, M. J. 1987. *Charisma and Community: A Study of Religious Commitment Within the Charismatic Renewal.* New Brunswick, N.J.: Transaction Books.

Shenker, B. 1986. *Intentional Communities: Ideology and Alienation in Communal Societies.* Boston: Routledge and Kegan Paul.

Siegler, G. 1992. "The Structure of Anti-structure: The Development and Organization of a Religious Community in a Small Western Town." Ph.D. diss., University of Nevada at Reno.

Stark, R. 1987. "How New Religions Succeed: A Theoretical Model." Pp. 11–29 in D. Bromley and P. Hammond, eds., *The Future of New Religious Movements.* Macon, Ga.: Mercer University Press.

Tolbert, E. M. (aka White, M.). 1970. *Responsibility in Eldership.* Alturas, Calif.: ISOT Press.

———. 1974. *Cursed or Blessed: The Dichotomy of Man.* Alturas, Calif.: ISOT Press.

———. 1976. *Articles of Faith.* Canby, Calif.: ISOT Press.
———. 1979. *A Family Called ISOT.* Canby, Calif.: ISOT Press.
———. 1982. *The Prophets Foretell.* Canby, Calif.: ISOT Press.
———. 1988. *New Covenant Celebrations.* Canby, Calif.: ISOT Press.
———. 1990. *Of Our Faith.* Canby, Calif.: ISOT Press.
Zablocki, B. 1980. *The Joyful Community: An Account of the Bruderhof, a Communal Movement Now in Its Third Generation.* Chicago: University of Chicago Press.

Chapter 8

Children of the Underground Temple

Growing Up in Damanhur

Massimo Introvigne

Family ties can have a disruptive influence on collective life, according to sociological studies of communal utopias (Kanter 1972). The individual's special attachments to a friend, a lover, or a relative can ultimately be detrimental to a communal living commitment. As a result, in the early nineteenth century "American communes were self-consciously and vociferously designing alternatives to the conventional family system" (Bainbridge 1997:143).

The reorganization of the family in communal groups usually commences with "social implosion" (Bainbridge 1978:51–52), in which ties to people outside the commune are cut or attenuated and ties within the commune are strengthened. Over time—as a computer simulation might clearly indicate—most of the members' external ties wither away and these former relationships are replaced with multiple ties to other communalists as these internal relationships grow richer and more intense (Bainbridge 1997:248–249). Social implosion creates a favorable situation for communal commitment, but a less favorable situation for recruitment efforts. As far as children are concerned, social implosion may facilitate their socialization into communal values, but it also makes the commune vulnerable to external criticism and creates a situation that evokes hostile reactions from the surrounding society. When the commune is large, however, the side effects of social implosion appear to be somewhat mitigated. If the commune has a large population, it is more likely, and indeed necessary, to maintain ongoing contacts with individuals and agencies in outside world, and this less insular stance has an impact on the children living in the commune.

Damanhur may be regarded as the largest Italian communal new religious movement, although it prefers to be called not a religious movement, but a community with its own philosophy and worldview. In this chapter, I examine Damanhur's childrearing and educational methods within the framework of the commune's recent conflicts with the anticult movement. I attempt to show how some of the effects of communal life on children deemed "negative" by anticult agencies are mitigated by Damanhur's open stance and frequent congress with its host society, the result of the community's sheer size. (The limited implosion thesis is largely confirmed, particularly where it predicts a comparatively easy socialization of the children in the community, a risk of conflict with external oppositional coalitions, and more external contacts in larger communes.) Since Damanhur is not well known outside Italy, I commence by describing its history and unique worldview.

Damanhur is arguably the largest communal group in the world today and is certainly the largest commune belonging to the ancient wisdom-magical tradition. Although in existence for some twenty years, Damanhur has been the subject matter of very few scholarly studies (see Introvigne 1990:87–90; Berzano 1991, 1994, 1998; Poggi 1992; Macioti 1994; Cardano 1997). Nevertheless, Damanhur has been featured in countless Italian and European magazine articles, TV programs, and pieces of anticult literature (see Sierra 1993; Gramaglia 1989:384–392; Gatto Trocchi 1993:59–72; and, for criticism of Gatto Trocchi, see Introvigne 1993). An interesting account by Jeff Merrifield, an English journalist, was published in 1998. Damanhur has its own publishing branches, Edizioni Horus and Editrice Damanhur, and has produced more than 150 books and booklets, mostly authored by its founder, Oberto Airaudi. The interest of the media increased enormously after 1992 when Damanhur's vast Underground Temple—successfully kept secret for fifteen years—was discovered (following the directions given by an embittered ex-member) and seized by the Italian authorities for having allegedly breached in the construction a number of zoning and tax requirements. The main legal case concerning the Temple was eventually won by Damanhur in 1996.

Damanhur: A Short History

Damanhur is situated in Piedmont, less than thirty miles north of Turin, a city famous in Italy for its magical traditions (see Introvigne 1995:151–186). The presence of what is now the largest Egyptian museum in the world, built during Napoleon's reign, has inspired a number of local occult groups based on Egyptian myth and rituals (see Bongioanni and Grazzi 1994).

Damanhur's founder, Oberto Airaudi, was born in Balangero, in the Lanzo valleys, north of Turin, in 1950. He (1968) presents himself as a precocious young man in his autobiography, fascinated by Turin's occult milieu. He visited a number of "pranotherapists" (healers claiming to use the force of "prana" by raising their hands or using physical manipulations) and learned the secrets of this profession, which was quite popular in Italy in the 1970s. Airaudi became a successful pranotherapist himself, with offices in a number of different small towns in Piedmont. He also established a practice as a spiritualist medium, coauthored a spiritualist manual (Airaudi and Montefameglio 1979), and acquainted himself with Turin's theosophical subculture. In 1974, he had enough friends and clients to found his own organization, the Horus Center, followed by the School of Pranotherapy.

Almost immediately after the establishment of the Horus Center, Airaudi announced to the members that they should live communally. In 1975, steps were taken to rent (and subsequently buy) a property in Valchiusella valley, which is between the villages of Baldissero Canavese and Vidracco. The valley is also situated between Ivrea (one of Italy's "technocities" and the home of the computer company Olivetti) and Castellamonte (a town famous for the manufacture of china). In 1976, a settlement was established under the name of an ancient Egyptian city, Damanhur, with two dozens pioneers. Damanhur was officially inaugurated as a community in 1979. By 1981, the previous by-laws had been modified in a new "constitution," a move suggesting that the community regarded itself as a "separated people" and even "an independent state." The constitution was revised in 1984, 1986, and 1987; in 1989 it was reissued as the Constitution of the Nation of Damanhur, later amended in 1992. Damanhur's self-definition as a state had been actively opposed by anticultists and some local authorities, and so the 1989 text opted for the word *Nation,* later amended to *Federation.* At any rate, Damanhur boasts its own "government" of its own and its own currency, the credito, whose value is based on the Italian lira and whose function is largely symbolic.

From Damanhur's inception, its "citizens" have worked partly in the community and partly outside in secular society, but they return home to the commune after their working day is finished. Moreover, Damanhur's citizens have insisted from the onset that their children should be home-schooled and instructed in the Damanhurian worldview. The majority of the original pioneers, with a few exceptions, were young adults who had finished high school. A few members held college degrees, and a small group included skilled workers with no high school training. Couples joined the commune, and children were raised in small units composed of a number of families. The education of these children became a key issue in the conflict that arose between Damanhur and the anticult movement, a conflict that was finally arbitrated by the Italian authorities, largely in favor of the community.

The growth of Damanhur has been continual. There were two hundred citizens in 1985 and four hundred in 1997. Since the constitution rules that a community cannot exceed 220 members, Damanhur is now a federation of a number of different communities, all located within a radius of twenty miles in the Valchiusella valley. There were, as of 1998, two communities, Etulte and Tentyris; an "autonomous region," Damjl; and two "federal regions," Rama and Valdaijmil. Unofficially, the visitor encounters a continuum of homes in the valley, each inhabited by ten to fifteen people, including children. Some services are centralized in Damyl, including the schools. Damyl also houses the "Open Temple," a roofless structure decorated with statues of Greek and Egyptian divinities, and a larger open area featuring symbols from different religious traditions where the Sunday market is held, when the community welcomes tourists and visitors for a weekly feast. Visitors are now admitted to Damyl on a daily basis, although some guided tours are offered only on Sunday.

The community's products are sold through secular commercial channels, including international duty-free shops as far away as Saudi Arabia and Abu Dhabi. Damanhur is renowned for its health food products, china, and jewelry. Paintings by community artists (including the founder, Oberto Airaudi) are sold to the general public. More surprisingly, Damanhur has a high percentage of computers (one every six citizens), and one of the community's resources is the sale of software. Although self-sufficiency is a stated goal, even today a sizable percentage of citizens have outside jobs. As a rule, youths may become citizens, if they so choose, at the age of eighteen. In exceptional circumstances, teenagers over fourteen may be admitted to citizenship. This provision is theoretical, since the youngest citizen ever admitted was seventeen. In addition to the four hundred citizens and children of citizens (all residents in the community homes), Damanhur is composed of some three hundred "associated members," who live in their own homes, mainly within the province of Turin, but who contribute money to the community and visit on the weekend and during special celebrations. At least another one thousand people are regularly in touch with Damanhur and attend the courses of the Free University of Damanhur (in Turin and elsewhere) but do not contribute donations or tithings on a regular basis and are not considered "members." The constitution suggests that citizens should deed all their properties to the community, but in fact members have chosen to reserve areas of private property for themselves, and the economic arrangements of Damanhur have passed through a number of different phases (see Berzano 1994:146, 150).

Damanhur's Worldview

There are no systematic lessons (similar to a Christian catechism class or Sunday school) whereby Damanhur's worldview is imparted to the children. Rather, children become socialized into it through daily life in the community and through interaction with adults. According to sociologist Luigi Berzano (1994:144), Airaudi's worldview shows elements of four different religious traditions: ancient Egyptian, Celtic (including Christian Celtic), occult (with elements derived from the Theosophical Society), and New Age. When asked, any citizen of Damanhur would insist that the community's worldview is absolutely new and original, but for scholars of religion the influence of a larger theosophical and occult tradition is plainly evident. Many ideas popular in the New Age appear in the community's literature. But unlike other New Age meccas in

Europe, Damanhur is not vegetarian; in fact its restaurant (which is open to the public) excels in the preparation of meat specialties, as well as serving wine from the Piedmont vineyards. Vegetarian meals are available, but Airaudi himself is not vegetarian and does not abstain from wine (although all citizens, according to the constitution, should abstain from tobacco and drugs, and this rule is strictly enforced).

Damanhurians object to being called polytheists. "Only one God exists," they claim, but it is impossible to contact Him directly. Since God remains largely unknowable, we can access Him only through *the* gods, the "Intermediate Deities" ("Gabbiano" 1988:104–110). Only nine "Primeval Deities" are self-generated; all the others have been created by humans, but, in a manner similar to Carl Jung's archetypes, they have taken on an independent existence. Not to be confused with these "Intermediate Deities" are the "entities": angels, nature spirits, and demons. Although today the entities are "subtler" than humans, the first human was a Primeval Deity who was the victim of a fall and lapsed into the present condition of imprisonment within the material body and material existence. Many Deities and entities voluntarily followed humans into exile, and we may call on these beings to help us when we try to return to our original subtler state. The theosophical origin of this belief system is quite apparent.

Damanhur's cosmology includes the early generation of three "Mother worlds": the world of human beings, of plants, and of nature spirits. These worlds are not capable of communicating with each other directly, but they do generate "Echo worlds" through which communication may occur. Each race of living beings has an "astral tank," or repository of all knowledge accumulated by the race throughout its entire history. This concept is similar to the "akashic memory" of the theosophical tradition. Human beings may get in touch, through particular techniques, with the human "race mind" (the astral tank of the human race), and they may also access useful information by tapping the race minds of animals. To this end, each human being may enter into a special magical relation with an animal by assuming its name. In fact, all the citizens of Damanhur are identified not by a family name, but by an animal name (Elephant, Kangaroo, etc.). The founder used to be called "Hawk," although for many years he has simply been called "Oberto." Each citizen is now often identified by two names, the first of an animal and the second of a plant, and these names are freely chosen by whoever wishes to use them. (Noncitizens may decide to pick up an animal name.) Normally, the names are reserved for adults, but some children (aged seven or older) have insisted that they receive their own animal names, and some of these requests have been granted. Animal names also serve the obvious purpose of marking the community's "otherness" and defining its boundaries as a separate society, a purpose also served by the customary greeting of "With you" (*Con te*) rather than the more conventional "Good morning" or "Good evening." (This is not a fixed rule. Citizens also use the usual Italian greetings.)

Damanhurians still dabble in spiritualism, parapsychological experiments, and other classical techniques of the occult-esoteric milieu, but as the community matures, increasing emphasis is placed on the use of a distinctive esoteric language (believed to be an ancient secret language rediscovered by Damanhur) that is written both in Latin characters and in ideograms. A musical and dance tradition corresponding to this language has evolved. Rituals and ritual costumes have been created, and rituals are performed in an effort to restore human beings to their original exalted condition. At the same time, these rituals are intended to heal Mother Earth and protect Her from threatened ecological disasters. Although observers may note that Egyptian symbols are somewhat predominant, Airaudi insists that the Egyptian religion is not more important than other traditions in building Damanhur's new synthesis. Egypt, he told me in a recent interview, has also been used as a convenient *external* symbol system in order to hide esoteric truths that Damanhur is not yet prepared to share with the outside world.

Not until 1992, and then as the result of an unpredictable series of external circumstances, did it become clear to outside observers that the main "work" of the citizens of Damanhur was not creating a self-sufficient community or performing certain rituals and dances in the Open Temple. Their major work was directed toward building their magnum opus, the Underground Temple. According to one of Damanhur's hidden doctrines, the completion of this subterranean Temple is magically linked to the salvation of planet earth. The Temple consists of a large number of secret passages in the very heart of a small mountain, protected by technologically advanced devices that open doors that lead, one after the other, to hidden rooms of extraordinary beauty and magnificence. The artworks (mainly stained-glass windows, frescoes, and mosaics) are reminiscent not only of Byzantine, Egyptian, and Greek designs, but also of Liberty's fabrics and the Art Deco period. There are literally miles of corridors and thousands of statues, windows, and paintings. In fact, each member of the community makes a statue of the animal to which she or he is mystically linked by name.

Before 1996, a visit to the Underground Temple was a privilege reserved for a small number of noncitizens, including state and local officials, social scientists, and some journalists. Since resolution of the legal problems connected with the Underground Temple, more requests for a visit have been granted, although citizens prefer to limit this privilege to people genuinely interested in the Damanhurian spiritual experience, not just to passing tourists. Entering the Underground Temple is, as sociologist Maria Immacolata Macioti (1994:5) writes, like "entering into a fairy tale."

The Temple experience became accessible for the children of Damanhur after 1992. Before the discovery, children did not know about the Underground Temple before they were accepted as citizens, although they frequented the aboveground Open Temple. Adults refrained from mentioning the Underground Temple before the children, and any inadvertent reference was explained away as a reference to the Open Temple; these measures were necessary to preserve the secret. Since 1992, children have experienced the Underground Temple on occasion. They are admitted only to the "artistic" events (as opposed to the more specifically religious or spiritual ceremonies). Children are the star performers, as well as part of the audience, in the concerts, dances, and other performances that take place in the Underground Temple. The religious roots of art are very strong, and artistic expression is a means to spiritual experience in Damanhur.

Oberto Airaudi does not turn fifty until the year 2000, and the group, although founded in the mid-1970s, is still in its early, charismatic phase. Incidents such as the forced disclosure of the Underground Temple to the outside world may accelerate Weberian processes of "routinization of charisma" and lead to new directions. Although Airaudi and his friends prefer to define Damanhur informally as a "community" rather than as a religion, it will be difficult for the group to resist the forces of institutionalization, particularly if Damanhur continues to be successful.

Family and Childrearing

The organization of the family in Damanhur has attracted considerable hostile interest. Couples may join the community and maintain their relationship, although they must live communally with other families in one of the valley homes. Many single members have joined Damanhur and have entered into one of the community marriages, stipulated as a contract that provides for a "provisional" marriage for one, two, or three years. When the contract expires, the marriage can be renewed or dissolved. Sensationalist news reports have interpreted the Damanhur system of marriage as "free love." Damanhur's citizens, however, protest that a significant percentage of the marriages are regularly renewed and that in contrast to the larger society's hypocrisy—where marriages are theoretically "forever" but in many cases end up in divorces—the practice of periodically reevaluating the marriage results in better couples and contributes to the stability of families. Conflicts between spouses, defections, and lurid (and blatantly inaccurate) anticult reports on Damanhur family life and sexuality have resulted in two child custody cases. Both yielded legal victories for the community. By a decree dated December 10, 1993, in a case decided by the Juvenile Court of Ivrea, a mother who had joined Damanhur with her daughter after divorce successfully retained her ten-year-old daughter, in spite of the objections of the former husband. The two experts appointed by the court concluded that Damanhur was more than an adequate milieu for rearing children. The father tried again to obtain custody of the girl through an application filed on March 17, 1994, within the context of his divorce case. The court granted the divorce on October 30, 1996, but awarded permanent custody of the daughter to the mother, commenting that "notwithstanding the communal lifestyle, the mother appears to be a daily and caring presence in the life of the girl." On August 30, 1993 the Juvenile Court of Turin granted to an aunt living in Damanhur the custody of her niece, whose parents were both drug addicts. On December 7, 1993, several disgruntled ex-members (represented by two lawyers well known as anticult activists) appeared on the *Maurizio Costanzo Show,* the most popular TV talk show in Italy, and accused Damanhur of routinely abusing children. Scholars, including myself, who have studied the community generally agree that the accusations are false and find the lurid style of the talk show deplorable.

Resentful ex-members have also accused Damanhur of "programming" the birth of each new child according to the economic situation of each unit and the astrologically propitious moment. In many tabloid articles Damanhur's birth control practices have, more simply, been reported as the couples of Damanhur "having sex only when Airaudi gives his permission." This is a caricature of Airaudi's role in the community in general and of Damanhur's birth control practices in particular, a caricature offensive to Damanhur's women and families. Birth control is indeed practiced in Damanhur. In 1998, there were eighty children under fourteen in a communal system of four hundred members (this latter figure does include the children). Discounting unmarried, widowed, and older members, each couple has an average of 0.72 children to care for. This figure does not, however, indicate fertility. The fertility ratio is around 1–1.2 children per couple, which is close to the average fertility ratio of northern Italy (one of the lowest in the world) and quite dissimilar to the ratio of other communal new religious movements, such as The Family, where large families are the rule. Nevertheless, Damanhur continues to receive more requests to join the commune that it can accommodate. Moreover, there are very few cases of second-generation Damanhurians who have left the commune where their parents remain. Consequently, the Damanhur community has not thus far regarded children as its most important asset, necessary for its continued existence.

Damanhur's childrearing is strictly unisex: there are very few differences (at least no more differentiation than is found in northern Italian society at large) between boys and girls in education or in dress. When Damanhur was founded, the basic unit for childrearing was the commune. Infant children were taken care of by the community and spent most of their time in a communal day care center. However, the development of strong special ties between children and mothers was not discouraged. The children's emotional bonds with their fathers appear to be somewhat weaker. As Damanhur grew from dozens to hundreds of members, the focus of childrearing shifted from the commune to the family unit. Within the unit, infant children develop a special attachment to their mothers and to the other adults in the unit. This "microcommunal" phase of childrearing prepares the children for the subsequent "macrocommunal" phase, when they start spending more time in the central communal day care center and then move on to preschool. Through receiving socialization first in the unit and next in the larger commune, Damanhur's children gradually internalize the group's unique values.

According to Rosabeth Kanter (1972), well-established communes are capable of involving children in commitment mechanisms at an early age. Although Kanter's model has been subsequently disputed (see, e.g., Zablocki 1980), some Kanterian mechanisms appear evident in Damanhur's childrearing methods, particularly since, in response to outside criticism (as well as a consequence of growth), the community started permitting its children to interact more frequently with non-Damanhurian children. The commitment mechanism of *sacrifice* becomes apparent when Damanhur's children compare their own lifestyle to the less austere lives of middle-class children, who may have TV sets in their bedrooms, unlimited junk food, and expensive toys. But Damanhur's children also understand that the *communion* (sharing and participating in group work or ritual that create a sense of belonging to the group as a whole) and *transcendence* (mechanisms that convey a sense of the group as a spiritual or charismatic community with a powerful meaning) are unique and valuable features of their experience. As mentioned earlier, children experience Damanhur's meaning system mostly through art and "games," but the playful nature of Damanhur's worship make it difficult for the observer to distinguish ritual from play. In fact, most of Damanhur's children seem to understand what the commune is all about before entering school, although it is only much later that they may eventually become citizens.

Education and Schools

Damanhur had its own day care center, preschool, and elementary school early in its history, and an intermediate school for children aged eleven to fourteen was inaugurated in 1994. After a few conflicts, the autonomy of these schools was accepted by local authorities, who are now satisfied with imposing an examination on Damanhur's children at the end of each two- or three-year school cycle. Damanhur's schools have opted for a yearly examination as an additional guarantee of the quality of their education and another opportunity for their children to interact with outside boys and girls of the same age. Yearly examinations, which are carried out by school authorities of the local district of Loranzé, have confirmed that the educational standards of Damanhur schools are high. The results scored by children are higher than average. In fact, the ratio of teachers (twenty-five for the school year 1997–1998) to pupils (fifty-one) in Damanhur's school system is almost unheard of in modern instruction and explains the good results. Although the local authorities explicitly require that the programs of the national Italian education system be strictly followed at Damanhur, the community has been authorized to add more hours of schooling devoted to computing and the use of Internet, more foreign languages, theater, art, poetry, and mythology. "Reconciling logic and myth, poetry and computers, emotions and economy" is advanced as the goal of the Damanhur school system, described as "a global experience with strong humanistic features" (Scuola Damanhuriana 1996:22).

Ten minutes at the beginning of each school day are devoted to "harmonization"—a light form of yoga—and the elementary school has a "harmonization room" where a musical session opens each day of school. Pupils are allowed to visit the harmonization room individually in their free time. Once they reach the intermediate school, Damanhur's spiritual vision becomes part of young boys' and girls' daily life, although it is not a formal part of the curriculum. Damanhur claims that, although their education is "based on Damanhurian principles," children are not indoctrinated or compelled to become Damanhurian; rather, they are guided to make their own informed choices in due time (Scuola Damanhuriana 1996:28). Anticultists may easily contend that children in the community's schools cannot avoid being indoctrinated, but Damanhur's claim to prepare children to make free but informed religious choices are very similar to the claims made by countless Catholic schools in Italy. In fact, Damanhur's children understand that a time will come when they will have to decide whether to join the community as citizens or leave, an impending choice that is of great concern.

Some years ago, Airaudi's own daughter, Valeria, left Damanhur, where she had worked as a preschool teacher. She claimed that certain incidents in the life of the community (including a member's suicide) were often explained to schoolchildren so as to imply that Damanhur's leaders are virtually infallible. Although she (1996:32) wrote that Damanhur's children are "wonderful," the citizens found her comments unfair and better explained as reflecting her personal conflict with her father. A fairy tale written by one of Damanhur's mothers intended to explain the suicide to the children was controversial even within the community. Some supported it as a positive way to deal with the children's reaction to the suicide. At any rate, the tale was a personal initiative and not representative of a general pattern in Damanhur's education.

On the basis of my own observations, the results of Damanhur's educational system are indeed impressive, and the community's children are on average more proficient than most non-Damanhurian pupils of the same age in foreign languages, Italian usage, and computers. Many of them have also developed unusual interests and abilities in a variety of artistic activities. However, Damanhur's communal lifestyle and schools, when combined, *do* teach children in a not-too-subtle way the community's worldview, and contacts with children outside the community—although existing and encouraged—have been somewhat limited for years as a result of hostile attitudes among Damanhur's immediate neighbors. Nevertheless, better relations are slowly developing between the community and its neighbors, and opportunities for Damanhur children to interact with outside children are becoming more frequent.

Growing up in Damanhur means becoming part of both a communal and an alternative socioreligious system, with all the advantages and problems commonly found in this kind of setting. Anticultists, a few disgruntled ex-members, and the local Catholic bishop (who, ironically, is famous for his liberal views) have strongly opposed Damanhur's family arrangements. The bishop (Bettazzi 1992:3) has declared that the family patterns of Damanhur are "against the common moral rules" and that children and grown-ups alike are "brainwashed" into Damanhur's esoteric worldview. Damanhur women arrived at the Regional Assembly building in Turin on October 14, 1991, to protest this kind of "defamation" and to assert their right to "planned motherhood" ("Noi siamo indignate" 1991). The community responded to the bishop's criticisms in 1992 by declaring that, although its arrangements might not comply with Catholic teachings, Damanhur's families have found a way of life that allows "equal dignity and reciprocal respects between women and men" (Comunità di Damanhur 1992). Ultimately, Italian authorities have resolved that, even though communal experiments such as Damanhur should be monitored as far as children are concerned, Damanhur has evolved a form of childrearing and education that is legitimate within a pluralistic society. The agreements between Damanhur and the local school board, the children's favorable results in the state examinations, and Damanhur's victories in the legal cases launched by ex-members all confirm that the Italian authorities have thus far favored Damanhur in arbitrating the conflict over children that wages between the commune and its critics.

References

Airaudi, O. 1968. *Cronaca del Mio Suicidio.* Turin: CEI.

Airaudi, O., and U. Montefameglio. 1979. *Lo Spiritismo.* Turin: MEB.

Airaudi, V. 1996. "Ci scrive la figlia di Oberto Airaudi." *Liberation Times* 78 (April): 32–33.

Bainbridge, W. S. 1978. *Satan's Power: A Deviant Psychotherapy Cult.* Berkeley and Los Angeles: University of California Press.

———. 1997. *The Sociology of Religious Movements.* New York: Routledge.

Berzano, L. 1991. "Religione e autoperfezionamento." Pp. 141–186 in M. I. Macioti, ed., *Maghi e magie nell'Italia di oggi.* Florence: Angelo Pontecorboli Editore.

———. 1994. *Religiosità del nuovo areopago: Credenze e forme religiose nell'epoca postsecolare.* Milan: Franco Angeli.

———. 1998. *Damanhur: Popolo e comunità.* Leumann, Italy: Elle Di Ci.

Bettazzi, L. 1992. "Parliamo di Damanhur." *Il risveglio popolare,* October 22: 3.

Bongioanni, A., and R. Grazzi. 1994. *Torino, l'Egitto e l'Oriente fra storia e leggenda.* Turin: L'Angolo Manzoni Editrice.

Cardano, M. 1997. *Lo specchio, la rosa, e il loto: Uno studio sulla sacralizzazione della natura.* Rome: SEAM.

Comunità di Damanhur. 1992. "Il vescovo di Ivrea male informato." Press release. October 18.

"Gabbiano" [Gagliardi, M.], ed. 1988. *La Via Horusiana: Il Libro: Princìpi e concetti fondamentali della scuola di pensiero di Damanhur.* 2d ed. Turin: Edizioni Horus.

Gatto Trocchi, C. 1993. *Viaggio nella magia.* Rome: Laterza.

Gramaglia, P. A. 1989. *La reincarnazione.* Casale Monferrato, Italy: Piemme.

Introvigne, M. 1990. *Il cappello del mago: I nuovi movimenti magici dallo spiritismo al satanismo.* Milan: SugarCo.

———. 1993. "A proposito di viaggi nella magia." *La Critica Sociologica* 106 (summer): 127–134.

———. 1995. *La sfida magica.* Milan: Ancora.

Kanter, R. M. 1972. *Commitment and Community: Communes and Utopias in Sociological Perspective.* Cambridge, Mass.: Harvard University Press.

Macioti, M. I. 1994. "Il tempio sotterraneo di Damanhur." *Ars Regia* 4(19) (July-August): 4–9.

Merrifield, Jeff. 1998. *Damanhur: The Real Dream.* London: Thorsons.

"Noi siamo indignate" 1991. Flyer distributed by Damanhur's women during their Regional Assembly protest, October 14.

Poggi, I. 1992. "Alternative Spirituality in Italy." Pp. 271–286 in J. R. Lewis and J. G. Melton, eds., *Perspectives on the New Age.* Albany: State University of New York Press.

Scuola Damanhuriana. 1996. *La finalità della Scuola damanhuriana nel percorso formativo dalla Scuola nido alla Scuola media.* Baldissero Canavese, Italy: Scuola Damanhuriana.

Sierra, J. 1993. "El secreto de Damanhur." *Mas allá de la ciencia* 50 (April): 38–51.

Zablocki, B. 1980. *Alienation and Charisma: A Study of Contemporary American Communes.* New York: Free Press.

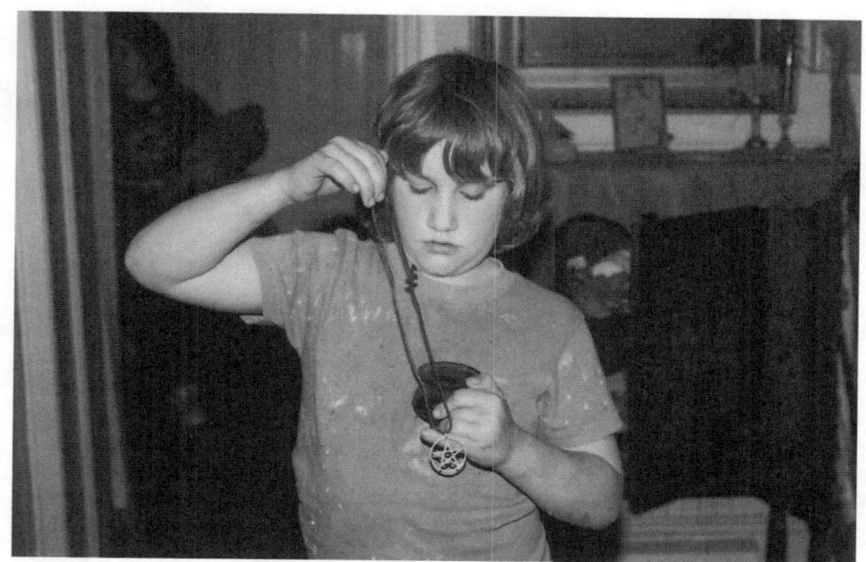

Wiccan boy with miniature cauldron and pentagram. *Photo courtesy of David M. Donahue*

Pagan boy on magic house in back yard. *Photo courtesy of David M. Donahue*

Twelve-year-old witchling with magical wand. *Photo courtesy of David M. Donahue*

Girls in the Osho Ko Hsuan School. *Photo courtesy of M. R. Tyler*

Children of Osho's international disciples at play. *Photo courtesy of M. R. Tyler*

Children celebrating the Damanhurian New Year. *Photo courtesy of Valter Maccantelli*

Damanhurian preschoolers enjoying lunch. *Photo courtesy of Valter Maccantelli*

Messianic Community parents and children in front of the Maples communal house on June 22, 1994, ten years after the raid. *Photo courtesy of Jeane A. Swantko.*

Michael Dawson with his father Isaac Dawson in the Messianic Community in Nova Scotia before the legal battles. *Photo courtesy of Jeane A. Swantko*

Messianic Communities' youths in "ten years-after-the-raid" celebration at Bellows Falls, Vermont, 1994. *Photo courtesy of Jeane A. Swantko and Edward Wiseman*

The Family's children in a Christmas play. *Photo courtesy of Lonnie Davis and Claire Borowik*

Mothers in the Family demonstrating outside the Argentinian embassy after the raid on their children in 1993. *Photo courtesy of Lonnie Davis and Claire Borowik*

Family children witnessing the homeless concerning the endtime. *Photo courtesy of Lonnie Davis and Claire Borowik*

The Family's second generation holding a red sackcloth vigil. *Photo courtesy of Lonnie Davis and Claire Borowik*

PART III

How Society Responds

LEGAL AND FREEDOM ISSUES

CHAPTER 9

Frontiers and Families

THE CHILDREN OF ISLAND POND

SUSAN J. PALMER

The term "child abuse" cannot be invoked as a talismanic invocation to support the exercise of State power which egregiously violates both First and Fifth Amendment Rights.
—Judge Frank Mahady, at the detention hearings after the raid on Island Pond

The short history of the Messianic Communities might fairly be described as bristling with controversy.[1] Since the early 1980s, this communal movement has been embroiled in an ongoing struggle with society over the right to raise its children according to its own prophetic tradition—and, indeed, over parents' basic right to keep their children at all. A series of custody disputes have drawn attention to medical and educational issues, but the primary focus of concern is, and has always been, on the group's biblically based disciplinary method, which several apostates have characterized as "child abuse." These escalating conflicts climaxed in 1984 in a well-publicized raid on 112 children by mounted police and social workers in Island Pond, Vermont. Even though this dramatic event was quickly resolved—Judge Frank Mahady dismissed all charges and deemed this emergency action unconstitutional—the controversy continues. At the time of this writing, the communities' home schools are under siege in Germany and a man and women in France have been imprisoned for several months without being charged and may eventually be tried for medical neglect leading to the death of their baby son, who was born with a congenital heart defect. In North America, two community fathers have been charged with custodial interference and contempt of court. Abduction and custody battles, initiated by defecting parents, continue to occupy the courts.

Media stories and outsiders' perspectives tend to fall into two camps: the *Village of the Damned* or the *Little House on the Prairie*. As a researcher sifts through news reports, court affidavits, ex-members' or current members' testimonials, sharply contrasting portraits of the Messianic Communities' family life emerge. These range from dark, Orwellian visions of cowering children with fathers brandishing paddles and threatening hellfire, to heartwarming portraits of quaintly dressed, God-fearing neopioneers who defend their loved ones from religious persecution.

The notion of children growing up in "cults" evokes both fascination and fear in the American public, whose responses range from "Aren't they quaint and adorable!" to "We must rescue them!" To understand the ambivalent opinions regarding this issue—particularly as it concerns the child-centered millenarian movement of this study—we should keep in mind two important, but mutually conflicting American obsessions: the frontier and the family.

Frederick J. Turner (1920), writing in 1893, considered frontiers the most distinctive factor in the American experience, setting their egalitarian stamp on American democracy and character. Their powerful appeal has been explained by Lillian Schlissel, Byrd Gibbens, and Elizabeth Hampsten (1989:241) as "spaces to separate from failure, escape from domestic despair . . . [since] generational conflicts had become so powerful that distance alone absorbed their violence!" Thus, frontiers offer a convenient escape from intolerable family relationships, and they provide new conditions within which better families can be forged.

Throughout American social history and literature, the family is constantly being redefined, idealized, and criticized, but something strange occurs when frontiers are considered in the context of families. As Schlissel et al. (1989:231) observe, "The field between them [becomes] charged, for the frontier suggests that which is expansive and unlimited, and family implies boundaries and a safe homecoming; thus there is tug-of-war in two directions." This tension between two cultural themes has been dramatized in cowboy films as a gender-based struggle involving the man, who is departing for the cattle drive or gunfight, and the woman, who wants him to settle down on the homestead and raise a family.

New religious movements (NRMs) might be described as voluntary families camping on the frontiers of orthodox religion and conventional society. People in NRMs inhabit volatile, rapidly changing environments because of the unpredictable forces of charisma, prophecy, persecution, and poverty that shape their futures. Given these dangers, the public might ask, why would sensible Americans venture out into that disordered space? Whereas adult conversion and its attendant risks presumably involve the element of choice, what will become of those children who are born on these new spiritual frontiers?

I argue that the intense concern expressed by the media and in the law courts over the fate of children brought up in the Messianic Communities is rooted in this familiar cultural tension. The human family has always been composed of a fragile assortment of human needs, in spite of the rhetorical efforts of social and religious bodies to imply permanence or solidity; but the family set on the frontier appears to be "an ephemeral paradoxical institution, doomed to extinction . . . probably within the space of a single generation" (Schlissel et al. 1989:238). Whereas the Messianic Communities' real-life child custody disputes stem from complex interactions between different interest groups, the themes underlying these church/state conflicts contain a powerful mythic quality that guarantees good copy and excites suspense. What will happen, the public wonders, to families who venture out into "cultland"—that weird, volatile, and potentially dangerous spiritual wilderness?

Schlissel and her colleagues (1989) supply three possible resolutions to this suspenseful question in their study of pioneers in the 1880s. In *Far from Home: Families of the Westward Journey* they reconstruct the struggles of four families, using letters and diaries, and propose three "myths" of the frontier family: the garden myth, the gothic myth, and the carnival myth. The shapes of all three myths can be discerned in sources of documentation on the Messianic Communities. The garden myth—the pioneer's quest for a simple, harmonious life in the bosom of nature, for a return to a long-lost Eden in the heart of the wilderness—fuels the stories that appear in the group's evangelistic *Freepaper* and in members' testimonials. The gothic myth—complaints of broken dreams, hardship, exploitation, and dystopian abuses—informs apostates' tales circulated in news reports and in anticult literature. Elements of the carnival myth—the traveler's experiences of mad, comic, creative chaos, of queasy fun and houses of illusion—can be found in insiders', as well as outsiders', accounts describing what lies across the other side of the commune's boundaries. As we study the Messianic Communities' determination to rear sinless children for Yahshua's Return—in spite of all the controversies and stigmatizing efforts surrounding them—we must confront our own ambivalence and nostalgia as twentieth-century parents—and face the gap between our fading cultural ideals and the complex realities of parenting in the fractured, pluralistic "new family" of today (Glendon 1985). Hopefully, after studying this NRM's religiously based ideals regarding children and discipline, as well as the political forces behind its conflicts with society, we might better understand the intense passions evoked by this utopian community.

The History

The Messianic Communities, better known as the Northeast Kingdom Community Church, is at once a communal society and a millenarian movement founded by Elbert Eugene Spriggs (known as Yoneq) and his wife, Marsha, in 1972 in Chattanooga, Tennessee.[2] Its roots are in the Jesus People Revival, and its belief system has much in common with fundamentalist Christianity, but members define themselves as the lost and scattered tribes of the ancient Jews who followed Jesus Christ and adopt Hebrew names accordingly. They believe their "church" (meaning "community") is undergoing a process of purification as the "pure and spotless bride" awaiting her bridegroom: the Second Coming, whom they call by the Hebrew name for Jesus, "Yahshua." By renouncing the world and moving into communes, members become part of the "body of the Messiah"; because of their obedience to "Our Master," they hope to avoid physical death. By increasing their ranks through conversions and childbearing, they are "raising up a people" in preparation for the *Yobel* (Jubilee) horn that heralds the return of Yahshua.

The communities have evolved a unique culture with an emphasis on craftwork and handiwork; since the mid-1970s they have created unique songs and dance forms and developed distinctive patterns of marriage and childrearing. Their Elders condemn abortion and homosexuality and uphold monogamy, premarital chastity, and home schooling. Teenagers' courtships are carefully supervised so as to preserve the youths' virginity for the wedding night. To commit adultery is to sever the link to the Messiah, and to his "body," or community, and is an excommunicable offense. The members' ideals of sexual purity are tied to their millenarian expectations and their hopes for physical immortality.

The church numbers around twenty-five hundred members, and roughly half are children (under eighteen and of the second and third generation). Communities have been established in Brazil, France, Australia, Canada, and recently in Germany, but the majority of members live in New England, mainly in Vermont or Massachusetts. In 1993, the community in Island Pond, Vermont, numbered fifteen households. By 1998, in response to a collective revelation, it had shrunk to two as families moved away to Bellows Falls, Rutland, or Burlington, Vermont; to Rhode Island; and to Hyannis, Massachusetts, to set up new communities.

Each local community or tribe is "covered" by a council of male Elders (one from each household). Decision-making appears to be a collective process based on hearing from the brothers and sisters "what's on their heart," on consulting the Bible, and on group prayer. Under the guidance of Apostle Spriggs, a rather informal hierarchy of Teachers, Elders, Deacons, Deaconesses, and Shepherds has formed. Marsha Spriggs has an important role as a spiritual counselor and role model for the women, and the Spriggses work together as a team, so that the leadership of this NRM could accurately be described as a "charismatic duo." Women wear head scarves on the Sabbath to demonstrate their submission to their husbands and to the male Elders, who, in turn, are "covered" by "Our Master" (Yahshua). The Spriggses are childless and have no permanent home, but they travel among the communities offering counsel and inspiration; they tend to maintain a low-key, elusive presence so as to encourage local self-sufficiency.

The community distributes the *Freepaper* to disseminate its religious message and invite the reader to become part of the "Body of the Messiah." Evangelical efforts surround the Grateful Dead's concerts, the Billy Graham Crusade, the Rainbow Gathering, and, recently, the Promise Keepers. Husband and wife teams drive up to these events in the community's distinctive double-decker bus, distribute the *Freepaper,* perform Israeli dances to the rhythm of handmade Celtic instruments, and offer home-baked bread and cookies. Individual "Walkers" are sent out on hitchhiking preaching tours. A recent trend has been for young married couples to move to a new city, find odd jobs, and set up Wayout Houses—temporary communal homes—to model a "small demonstration of the life" to potential converts. Church members say their goal is to be more visible in highly populated areas and interact more with their neighbors, inviting them into their homes. They also operate restaurants as "Courts of the Gentiles."

Childrearing Practices

Roughly half the membership is composed of children, including youthful, unmarried, second-generation members. Some of these children are brought in by new converts, but the overwhelming majority are born into the community. Although no membership surveys or attrition figures are available, the community appears to have a high rate of attrition among its adult members, but a very low rate among the second generation.[3] One Elder said: "The number of brothers and sisters born into the Body who have left? I can count them on one hand!"

Perceiving the "generation gap" as tearing a hole in society, Messianic Communities' women and men reject this gap in some ways and yet affirm it in others. They draw clear margins between the generations, insisting that children obey their parents, are owned by the parents, and are not equivalent in power to their parents. And yet members blur the lines and narrow the gap in other ways. All ages espouse the same values, listen to the same stories, and share the same social life and work. Fathers in their twenties grow the long beards of grandfathers; girls marry in their late teens and take on the same roles as their mothers. Five-year-old girls wear the same style of pinafore as their grandmothers, who retain their girlish flowing hair, yet let the gray grow in. Thus, the age sets are at once formally hierarchical and informally egalitarian.

Children are present at nearly all ritual and social events, and are often the center of attention at the morning and evening "sacrifice" (religious service), where they form a circle, dance, and frequently sing:

> We are thankful to be chosen to be part of a people
> Who no longer live for themselves, but for Him
> Who gave up his life, so that we could live together
> Free to demonstrate the love He's put inside of our hearts.
> We rejoice in this.
> We are forgiven people.
> And we give thanks to Him. How can we help but praise Him?
> We rejoice in our Master's loving-kindness.

All participate in prayer and confessions and listen to the Elders' teachings. Sometimes the children show their drawings and letters or gifts received from friends in a sister community. At one occasion I attended, Island Pond children opened presents of shells, cards, pencils, and notepads sent by the children of the community in Sus, France.

On Saturday at "sundown" (members avoid references to numerical time), the main Shabbat event is the children's story, in which one of the Elders relates a Bible story, embellished with mime and references to American history. Children are eager participants, answer questions, and act out events; then all return to their own households to drink from the Victory Cup (a large clay goblet containing homemade wine used in the same fashion as the chalice in mainstream Christianity) and confess their selfish actions during the week.

Challenging Rosabeth Moss Kanter's (1972) theory of "defamilialization," in this commune the biological family is not undermined but is actually *reinforced* by commitment mechanisms that appear designed to strengthen bonds *within* the nuclear family. The husband-wife relationship is supported by the community, and members take turns baby-sitting, so that the couple can have one evening a week to go out. On Shabbat, time is set aside for nuclear families, who stay in their quarters and sleep in or read. Fruit cobblers and tisanes are laid out the night before, so that there is no need for the women to descend into the communal kitchen. Parents exhibit constant physical affection for their children, who sit on their laps and are circled inside their arms, and children hold hands and hug one another. It is considered unseemly, however, for couples to demonstrate physical affection in public.

Each family has at least two rooms: one bedroom for the parents and one or more for the children. Babies sleep in cots beside the parents' bed. Older children often choose to sleep with their friends or peer group. Children's bedrooms are nostalgically attractive, with carved wooden furniture and hand-painted bureaus. Mothers make patchwork quilts, handmade curtains, and dried flowers, and they paint watercolors from nature, often illustrating Bible verses, to decorate the walls.

Children attend home-schooling, or "training," sessions four days a week, where they learn reading, writing, arithmetic, history, and geography. Science classes are called "creation," and Darwin's theory of evolution is ignored. Hours are flexible, and summers are devoted to community life, with canoeing, swimming, hiking, and sailing. Children learn to read early, often by age four or five, but by age thirteen they abandon formal academics and are apprenticed to adults who train them in crafts and specialized labor. Children perform plays, skits, and Christmas tableaus and read Bible stories. No television or outings to movie theaters are permitted.

Children dress as smaller adults, with girls wearing long braids, skirts, or bloomers and boys cutting their hair at shoulder length, tied in a clump with headbands. Boys learn carpentry and girls learn cooking and sewing, but both sexes can prepare food and make candles, soap, and paper. Little girls quarrel over the privilege of feeding and holding babies. Children are integrated smoothly into daily chores, cleanups, and food preparation. Community children are curious about outsiders and tend to stare unself-consciously at newcomers. They are very friendly toward outside kids and invite them to pick strawberries and play ball. They exhibit highly developed social skills.[4]

Toys are prohibited. The declared aim is to discourage "fantasy" but to encourage the "imagination." Trucks, dolls, and teddy bears are discouraged, but building blocks, Legos, Tinker Toys, balls, carpentry tools, writing materials, and sewing kits are available. Santa Claus is dismissed as "fantasy," but the community's own religious beliefs are held to be literally true. Children do not receive allowances or candy. For their recreation, noncompetitive games are organized on Sunday afternoons, and Thursday night dance classes are held. The children receive extensive musical training on instruments and memorize and compose songs. The teenagers entertain themselves by forming small musical groups with acoustic instruments—guitars, hammer dulcimers, harps, flutes, and drums—and they play traditional Celtic and Israeli dance music. The communities' religious services feature storytelling and are playful and entertaining for children.

Fathers are as actively involved as mothers in raising children. Fathers take their children for daily walks, read stories at night, and teach their sons work skills during the day. On the evening of the Shabbat, as I walked along the path through the woods to the gathering, I saw many fathers carrying toddlers on their shoulders or babies in backpacks. The men frequently meet to discuss problems and policies in childrearing, even discussing various cures for diaper rash. In the Messianic Communities, childrearing is a manly vocation.

Teenagers who are courting spend time together for several months under their parents' supervision while living in separate households. If they decide to marry, both sets of parents must agree, and each member of both households must say a "hearty Amen." Youths marry and become parents at an early age. Handling rebellious teenagers is a recent concern, aired at a June 22, 1994, celebration in Basin Farm. The community in Boston discovered a teen "underground" where teens were forming cliques, saying cruel things behind each others' backs, and closing ranks against parental intervention.[5] The afternoon was devoted to hearing the confessions and repentances of guilty teens, which I interpreted as a Kanterian (1972) "mortification mechanism" applied to the second generation.

Children do not participate in the group's evangelistic activities; they remain at home with "watchers" when the parents go out on short missionary tours. They are protected from exposure to Western materialism, and their bodies are covered modestly. Girls and boys even wear sleeves and pantalets when swimming. Parents teach their children the basic facts about sex and death but do not want them exposed to the glamorized or sensationalized depictions of either that appear on television.

According to the communities' literal interpretation of Matthew 18:3 ("Except ye be converted and become as little children ye shall not enter into the Kingdom of Heaven"), childhood is a period of innocence and natural faith (this view is reminiscent of that of medieval authors and nineteenth-century Romantics). Shulamith Shahar (1990:19) observes that "the idea that Thanatos and Eros have no place in the cosmogony of the child" is found in many medieval manuscripts, such as those of Gilbert of Nogent and John Bromyard and in *Le Roman de la Rose.* The notion that when the child becomes aware of the profound realities of death and sex, the paradise of childhood comes to an end can be traced throughout the history of Western literature (Shahar 1990). Messianic Communities parents shelter their children inside the walled "garden" of their sectarian commune and literally believe, given the imminence of Yahshua's return, that their children may not need to undergo the throes of death. One Elder declared: "God is just sick and tired of watching people die! Our children will be so pure they will gladden Our Father's heart with their perpetual life!"

Thus, children play a central role in the Messianic Communities' eschatological drama. Members believe that it is up to them to "raise up a people" and prepare the "pure and spotless bride" (their community) before Yahshua returns and ushers in the millennium. The Elders received a prophecy that during the seven years of the Tribulation 144,000 pure virgin males in the third generation (12,000 from each tribe and 2 from every household) will set out to preach and be ruthlessly martyred. Two will be killed and resurrected on the streets of Jerusalem. These young men will be "sealed with the seal of God, wielding magical powers, able to call down plagues and to predict the acts of God." One Elder explained that the power of the younger generation "is way beyond *us;* we certainly don't have that kind of self-control. They have to be raised for that—and not by watching MTV or by reading cartoons about talking animals!"

The theology behind the Messianic Communities' childrearing contains more than a hint of eugenics—of a purification process throughout the generations to create (as one brother put it) a "grade A humanity." Parents expect their children to be less materialistic, more spiritually refined, and more attuned to Yahshua's voice than to their own generation. One father of six said: "I had girlfriends before I came into the community, and we were not celibate! Sometimes I have flashbacks of the past, something just pops into my head—but they were relationships that were never meant to be! Our children will not have that problem. They will have one wife, one husband. They will be single-minded and pure."

The Issue of Corporal Punishment

Since the group's disciplinary practices have been a major source of controversy and a burning issue in court custody battles, it is important to investigate the theory and practice concerning "the rod." According to Spriggs's guidelines, if a child does not obey on *first command,* he or she must be disciplined because it is imperative that the child be trained to obey the parents so as to stay alert, ready for "Yahshua's call." The spanking must be administered in a calm "spirit," with no need for prior rationalizations. Some small concessions, however, have been made to external censure (or internal mistakes and excesses). The child must be under twelve, and it must be the child's *own* parents who administer the spanking (unless they appoint a teacher or guardian), and they must take care to leave no marks. Usually the discipline consists of no more than a few stinging blows with a flexible reed, such as a balloon stick, on the bottom or the palm of the hand. Then the child receives a hug and is forgiven.

Although corporal punishment of children is part of the group's Bible fundamentalist heritage (see Ellison and Sherkat 1993) and Proverbs 22:6 and other Bible verses are often quoted to justify the use of the rod, within the community an idiosyncratic theodicy and set of rituals have evolved around this childrearing practice. Corporal punishment appears to function as a kind of moral purification ritual, since members believe they are cleansing the child of guilt, so that their children will achieve eternal life—in this case physical immortality. From this theological perspective, without the rod, the child "dies unto sin." From a sociological perspective, the rod corresponds to Kanter's mortification mechanism, since it humbles the individual and facilitates adjustment to communal life.

Eugene Spriggs appears to encourage this strong stand on discipline. On June 23, 1994, he gave a speech at the Basin Farm celebration in which he shared fond memories of his own father, who "lit into him," and of a schoolteacher who "gave it to him." "A parent who doesn't discipline his child isn't a true parent," he concluded.

I have been asked on many occasions to express an opinion concerning the severity of these disciplines. I always state that, since I have never personally witnessed the chastisement of children, I cannot judge. Certainly, the people I have spent time with strike me as kind and loving parents, and their children are high-spirited and trusting, so it is difficult to believe some of the affidavits I have read for the courts.

Communal groups have always been a locus for custody disputes, but the Messianic Communities, because of their anachronistic methods of child discipline, rejection of modernity and pluralism, neoconservative roles for women, and apocalyptic expectations, provide fertile ground for lawsuits, yellow journalism, and persecution.

A History of the Raid on Island Pond

The Messianic Communities' long, drawn-out battle over the custody of their children began in 1982 when three sets of parents went to court over the custody of eleven children. The judges awarded custody (in each case) to the fathers residing outside the community. One of the judges, Frank Mahady, expressed his opinion at the time that the children were trapped in "some sort of holy war" between the parents.[6]

One of these custodial fathers, Juan Mattatall, turned out to be the church's most bitter career apostate. He had contacted Galen Kelly and Priscilla Coates of the anticult organization the Citizen's Freedom Foundation (CFF) when he first left the community, and with their support he was awarded custody of his five children. His youngest daughter, Lydia, however, was overseas in France living with Eugene and Marsha Spriggs.[7] Mattatall accused Apostle Spriggs of kidnapping Lydia. Cindy Mattatall, the mother, appeared before Judge Mahady in a series of hearings and made secret arrangements to fly with her children to Europe. The CFF helped Juan Mattatall track down her passport number and her date of departure. According to a member's report, "The New Jersey State Police, Juan, and some people from the ACM [anticult movement] came in and held her at gunpoint in the middle of the night and took the children away, even the baby who was nursing when they broke in."

Lydia Mattatall returned to North America with the Spriggs in 1982. Cindy Mattatall traveled to Nova Scotia to meet them. The Royal Canadian Mounted Police (RCMP) ordered a road block, seized Lydia Mattatall, and handed over to her father. He moved to Burlington, and a story appeared on the front page of the *Burlington Free Press* showing the triumphant father reunited with his blond, mop-haired kids. He hired a nanny and attended a local church, where he stood in the pulpit and spoke of how he had rescued his kids from the cult, and "now the next step was to rescue his wife." He brought the children to Island Pond to visit their mother on two occasions after he received a court order to do so, but he arrived in a camper with CFF workers and parked right outside the Island Pond Maples household for the night. He handed out whistles to each of the kids, promising to come to their rescue if they were abused.[8]

In the wake of Mattatall's court victory, a network of journalists, social workers, and anticultists began to seek out defectors and search for corroborating evidence of child abuse. Priscilla Coates of the CFF met with the Vermont attorney general's staff and provided names of defectors. The state of Vermont paid for Conrad Grimms (the acting director of Social and Rehabilitation Services in Newport, Vermont), and Peter Johnson of the Vermont State Police to travel around the country between 1982 and 1983 tracking down ex-members, who were now living in seven different states, to interview them for child abuse stories. These interviews were used in the eighteen affidavits that became the basis for the raid. One of these, the Moran affidavit, featured the stories of fourteen defectors. Six recounted stories that were remarkably similar, and all six happened to have been deprogrammed by Galen Kelly.[9]

A network of concerned parties went to the attorney general's office in Montpelier and handed over social services' files and police reports. Judge Wolchik issued a search warrant, which was brought to Governor Richard Snelling, who summoned top officials for a meeting (Hoffman 1994:2). Galen Kelly and Priscilla Coates produced data on two cases of child beating fatalities that had occurred in Michigan and West Virginia NRMs completely unconnected to the Island Pond community, and these were cited to justify emergency measures (Malcarne and Burchard 1992:82).

On June 22, 1984, at dawn, ninety Vermont state troopers arrived in their cruisers at the homes of the community in Island Pond, armed with a court order and accompanied by fifty Social Rehabilitation Services workers. They searched the households and took 112 children into custody. The parents were allowed to accompany them, and the families were bused to Newport. Judge Frank Mahady, after holding forty individual detention hearings in one day, ruled that the search warrant issued by the state was unconstitutional. All the children were returned to their parents without undergoing examinations for signs of physical abuse.

Interpretations of the raid, its meaning, and its outcome were conflicting. Judge Mahady pronounced the raid, "a grossly unlawful scheme" (Dunbar 1994). He commented that the state's motive was not the issue, for "even when the state acts in a noble cause, it must act lawfully" (Kokoszka 1994). Judge Wolchik, who had signed the search warrant for the raid, later admitted at a confirmation hearing in 1986, "I now believe that I relied on false or unreliable information." Many journalists, however, criticized Mahady's decision. The editor of the Orleans County, Vermont, *Chronicle,* Chris Braithwaite (1983), produced an article, "Have We Lost the Children?" that deplored Judge Mahady's ruling. For others, the moral of the failed raid was a call for more draconian and intrusive measures against "cults" suspected of child abuse (see Malcarne and Burchard 1992). Dramatic as the raid was, it was followed by several equally dramatic—but small-scale—custody battles involving high-speed chases and alleged kidnappings. These stirring events provided the raw material for frontier myths.

The Messianic Communities' reputation as the "cult that steals little children" is largely due to the activism of Laurie Johnson, who embarked on an eight-year search for her two missing boys, Seth and Nathan; they disappeared in 1989 with their father, Stephen Wootten, shortly after she had launched a custody suit following her defection from the community. Seth and Nathan Wootten's faces have appeared on Child Find and Childseekers posters, with the caption "It is believed that the cult is assisting in the concealment of these and other children sought by custodial parents and authorities." Johnson appeared on the *Jerry Springer Show* in 1995 and invited viewers to send money to the "Friends of Nathan and Seth" foundation. She also hired a colorful team of private investigators from Philadelphia who run an agency by the name of CRIB (Children's Rights Investigation Bureau); its insignia closely resembles that of the FBI. These investigators rode Harleys, wore cowboys outfits, and toted pistols and handcuffs. Community members complained that these investigators would circle around on the motorbikes to "spy on our gatherings and say bad things about us to visitors" (personal communication). In February 1996, the community in Winnipeg, Manitoba, was searched by police and youth protection officials for Seth and Nathan. In April 1997, Wootten and the boys were picked up by the FBI in Florida. Steve Wootten is awaiting trial, and Laurie Johnson was reunited with her sons after hiring Rick Ross to provide them with "exit counseling."[10] The charges against Wooten were dismissed in the 1998 trial.

Another custody battle that reached epic proportions was the well-publicized *Seymour* v. *Dawson* case in Canada. Edward Dawson joined the community in 1986, leaving his three-year-old son, Michael, in the care of the boy's mother, Judy Seymour. After a few months, she gave the boy to Dawson's sister and her husband to be raised on their farm and signed an unnotarized agreement granting them custody. Dawson then took Michael to live with the Messianic Community in Nova Scotia after his mother had visited the place and agreed to the move. In August 1987, Dawson and his son were feeding the chickens on the community's Myrtle Tree Farm in Nova Scotia when a police car and social services workers appeared unannounced and insisted on inspecting Michael for signs of abuse. On September 24, 1987, Michael Dawson was taken into custody for forty-four days and placed with a foster family. Doctors and psychologists examined the child but found no evidence of abuse, so he was returned to his father. Social services officials appealed the court's decision, and Dawson went to the appeals division of the Supreme Court in Nova Scotia while his case was ongoing in the Family Court.

In 1987, Judy Seymour sued for custody of her son. Meanwhile, during the Family Court proceedings, Dawson had made his son unavailable to the court. Dawson was held in contempt of court and put in jail. Working with his lawyer, Jean Swantko, a former public defender from Vermont, he appeared in Halifax before a tribunal. On February 5, 1988, the Supreme Court ordered his immediate release and deemed him a fit father.

In 1992, Seymour and her lawyer arranged an ex parte hearing with the judge in Nova Scotia, where a local deprogrammer (and licensed real-estate broker), Stephen North claimed that the Northeast Community Church bore the unmistakable earmarks of a "cult" (on tape he declares, "Sleep deprivation is very involved with these groups"). His expertise seemed to impress Judge Black of Kentville, Nova Scotia, who issued an order on March 10, 1992, granting Judy Seymour "interim liberal access" for the weekend and ordering Dawson to appear in court the following week. Dawson refused to let the mother take the boy off unaccompanied, and Dawson failed to appear in court, for he had already crossed the border and taken his son to live in a community household in California.

Dawson was apprehended by the FBI in spring 1994 in California, placed in a maximum security prison for three months, and charged with abduction and disobeying of a court order. In the 1994 trial, Dawson was acquitted of abduction, and on a 1995 appeal the charge of disobeying a court order was dismissed. The court then won a new trial on the charge of abduction. In November 1997, Dawson represented himself at a two-week jury trial where Michael, then fourteen, testified concerning his traumatic experiences of the past—police seizures, foster homes, and psychological examination—and Dawson received a verdict of "not guilty." Michael is currently living with his mother, who has de facto custody in Montreal.

The Messianic Communities continue to elicit controversy and stimulate new investigations. Every time a new commune is established, watchdog groups circulate information packets produced by the (now defunct) Citizen's Freedom Foundation to local authorities. In 1994, in Hyannis, Massachusetts, for example, social workers paid an unannounced visit to the community and argued with the parents who refused to allow them to speak to the children in private or disrobe them to look for bruises. The social workers had been prompted by Bob Parton of the New England Institute of Religious Studies, who had contacted the Department of Social Services in Hyannis, Massachusetts, and filed a petition with the court stating that these children were in need of care, citing as evidence a report from a former member concerning child beatings. A hearing took place at the Barnstable County Courthouse on June 20, 1994. Among the young parents asked to identify their own baby boy, Tabor, were Jeff Whitten and Jennifer Johnson, who as children had themselves been taken into custody in the raid of 1984. All charges were dismissed for lack of evidence on November 8, 1994.

An investigation was made into the community in Rutland, Vermont, as part of the *Lavin* v. *Lavin* custody dispute over the four Lavin daughters. On May 11, 1994, Rutland Family Court awarded physical custody to the father, who was living outside the community. All four girls have since chosen to live unofficially with their mother inside the community. They do so with their father's blessing, since he is now sympathetic to their religious goals. When interviewed on television, he said his daughters had a "better life" inside the group. The court-appointed psychologist in the case found the communities' childrearing practices "safe" and "developmentally sound."[11]

Schlissel's Three Myths of the Frontier

Having traced the real-life conflicts between this NRM and its host society, we might ask how this history sheds light on the challenge that alternative, religiously based patterns of childrearing pose to American ideas (and ideals) of the family. We can usefully examine this challenge as a tug of war between two American quests—the search for the right frontier that will bring freedom and fortune and the dream of the loving family as a safe haven—and the three myths that bind them.

The garden myth, according to Schlissel et al. (1989), conveys the pioneers' aspirations to settle in fertile land where they expect to find order and the blessing of fruitful toil, a dream of family, land, and inheritance in balance. The church's *Freepaper* offers many examples of this myth in the form of testimonials of finding love and better family life in the Body of the Messiah. *Back to the Garden* (n.d.:n.p.) claims, "He has given us the opportunity to come back to the garden through obedience to His words." Like many utopian communes past and present, this community offers the potential convert perfect love, new marriages that restore the innocence of Adam and Eve before the Fall, an intimate and egalitarian communal life, harmony with nature, and meaningful work with the hands. On the secular side, apostates such as Mattatall, Johnson, and Seymour who have wrested their children from the scary maw of a "cult" describe their triumphant and thankful return to the middle-class garden of single-parent-family normalcy.

The carnival myth portrays the frontier as a liminal space for bursting out and breaking bounds, a place where humor and hilarity compensate for hardship, as in the Gold Rush frontier towns famous for their eccentricities, gambling, and speculations. NRMs offer youths a self-imposed rite of passage where everything that is determined by social-hierarchical inequality is suspended. People who in "straight society" are separated by impenetrable hierarchical barriers may enter into free, familiar contact inside the carnival space of a mystical community.

Elements of the fantastic and the festival that are borrowed from American counterculture appear in the Messianic Communities' *Freepaper.* The community's double-decker bus is often seen parked at the Rainbow Tribe, at the Bread and Puppet Circus, and at Grateful Dead concerts amid crafts peddlers, tie-dye T-shirts, jugglers, face-painting stalls, African drummers, and other extravagances. The movement's founder, Elbert Spriggs, is (significantly, if inaccurately) described in anticult literature as a former "carnival barker." Although the group's missionaries appear to be just another sideshow in these carnivals, they denounce the outside world as a frightening and queasy roller-coaster to destruction. In "Oh What a Night!" (*Freepaper: The 60's* n.d.:n.p.) a member recalls: "I used to live in a land called Rock and Roll fantasy. . . . The LSD, the granules of cocaine, the THC, Quaaludes—so heavenly, very mellow yellow & orange & blue— . . . but oh the terror of it all! I was coming down, down, down . . . must face tomorrow 150 bucks poorer, that night in Interstate 59."

The gothic myth of the frontier generates tales of heartbreak and loneliness, of broken promises and human failure. Examples of this type can be found in the stories of embittered ex-members and in the propaganda circulated by the anticult movement. Michael Woodruff (1984:3) warns worried relatives of "testimonies . . . some 200 pages of affidavits [that] tell us of systematic, frequent, and lengthy beatings of children by parents and church elders with wooden and iron rods and paddles, often drawing blood . . . stripped naked and beaten for several hours."

A striking example of the gothic myth is found in "The Children and the Cults," by journalist Barbara Grizutti Harrison (1984), a disaffected Jehovah's Witness. Harrison (1984:58, 59) asserts that "the cult is robbing children of their childhood" and describes the youths of Island Pond as far more sinister than pathetic: their facial expressions are "not like other children" but are "praeternaturally grave." She associates these youths with the zombielike, homicidal, telekinetic extraterrestrial children of the sci-fi film *Village of the Damned.* She (1984:68) even endows the Island Pond young with negative magical powers: "An elder . . . stared at me unblinkingly and told me about the Lake of Fire. . . . I felt virulent hatred focused on me like an invasion of the body. . . . My heart was being attacked. . . . The women, their voices sweet, chanted about the Lake of Fire. The children watched. Three hours later I was admitted to the North Country Hospital for chest pains." Invited by the community to "come and stay for three days," Harrison was immediately on guard:

"Three days is the standard period for what is variously known as 'brainwashing,' persuasive coercion or mind control," she (1984:60) writes triumphantly.

But secular family life is equally grim and gothic from the current members' perspectives. Their testimonies describe their wanderings through the bleak landscape of American family life before they found love in the Body of the Messiah. In a *Freepaper* article "Born to Be Wasted" (n.d.:60), a brother complains: "Yeah, we were all wasted! In one way or another. My life and my conscience started being laid waste . . . when I was born. . . . A year later my Mom split with my sister leaving us three boys with an alcoholic dad who dropped us all off six months later and attempted suicide." In another testimonial, an anonymous sister describes her guilt and horror following a traumatic abortion: "He [Yahshua] delivered me out of that society that rapes its victims . . . encourages the murder of innocent babies. . . . My conscience . . . was snuffed out by the sick reasoning and social pressure that directed my life" (*North Island Freepaper* n.d.:46).

A common variation on the gothic myth is the child who is lost on the frontier; this variation is replete with tales of abductions, mysterious disappearances, and brainwashing—a modern version of soul-snatching. The headlines of news reports outlining the Laurie Johnson and Judy Seymour cases are calculated to chill a parent's heart: "Mom Seeks to Save Kids from Cold Hands of Cult"; "Family Desperately Seeks Two Children" (*Palladium Times*, Monday, December 16, 1991:2); "Church Tore Family Apart" (*The Winnipeg Sun*, Friday, April 2, 1993). A particularly bizarre example of this theme is the persistent rumor of the mysterious disappearance of millionaire's son Lyndon Fuller into "the cult."

Lyndon Fuller, the twenty-four-year-old son of the Fuller Brush manufacturing family, escaped from the psychiatric ward of a hospital in Berowick, Nova Scotia, in 1991 and vanished without a trace. A rumor spread throughout the towns of Berowick and Barrington Passage that the millionaire's son had disappeared into the Messianic Communities' Myrtle Tree Farm—in spite of the fact that he had never shown an interest the community's religion or ever had any contact with its members. The Royal Canadian Mounted Police planted officers in a neighbor's attic for months to watch the vehicles that came and left the farm. Deprogrammer Stephen North was spotted by members in a field studying the farm through binoculars. Helicopters hovered overhead. The community's double-decker bus was stopped and searched on the highway. The case remains open, and rumors still abound in Nova Scotia.

Conclusion

Considered within the folklore of frontiers and families, this NRM presents a puzzling paradox. It is a nostalgic retreat into the past, a return to the certainty, the simplicity, of early days. Yet it is also an abrupt departure for adventure, a radical rejection of parents and of mainstream American culture. This

NRM is reassuringly familiar, conjuring up yellowed photographs of Mormon pioneers or museum displays of Shaker furniture. At the same time, it is profoundly alien, aspiring toward an uncertain apocalyptic future. It is a strange, unsettling reaggregation of familiar cultural elements.

For outsiders, the Messianic Communities' gleeful anticipation of world destruction is disquieting. Its claim to be the elite, chosen people has an unfashionable ring in an era promoting such buzzwords as *multiracial* and *multiculturalism.* The apocalyptic element is felt to present a threat to children's safety, although church historians could point to tens of thousands of "world's ends" that have come and gone without anyone getting scratched and children who sing militant hymns such as "Onward Christian Soldiers" in Protestant churches or read the violent poetry in Revelation without exciting concern.

Is there is a lesson to be learned from this long history of conflict? If there is, we must first distinguish the Messianic Communities from other NRMs prosecuted for child abuse. The latter ranges from Christians to Hindus, from Black Hebrews to therapy groups (Melton 1986:255–258). The few existing studies on family life inside NRMs suggest an enormous range of childrearing practices and parental attitudes.

Shahar's (1990) critique of Philippe Ariès's theory in *Centuries of Childhood* would apply to media stereotypes of cults as places where children are almost routinely abused, neglected or sexually exploited. Stephen Wilson (1984) points out that childrearing methods and popular notions of child development have varied considerably throughout the centuries, among neighboring kingdoms, and even within different classes or guilds during the same period in Europe. In investigating childrearing methods in the Middle Ages, "certain historians," he (1984:181–198) complains, have tended to rely on the only records that are available; they delve into court registers and report cases of maternal cruelty or infanticide or search the records of foundling homes for reports of abandonment, "which usually are concerned with criminal or deviant behaviour—transgressians of the moral code of the day." Shahar (1990:6) argues that, whereas "these cases have been documented and are worthy of research, . . . it is clear they represent deviations from the norm which were unacceptable to society . . . [but] they have been cited to suggest generalizations about parent-child relations."

Lawrence Foster (1981) quotes historian Frank Manuel when summing up the significance of nineteenth-century communal experiments in gender: "The utopia might well be the most sensitive indicator of where the sharpest anguish of an age lies." In this light, the patterns of parenting in NRMs are like distorted reflections of our own parental failures and excesses. Lewis Poteet (1989:12), in his study of the "cult" in Nova Scotia, observes: "In fact during one of the heated newspaper attacks on them, there were side-by-side stories which castigated the cult for beating its children and simultaneously announced that the local school board was going to suspend the long-established custom of caning disobedient pupils 'at the end of next year.'" He (1989:10) concludes with a fascinating insight: "The commune has affinities with the culture as it *might like to see itself,* not as it actually is. . . . The members of the Cult have put their feet down in footprints made by an earlier community."

The frontier family is remembered with nostalgia as a model of ordered simplicity, and yet it was neither simple nor orderly, but full of changes and abrupt transitions. In all the permutations of the Messianic Communities, the extended voluntary and spiritual families recapitulate the evolution of the modern family—only they run it backward. In this history of self-willed dislocations, discontinuities, and custody battles, we can discern the outlines of our own family histories. What Schlissel et al. (1989:xvii–xviii) find significant in their pioneer families we might apply also to the Messianic Communities' families: "They are us in other clothes, where we began and where our dreams were given form. On the broad spaces of the unformed frontiers, in the curious destinies of these families, is something that speaks to us of what it means to be a family in America today."

Notes

1. The Messianic Communities were originally known as the Vine Community Church during the formative years in Chattanooga, then as the Northeast Kingdom Community in Vermont, and, most recently, as the Apostolic Order in Europe. The communities are known to each other as "tribes," each bearing its own Hebrew name.
2. I met and interviewed Apostle Spriggs with my colleague John Bozeman at the Basin Farm in 1994. The impression I gained was of a warm but shrewd person, a "laid-back" hippie or an artisan with a vision, evidently an outstanding Bible studies teacher and a skillful group facilitator with a strong visual or artistic bent. I want to convey my own impressions of Apostle Spriggs, since the media and the former Citizen's Freedom Foundation have portrayed him as a "carnival barker" and relied on the tired stereotype of the power-hungry "cult leader." In my experience every religious innovator/NRM founder has a different and distinct personality, personal life, and modus operandi. To my knowledge, J. Gordon Melton and John Bozeman are the only other scholars who have had the privilege of meeting Elbert Spriggs.
3. Although the Elders have not been receptive to the idea of a questionnaire, my impression as a participant-observer is that members come and go—and return—with great frequency, although the attrition rate was even higher, I was told, in the early years in Chattanooga.
4. My own son and daughter were welcomed and befriended by the children of Island Pond even before I "came out" as a scholar of NRMs. Thus, we were received as potential "joiners" rather than as possibly outside allies. After we spent our first weekend with the community in 1989, I had a hard time separating my children from their new friends, and they resisted getting into the car when it was time to leave. I was amused to hear their account of their friends taking them to dig up a "treasure chest" filled with candy, toys, and quarters, buried in a grove of trees at the foot of the garden, since I had just been listening to the Elders explain why they did not allow their children to have these things (see Palmer 1994). When I tried to enlist my children as my research assistants on our next trip, I made the mistake of listening too eagerly to their stories. They immediately clammed up: "We're not your spies, Mummy. They're our *friends*!"

5. One Elder, evidently nervous about the presence of myself and John Bozeman at this confrontation, explained that their youths were starting to behave "just as bad as teenagers in the churches!"
6. *Gregoire* v. *Gregoire* (1983).
7. Members claim that Cindy Mattatall gained her husband's consent prior to this arrangement, but when he was disciplined by the community in Boston, he decided to claim his daughter was "kidnapped."
8. This story was told to me by Eddie Wiseman and his wife, Jean Swantko.
9. Galen Kelly is a deprogrammer who was sentenced to seven and a half years in 1993 for kidnapping a woman "cult member." See *Times Herald Record* (Middletown, N.Y.), September 25, 1993.
10. Rick Ross is a well-known deprogrammer who advised the FBI during the siege of the Branch Davidians at Waco, Texas. In 1993, he was charged and found guilty of the unlawful imprisonment of Jason Scott, who had joined a Pentecostal church in Bellevue, Washington, against his mother's wishes (*Journal American,* July 3, 1993, A1). Later Ross made an out-of-court settlement with Scott, in which he owed him several hours of exit counseling.
11. See "The Assessment of the Potential Impact of the Messianic Community on the Welfare and Best Interest of the Children," a psychological report submitted as evidence by Dr. Craig Knapp for *Lavin* v. *Lavin* (1994).

References

Back to the Garden: Freepaper. N.d. Island Pond, Vt.: Parchment Press.

"Born to Be Wasted: A Teenage Wasteland." N.d. *Freepaper.*

Braithwaite, C. 1983. "Island Pond Cult Loses Custody Fight, Business." *The Chronicle* (Orleans County, Vt.), May 25, 1.

Dunbar, B. 1994. "Ten Years After the Raid." *The Chronicle* (Orleans County, Vt.), June 24, 30–37.

Ellison, C. G., and D. E. Sherkat. 1993. "Conservative Protestantism and Support for Corporal Punishment." *American Sociological Review* 58: 131–144.

Foster, L. 1981. *Religion and Sexuality: Three American Communal Experiments of the Nineteenth Century*. New York: Oxford University Press.

Freepaper: The 60's. N.d.

Glendon, M. A. 1985. *The New Family and the New Property.* Toronto: Butterworth.

Harrison, B. G. 1984. "The Children and the Cults." *New England Monthly* (December): 56–69.

Hoffman, J. 1994. "Island Pond Raid, 10 Years Later." *Sunday Rutland Herald and Sunday Times Argus* (Barre-Montepelier, Vt.), June 19, 1–3.

Kanter, R. M. 1972. *Commitment and Community: Communes and Utopias in Sociological Perspective.* Cambridge, Mass.: Harvard University Press.

Kokoszka, L. 1994. "Time Mellows Communities Caught in Raid." *Caledonian Record* (Vt.), June 22, 1–8.

Malcarne, V., and J. Burchard. 1992. "Investigations of Child Abuse/Neglect Allegations in Religious Cults: A Case Study in Vermont." *Behavioral Sciences and the Law* 10: 77–88.

Melton, J. G. 1986. "Report of Survey on Cult-Related Violence." Santa Barbara, Calif.: Institute for the Study of American Religion.

North Island Freepaper: The Answer Is Blowin' in the Wind. N.d.
Palmer, S. J. 1994. *Moon Sisters, Krishna Mothers, Rajneesh Lovers: Women's Roles in New Religions.* Syracuse, N.Y.: Syracuse University Press.
Poteet, L. J. 1989. "The 'Cult' Meets the Cultures of Nova Scotia's South South Shore." *Nova Scotia New Maritimes* 11: 10–13.
Schlissel, L., B. Gibbens, and E. Hampsten. 1989. *Far from Home: Families of the Westward Journey.* New York: Schocken Books.
Shahar, S. 1990. *Childhood in the Middle Ages.* New York: Routledge.
Turner, F. J. 1920. "The Significance of the Frontier in American History." In H. P. Simonson, ed., *The Frontier in American History.* New York: Frederick Ungar.
Wilson, Stephen. 1984. "The Myth of Motherhood a Myth: The Historical View of European Child-Rearing." *Social History* 9 (2).
Woodruff, M. 1984. "Cultism and Child Abuse: Cases of Convergence." *Cult Observer* (September): 4.

CHAPTER 10

Social Control of New Religions

FROM "BRAINWASHING" CLAIMS TO CHILD SEX ABUSE ACCUSATIONS

JAMES T. RICHARDSON

Social control of new religious movements (NRMs)—popularly known as "cults"—has taken many forms in the United States since such groups became defined as a social problem. This chapter summarizes some of the earlier efforts at social control attempted mainly by defectors from these movements and examines the use of a major new tactic—child abuse allegations—that has become the "ultimate weapon" to inhibit the growth and prosperity of exotic religious groups. The chapter then comments on the success of these various methods of social control, as well as on some of the consequences of using child abuse allegations.

The Early History of Social Control Efforts

When new religious groups first came to public attention in the United States in the late 1960s, there appeared to be a general feeling that this new trend—of youths moving into communes in northern California—was preferable to youth hanging out on street corners or marching in demonstrations. Soon, however, Americans discovered that some of these communes were actually "high-demand" organizations, promoting beliefs, values, and behaviors that conflicted with those of the dominant culture. The recognition that many American youth were quite serious about their new religious affiliation came as a surprise to many (Richardson 1985b; Robbins 1988).

This new perception of the groups as constituting a *threat* was mainly the result of two converging factors: the social location of the target population for converts—well-educated, affluent American youths (Wuthnow 1978, 1986)—and the relatively vulnerable political situation of the newer religions. The social origins of most participants in the new groups meant that their families and friends were often well positioned to bring public attention to the new phenomenon of young people joining exotic religions. Thus, the parents and other interested parties were able, with the help of the media, to have the new religious movements defined as a social problem. In short, some disenchanted but relatively high-status parents knew exactly what "buttons to push" to galvanize politicians, government agencies, and journalists into action. There was a confluence of interest among disenchanted parents, government officials, journalists, and others, many of whom desired to exercise control over new religions. The target groups could often do very little to fend off such attentions and refute allegations of wrongdoing because of their weak political position and their limited financial resources.

The Unification Church (the "Moonies") and the Children of God in particular attracted early negative attention from parents who did not want their sons or daughter to give up promising careers and conventional lifestyles to proselytize or fund-raise on the streets of U.S. cities or (even worse) to be sent to foreign missionary fields. These two religious movements became the focus of the early anticult movement in the United States, as concerned parents and sympathizers networked to counter a perceived growing social problem (Shupe and Bromley 1980, 1994).

Accusations of Brainwashing and Other Early Social Control Efforts

Social control tactics employed against NRMs have often been based, directly or indirectly, on accusations of "brainwashing," as well as on allegations of "mind control." This new fashionable concern was the alleged exploitation of youthful participants through sophisticated psychotechnology supposedly derived from the experiments of communists in China and the former Soviet Union (Solomon 1983; Richardson and Kilbourne 1983; Barker 1984; Fort 1985; Anthony 1990; Richardson 1993).

Public opinion research reveals that this view of NRMs as exploitative has become widespread (Bromley and Breschel 1992; Richardson 1992), in part because of media accounts that have adopted the typical atrocity tale format to describe "cult" fund-raising and recruitment strategies (Bromley, Shupe, and Ventimiglia 1979). The widespread notion that cults routinely brainwash potential recruits and then maintain them as participants and fund-raisers through the ineluctable process of mind control has fueled many different efforts at social control by government agencies and other interest groups (Bromley and Robbins 1993; Richardson 1995a, 1996).

Government Control Efforts

A major inhibitor of direct control in the United States has been First Amendment protections afforded to religious groups. Although not inviolate, this protection has had a deterrent effect on U.S. government agencies, whose exertion of authority over NRMs appears mild and tentative compared to that occurring in some other Western societies not "hindered" by such a constitutional protection (Beckford 1985; Shupe and Bromley 1994; Richardson 1995a, 1995b). Even so, despite early failures, there has been a recent expansion of state control over minority religions in the United States, with the legal system showing a willingness over time to allow more stringent control over religious groups (Bromley and Robbins 1993; Richardson 1995a). Freedom of religion has been "flanked," allowing new kinds of control to be exerted, usually justified with notions of brainwashing. In spite of this, some of the newer religions have persisted and even thrived in the face of what they have experienced as persecution. Eileen Barker (1983) notes how opposition sometimes affirms theological positions, enhancing internal commitment to the group. Negative press paradoxically can function as publicity, attracting new members.

Nevertheless, the sustained punitive nature of social control has had a deleterious effect on the proliferation of NRMs. There does appear to be a declining interest among young people in alternative spirituality, certainly compared to the late 1960s and early 1970s. This might be due to the diminishing target population, and to economic conditions, but certainly the bad press and stigmatizing efforts surrounding the new religions have had their effect as the anticult movement has gathered strength and spread around the world (Bromley and Shupe 1994).

The punitive control of NRMs, based mainly on brainwashing accusations, has led to the "deformation" of some groups (Richardson 1985a), since they have found it necessary to allocate many of their resources to defense tactics at the expense of promoting the group's message or supporting its chosen lifestyle. In the United States this deformation has often taken the form of legal defense against various legal claims. Some groups also have undertaken civil actions, and others have filed suits to force a federal or state agency to apply its rules and regulations in ways more advantageous to the group (Richardson forthcoming). These earlier social control efforts, however, might be dismissed as minor irritants compared to the most recent tactic—child abuse accusations.

Social Control Through Child Abuse Accusations

Those new religions that have managed to survive the early social control efforts have gradually matured in a predictable fashion. Members have aged, many have married and produced children, and the organizations have become institutionalized, less charismatic, and more "domesticated" (Richardson 1985a). Their energies have turned inward to support their growing families, and their earlier radical stances have softened as they have found it expedient to adopt a more ordinary, respectable lifestyle.

This newfound respectability, however, has rendered them vulnerable to a major new social control tactic. The very presence of children in many of these groups can make them a target, a phenomenon that must be understood within the context of contemporary Western society's deep preoccupation with the welfare of children (Best 1990). Child protection agencies, recently developed, will swing into action when child abuse is alleged, often backed by police authority and the media, not to mention health care workers and child therapists. Government agencies respond promptly to such claims as a result of recently enacted laws that require immediate action when child abuse is reported (Carney 1993; Ellison and Bartkowski 1995).

The bureaucratic imperatives of these new, untried agencies require that they justify their existence, expand their roles, and clarify the meaning of the (often vague) statutes they must enforce, while simultaneously striving to put an end to child abuse. Thus, networks have formed among different groups with common interests: those claiming that child abuse was rife in new religious groups, those enforcing the laws, and those working in the new child protection area. The existence of the new mandatory reporting and investigation laws means that the power of the state can be used against anyone or any group. This awe-inspiring power can be unleashed by any person making the claim that child abuse is occurring.

This new situation has led to a dramatic increase in accusations of child abuse leveled against members of minority religions. A spate of cases alleging the neglect, manslaughter, or murder of children have been brought against a handful of parents and leaders. The most publicized situations involve the withholding of modern medical treatment from sick children. The Church of Jesus Christ, Scientists has borne the brunt of such charges because the public's concern for the welfare of children has sometimes overridden state exemptions and federal laws explicitly allowing the use of "spiritual healing" (Richardson and DeWitt 1992).

Individual members of NRMs have been charged with abusing *specific* children, usually their own. The 1983 Stonegate case briefly described in Barker (1989), Wentzel (1990), and Vanessa Malcarne and John Burchard (1992) involved the death of a child who was beaten until he died from shock and loss of blood. This case demonstrated that child abuse laws can be applied against members of religious groups effectively, for both the mother and the group leader were found guilty of the charges brought in the case, and the group disbanded.

"Collective" Child Abuse Accusations

Quite a different claim, however, has currently been directed against NRMs. This new claim is that *all children in certain groups are being harmed just by being in a group that adheres to certain beliefs and practices thought by some to be harmful to children.* The somewhat outmoded notion that cults brainwash their members so as to exploit them has sometimes been replaced by claims that the cults today are exploiting the children of the parents—who are presumably too brainwashed to notice or care.

Many child abuse claims were initiated within the context of custody disputes between ex-members and their spouses who chose to remain with the children in the communal setting. This was the situation that sparked the well-known 1984 case of the Northeast Kingdom Community Church in Island Pond, described by Wentzel (1990), Malcarne and Burchard (1992), Bozeman and Palmer (1997), and Swantko (1998). Efforts to exert control over the Branch Davidians in Waco, Texas, gained impetus through child abuse allegations that were made in the context of a custody dispute (Ellison and Bartkowski 1995). Such information lent support to a more general claim that the Davidians were involved in various kinds of child abuse behaviors within the group. This claim was used to justify the FBI assault in 1993 on the compound but was deemphasized after the assault resulted in the deaths of eighteen children (Ellison and Bartkowski 1995).

Specific Types of Alleged Child Abuse

Allegations of *collective* or *mass* child abuse fall into at least four categories. The first concerns *religious home schooling,* which is regarded by some as a process of indoctrination that instills prejudice and intolerance in children and produces youths who are ill-equipped to compete in the secular marketplace or to enter higher education.

The second category of collective child abuse accusations focuses on the *corporal punishment* of children commonly practiced in some communities emerging out of Christian fundamentalism. These traditional punitive measures are perceived as physical abuse by many in our society. A few isolated but widely reported cases of child mortality resulting from corporal punishment, as in the Stonegate case, have fueled the emotions of the general public, encouraging control agents to exert themselves when allegations of *collective* child abuse are made.

The third category involves concern about the *low living standard,* real or alleged, of many recently formed communal or missionary movements. This may be the consequence of an absence of funds or the rejection of mainstream aspirations to support a typically middle-class lifestyle (including dietary habits, plumbing, and shelter). Aside from the questionable veracity of this claim in some cases, these accusations are legally problematic because in America large numbers of children growing up in secular families or mainline religions live in poverty. To apply child abuse laws to religious minorities because of their low living standards raises obvious "equal opportunity under the law" questions if other communities with equally low living standards are not also targeted.

The ultimate weapon of the collective accusations is, of course, claims of *sexual abuse* perpetrated against children. This intensely stigmatizing and damaging charge has been laid against religious groups in recent years in several countries. Any new or communal religious group is vulnerable to this kind of claim if it has any children at all. These NRMs are especially vulnerable if they live in relative or perceived poverty, practice home schooling, or uphold corporal punishment. Some groups combine two or more of these patterns, which understandably compounds the concern of child protection workers, making them more prone to take action when accusations are made.

New Religions and Sexuality

Communal living is not generally regarded in a positive light in American society, the assumption being that "communal" implies sexual freedom, if not license. The idea of a hippie commune brings to mind a picture of half-clad marijuana-smoking youths living in sexual promiscuity. Communal groups during the 1960s and 1970s were often accused of sexual deviance, even though studies showed that many of these groups exerted strict control over their members' sexuality through rules governing courtship, cross-sexual contact, and marriage (Richardson, Stewart, and Simmonds 1979). Many groups practiced celibacy or limited sex between spouses for procreative purposes only (Rochford 1985). Even so, rumors persisted that the new religious communes were engaged in bizarre and unwholesome sexual practices that veered toward license, not self-restraint. Other groups developed religiously validated patterns of "free love." The followers of Bhagwan Shree Rajneesh were one of the most notorious of the new religions to engage in flagrant expressions of heterosexuality (Carter 1990).

The Children of God/The Family

One of the most well known of the new religions is The Family, formerly known as the Children of God (COG). Although the group espouses a Christian fundamentalist belief system, its sexual ethics are remarkably flexible and justified through the founding prophet's theological innovations (Richardson and Davis 1983). The group sanctions sex between single heterosexual members and sex outside the bonds of matrimony, and for a few years the COG sanctioned the use of sex as a recruitment tool: an Evangelical ministry referred to as "flirty fishing" (Richardson and Davis 1983; Wallis 1979).

The COG has become relatively domesticated in its sexual ethics in recent years and has changed its name to The Family—perhaps in an effort to escape its rather lurid past. The new name also suggests that the group has evolved into a large collectivity of families. Out of nine thousand members worldwide, more than five thousand are children, as of 1994 (Richardson 1994).

The COG's early controversial practices are well chronicled in its own voluminous literature, as well as in many anticult publications and scholarly treatments. In the course of this history of sexual experimentation, some of the early COG literature seemed to sanction sexual activity for young children, which makes the group vulnerable to claims that child sex abuse has occurred and is still occurring. Also, the large number of children in The Family increases the likelihood that such accusations will be made as more defections occur that involve child custody disputes.

Child Abuse Charges Against The Family

Several ex-members of the COG, in collusion with the anticult movement, have mounted charges against The Family in different countries: Argentina, Australia, Spain, Peru, Norway, France, the United States, and the United Kingdom. These charges have led to large-scale raids on The Family's communal homes in some of these countries. Hundreds of children have been seized in these raids in efforts to rescue them from the "sex-for-salvation cult" and place them as wards of the state or return them to their relatives outside the commune. Members of minority religions usually fare poorly in such conflicts (Tyner 1991).

A similar pattern has occurred in several countries with Family communal homes: some of the agencies and detractors circulate lurid passages from the group's literature and claim that children are encouraged to be sexually active in the group and that sex with minors is presently occurring. A comparison among the raids that were staged in Argentina, Spain, Australia, and France suggests that a campaign of international proportions has been waged against The Family by some of its detractors.

The Family in Argentina

In October 1989, Buenos Aires police staged a raid on The Family's commune. Adults were taken into custody, and children were placed as wards of the state. Some of the police threatened members with machine guns as they launched the raid without prior warning to the group, but with electronic and print media representatives present. Police claimed drugs were found on the premises, but observers reported seeing police officers planting bags of white powder in bedroom drawers. The judge presiding over the case specifically refuted the drug charges, noting that there was no historical evidence that the group sanctioned the use of drugs.

Social workers and physicians found no evidence of sexual abuse in the course of their examinations. The children passed educational tests with high scores, impressing judicial authorities and teachers. Court officials who visited the homes after the raid issued favorable reports concerning the children's education. As a result of these investigations, all criminal and civil charges against The Family were eventually dropped. The children were returned to their parents, and the authorities made positive statements about the group's childrearing methods. Nevertheless, a fresh raid was launched four years later.

On September 1, 1993, Buenos Aires police raided several Family homes, taking 137 children into custody and arresting 21 adults. The raids were apparently motivated by one particular magistrate who had become convinced by former COG members from outside the country that great abuses were taking place in Family communities. The episode became an international incident, as members of The Family demonstrated outside many Argentine embassies in other countries, attempting to draw attention to the plight of their imprisoned members. On December 13, 1993, the Argentina Court of Appeals of San Martin ordered the release of all imprisoned members of The Family and returned all children to their parents. The three-hundred-page opinion was very critical of both the magistrate (it declared him incompetent) and of the career apostates from outside the country who had initially promoted the charges (Richardson 1996). The issue as of 1998 is unsettled, as the case is under appeal in the Argentina Supreme Court.

Spain and The Family

In July 1990, police and social workers in Barcelona raided the communal home of The Family, arresting ten adults and taking twenty-one children away from their parents and holding them for eleven months in state institutions. The children were not allowed any contact with their parents for the first two months and were subjected to numerous examinations by psychologists. When parents were allowed to visit their children, they did so under tight supervision and were not allowed to read from the Bible or leave a Bible in their children's keeping.

After eleven months, the children were released to their parents, but with direction by the court to enroll them in public schools, thereby enforcing the abandonment of the group's home-schooling program. Another order required that each individual family live in its own residence, a direct strike at the group's communal way of life. The strong action taken by authorities in the case was provoked by complaints filed by ex-members, who accused the group of neglect and aberrant sexual practices, including sex with young children. These ex-members were backed by anticult organizations in Spain and in England.

When the case was finally decided on May 22, 1992, it was a resounding victory for The Family. Independent psychologists who examined the children over their eleven-month incarceration concluded that there was no evidence of trauma other than anxiety over the forced separation from their parents and no evidence of abuse or neglect to justify a continued separation. The president of the panel of judges hearing the civil case absolved Family members from all charges and criticized in strong language the handling of the episode. The judge alluded to the Spanish Inquisition in discussing the actions of authorities in the case, and compared the conditions in the institutions in which the children were held to Soviet concentration camps. In a seven-page ruling, the judge stated there was no evidence that the children had been harmed by communal life or home schooling. He noted that the psychiatric reports unanimously concluded there was no mental illness or any type of psychosis present in the children. The Family may have found itself to be in a stronger position in its relationship with society than before this episode, although the turmoil caused by the raids made this a costly victory.

Australia and The Family

In May 1992, several communal homes belonging to The Family near Melbourne (Victoria) and Sydney (New South Wales) were raided simultaneously. A total of 153 children were taken into custody amid an immense amount of publicity concerning accusations of aberrant sexual behavior in the homes. The raids were preceded by lengthy investigations and surveillance of the same homes. Officials in Victoria decided to stage the raids in May 1992 because of a planned exposé on The Family that a popular TV program was planning to air. Officials feared that after the program was shown, The Family would flee the area. Thus, Victoria officials, giving less than forty-eight hours' notice, urged New South Wales child care officials to participate in the raids. In Victoria the TV channel knew the exact timing of the raids and had cameras present, with a media helicopter hovering above the homes as they were raided.

In Sydney the case was resolved relatively quickly, after a thirty-one-day hearing in which one of the representatives of the Department of Community Services (DCS) stood in the witness box trying to explain why the DCS had taken the action it had. A settlement was achieved after the DCS agreed to a unique form of mediation with a former High Court judge serving as mediator. The settlement involved a withdrawal of official charges by the DCS of sexual abuse, coupled with an agreement to allow some evaluation of the children's home schooling, as well as making sure the children had some exposure to the wider society through obligatory riding and ballet lessons where they would meet other children.

In Melbourne the case took much longer to resolve, mainly because the state had refused to furnish legal aid to the group's parents, claiming funds were not available (Giddings 1993). The magistrate in the case stated that he would not proceed until the group parents had adequate legal representation, so the case was at an impasse for a year. Then a decision was made by the agency bringing the charges, Child Services Victoria (CSV), to partly fund The Family's legal defense, so that the case could go forward.

Efforts had been made by The Family and its attorneys to settle the case in a similar fashion to the one in New South Wales, but these efforts were strongly resisted by the CSV, and a court-ordered mediation attempt failed. In the meantime, however, the ninety-three children were still technically wards of the state and could not be moved without permission from the court. Eventually, the Victorian state government forced the CSV to settle the case on terms similar to those developed in the Sydney case.

These cases resulted in a major embarrassment for most of the child services and police authorities who had participated in the predawn raids (Goddard 1994a, 1994b). They became the brunt of a great deal of negative publicity, including strong editorials criticizing their interventions. Discussions were held in both state parliaments concerning the authorities' handling of the case and their staggering costs. Estimates were made public that the New South Wales action had cost nearly $5 million (U.S. $3.5 million) before it was mediated and that the Victorian case had cost as much as $10 million. Civil actions have been filed in New South Wales seeking damages on behalf of some of the children. This action is still pending as of 1998, but it could result in large damages being paid to Family members whose children were taken in the raid.

The Family in France

At 6:00 A.M. on June 9, 1993, two Family communes in Lyon and Equille, near Aix-en-Provence, were raided, as well as some private homes of associate members not living communally. Some ninety children were taken in the raids, and all adults were arrested and held for forty-eight hours. As many as two hundred police were involved in the raids, some heavily armed with automatic weapons. Media representatives were also involved, covering the procedures of this effort to rescue children from what they dubbed a "sex cult."

The raids were provoked by accusations of child abuse and prostitution brought by the major French countercult group L'Association pour la Défense de la Famille et de l'Individu and individual detractors. The children in Lyon were returned to their parents within a week, but in Equille they were held for fifty-one days. All adults were released in both cities, and the resolution of the criminal charges and custody issues are still pending as of 1998.

Conclusion

Allegations of child abuse are powerful, and their effect can be quite punitive (Black 1976), especially if the claims are made in a situation where there is preexisting animosity toward a new religion. The effect on the targeted group can be devastating. Once children are removed by the state and their parents arrested, the group has little recourse but to allocate all available resources to fighting the charges in an effort to regain the children and release the adults from prison. And the group may have few resources to allocate, a situation with significant consequences (Cooney 1994). The group must also cope with the accompanying media barrage of negative publicity. Regardless of whether the charges have any substance, the impact can be profound. The group must adjust its priorities and alter its very shape, a short-term response that may well have long-lasting repercussions. In this way, the group's organizational life becomes "deformed" by the necessity of dealing with such pervasive external pressures (Richardson 1985a).

Nevertheless, this strategy of social control can backfire. A number of problems arise with this type of claim. One major issue that has become a controversy of major proportions concerns the very *definitions* of child abuse and child sexual abuse (Gelles and Cornell 1983; Wakefield and Underwager 1993; Ellison and Bartkowski 1995). Deciding what does and does not constitute abuse is often a difficult problem. Also, recent research has brought into sharp relief the suggestibility of children and the unreliable procedures sometimes used in such cases (Goleman 1993). Tied to this issue is the steep rise in claims of child abuse associated with custody battles in our society. This development compounds the usual difficulties in determining the facts of claims of child abuse.

Another key definitional issue is that most child abuse laws were not designed to deal with large-scale *collective* accusations. Such laws typically require that *individuals*—not a group—be charged with child abuse. When all the children of a group are taken into custody, the implication under the law is that they were all abused, which requires specific evidence for each child, as well as specific knowledge concerning the abusers.

Accusations of collective child abuse "in a cultic setting" (Malcarne and Burchard 1992) were not contemplated when the laws in the United States and most other countries were designed (Carney 1993). Such laws were not written to support the assumption that child abuse occurs by virtue of a child's growing up in certain social, religious, or economic circumstances. Indeed, recent U.S. laws concerning child abuse were deliberately designed to *avoid* claims that abuse resulted from living in poverty. Such considerations notwithstanding, individually oriented laws have often been stretched to fit the new communal religions.

The communal, sectarian, and often isolated nature of the groups in question makes it very difficult for authorities to gather the information needed to assess grievance claims. Current laws dealing with child abuse are based on the assumption that the claims can be readily investigated through social contacts: using corroborating testimony of teachers, neighbors, or friends of the family (Malcarne and Burchard 1992). Child abuse laws, moreover, assume a reasonable degree of cooperation on the part of the accused (Hardin 1988).

In cases involving religious communes that have withdrawn from society, the investigation often proves difficult, especially if the group chooses not to cooperate. Religious communities may not defer, for theological reasons, to secular authorities in the way that ordinary citizens might. There may be very few outsiders who have had any opportunity to witness the treatment of children because the group may practice home schooling and take care of its own medical needs. For these reasons, typical child abuse laws do not function well when applied to religious communes. Malcarne and Burchard (1992) have recommended how new laws to protect children in a "cultic setting" might be devised, but the prospect of passing laws about "collective child abuse" raises many difficult issues (Carney 1993).

There are other practical problems encountered by parties accusing NRMs of child abuse. Such actions bring in third parties who may not necessarily share the perspectives and interests of the government child care workers, therapists, critical ex-members, or anticultists who originally made the claim of abuse. Once charges have been made, the case will be heard in relatively public legal proceedings, resulting in "checks and balances" that may work in favor of the targeted group. The relative independence of the judiciary in many countries can impede efforts to expand the influence of government agencies responsible for children and can undercut the influence and credibility of the anticult movement

(Richardson 1996). Reports from professional psychologists, psychiatrists, and others may be made a part of the court record and eventually publicized in media accounts. Testimonies of parents and children from the group may appear in the news. The decisions of judges are also often made public. By using the legal system, the accusers risk the possibility that the way that the media frame the specific episode involving a particular NRM may change as more information and new perspectives become available (van Driel and Richardson 1988; Richardson 1996).

The raids on The Family are an interesting test case for this new strategy to combat NRMs. None of The Family's children taken in the several raids became permanent wards of the state because evidence of abuse was lacking. This development was not anticipated by the government child care functionaries and police authorities who directed and participated in the raids or by the anticult leaders who were involved in promoting the raids.

Certainly, these episodes can have long-term consequences for some the major protagonists. Members of NRMs have suddenly become aware that they and their children can be made to suffer at the hands of state authorities. The experience of having one's children snatched away in predawn raids by squadrons of armed police conveys an awe-inspiring message of the power of the state. This cannot but affect the way new religions define themselves, as well as the way they perceive the government and various agents of the state. Parents may interpret the actions of the law as a cosmic struggle between the forces of God and Satan for the ownership of their children. It also seems reasonable to assume that court-ordered scrutiny of NRM childrearing methods will have a significant impact on future patterns of education and childrearing. Research on this issue needs to be done to see if, in fact, the groups will "win the battle but lose the war" as they modify their child care and educational policies to accommodate secular authorities and conform more closely to mainstream standards of childrearing.

Only time will tell if accusations of collective child abuse will become a useful tactic of social control in the future. There may be more efforts to modify laws to facilitate the investigations of these cases involving communal religious groups. If radical measures such as those recommended by Malcarne and Burchard (1992) are taken seriously, this issue could escalate from the legal to the political sphere. If this occurs, then we could witness major changes in the law that would not only have a major impact on the future of many new religious groups but would also carry important legal implications affecting mainstream religions and secular families.

References

Anthony, D. 1990. "Religious Movements and 'Brainwashing' Litigation: Evaluating Key Testimony." Pp. 295–344 in T. Robbins and D. Anthony, eds., *In Gods We Trust.* New Brunswick, N.J.: Transaction Books.

Barker, E. 1983. "With Enemies Like That: Some Functions of Deprogramming as an Aid to Sectarian Membership." Pp. 329–344 in D. Bromley and J. Richardson, eds., *The Brainwashing/Deprogramming Controversy.* Lewiston, N.Y.: Edwin Mellen Press.

———. 1984. *The Making of a Moonie: Choice or Brainwashing?* Oxford: Blackwell.

———. 1989. *New Religious Movements.* London: Her Majesty's Stationery Office.

Beckford, J. 1985. *Cult Controversies.* London: Tavistock.

Best, J. 1990. *Threatened Children.* Chicago: University of Chicago Press.

Black, D. 1976. *The Behavior of Law.* New York: Academic Press.

Bozeman, J. M., and S. J. Palmer. 1997. "The Northeast Kingdom Community Church of Island Pond, Vermont: Raising Up a People for Yahshua's Return." *Journal of Contemporary Religion* 12 (2): 181–190.

Bromley, D., and E. Breschel. 1992. "General Population and Institutional Support for Social Control of New Religious Movements: Evidence from National Survey Data." *Behavioral Sciences and the Law* 10: 39–52.

Bromley, D., and T. Robbins. 1993. "The Role of Government in Regulating New and Unconventional Religions." Pp. 205–240 in J. Wood and D. Davis, eds., *The Role of Government in Monitoring and Regulating Religion in Public Life.* Waco, Tex.: J. M. Dawson Institute of Church-State Studies, Baylor University.

Bromley, D., and A. Shupe. 1994. "Organized Opposition to New Religious Movements." Pp. 177–198 in D. Bromley and J. Hadden, eds., *Handbook of Sects and Cults in America.* Greenwich, Conn.: JAI Press.

Bromley, D., A. Shupe, and J. Ventimiglia. 1979. "Atrocity Tales, the Unification Church, and the Social Construction of Evil." *Journal of Communication* 29: 42–53.

Carney, T. 1993. "Children of God: Harbingers of Another (Child Law) Reformation?" *Criminology Australia* 5: 2–5.

Carter, L. 1990. *Charisma and Control in Rajneeshpuram.* Cambridge, U.K.: Cambridge University Press.

Cooney, M. 1994. "Evidence as Partisanship." *Law and Society Review* 28: 833–858.

Ellison, C., and J. Bartkowski. 1995. "'Babies Were Being Beaten': Exploring Child Abuse at Ranch Apocalypse." Pp. 111–149 in S. Wright, ed., *Armageddon in Waco.* Chicago: University of Chicago Press.

Fort, J. 1985. "What Is Brainwashing and Who Says So?" Pp. 57–63 in B. Kilbourne, ed., *Scientific Research and New Religions: Divergent Perspectives.* San Francisco: Pacific Divisions of the American Association for the Advancement of Science.

Gelles, R., and C. Cornell. 1983. "International Perspectives in Child Abuse." *Child Abuse and Neglect* 7: 375–386.

Giddings, J. 1993. "Legal Aid in Victoria: Cash Crisis." *Alternative Law Journal* 18: 130–132.

Goddard, C. 1994a. "Governing the 'Family': Child Protection Policy and Practice and the 'Children of God.'" *Just Policy* 1: 9–11.

———. 1994b. "Still in the Dark over the Family Raids." *The Age* (May 6): 17.

Goleman, D. 1993. "Studies Reveal Suggestibility of Very Young as Witnesses." *New York Times,* June 11.

Hardin, M. 1988. "Legal Barriers in Child Abuse Investigations: State Powers and Individual Rights." *Washington Law Review* 63: 493–605.

Malcarne, V., and J. Burchard. 1992. "Investigations of Child Abuse/Neglect Allegations in Religious Cults: A Case Study in Vermont." *Behavioral Sciences and the Law* 10: 75–88.

Richardson, J. 1985a. "The 'Deformation' of New Religious Groups: Impacts of Societal and Organizational Factors." Pp. 163–175 in T. Robbins et al., eds., *Cults, Culture, and the Law.* Chico, Calif.: Scholars Press.

———. 1985b. "Studies in Conversion: Secularization or Re-enchantment?" Pp. 104–121 in P. Hammond, ed., *The Sacred in a Secular Age.* Berkeley and Los Angeles: University of California Press.

———. 1992. "Public Opinion and the Tax Evasion Trial of Reverend Moon." *Behavioral Sciences and the Law* 10: 53–63.

———. 1993. "A Social Psychology Critique of 'Brainwashing' Claims About Recruitment to New Religions." Pp. 75–97 in D. Bromley and J. Hadden, eds., *Sects and Cults in America.* Greenwich, Conn.: JAI Press.

———. 1994. "Update on The Family: Organizational Change and Development in a Controversial New Religious Group." Pp. 27–46 in J. Lewis and G. Melton, eds., *Sex, Slander, and Salvation: Investigating The Family/Children of God.* Stanford, Calif.: Center for Academic Publications.

———. 1995a. "Legal Status of Minority Religions in the United States." *Social Compass* 42: 249–264.

———. 1995b. "Minority Religions, Religious Freedom, and the New Pan-European Political and Judicial Institutions." *Journal of Church and State* 37: 39–59.

———. 1996. "'Brainwashing' Claims and Minority Religions Outside the U.S.: Cultural Diffusion of a Questionable Concept in the Legal Arena." *Brigham Young Law Review* 1996: 873–904.

———. 1999. "Law and Minority Religion." *Nova Religio* 2 (October) 3–107.

Richardson, J., and R. Davis. 1983. "Experiential Fundamentalism: Revisions of Orthodoxy in the Jesus Movement." *Journal of the American Academy of Religion* 51: 397–425.

Richardson, J., and J. DeWitt. 1992. "Christian Science Spiritual Healing, Public Opinion, and the Law." *Journal of Church and State* 34: 549–561.

Richardson, J., and B. Kilbourne. 1983. "Classical and Contemporary Applications of Brainwashing Models." Pp. 29–45 in D. Bromley and J. Richardson, eds., *The Brainwashing/Deprogramming Controversy.* Lewiston, N.Y.: Edwin Mellen Press.

Richardson, J., M. Stewart, and R. Simmonds. 1979. *Organized Miracles.* New Brunswick, N.J.: Transaction Books.

Robbins, T. 1988. *Cults, Converts, and Charisma.* Newbury Park, Calif.: Sage.

Rochford, B. 1985. *Hare Krishna in America.* New Brunswick, N.J.: Rutgers University Press.

Shupe, A., and D. Bromley. 1980. *The New Vigilantes.* Beverly Hills, Calif.: Sage.

———, eds. 1994. *Anti-Cult Movements in Cross-Cultural Perspective.* New York: Garland.

Solomon, T. 1983. "Programming and Deprogramming the 'Moonies': Social Psychology Applied." Pp. 163–182 in D. Bromley and J. Richardson, eds., *The Brainwashing/Deprogramming Controversy.* Lewiston, N.Y.: Edwin Mellen Press.

Tyner, M. 1991. "Who Gets the Kid?" *Liberty* (May-June): 8.

Van Driel, B., and J. Richardson. 1988. "Print Media Coverage of New Religions: A Longitudinal Study." *Journal of Communication* 38: 37–61.

Wakefield, H., and R. Underwager. 1993. "The Alleged Child Victim and Real Victims of Sexual Abuse." In J. Krivacska and J. Money, eds., *Handbook of Forensic Sexology.* Buffalo, N.Y.: Prometheus Books.

Wallis, R. 1979. "Sex, Marriage, and the Children of God." Pp. 74–90 in R. Wallis, ed., *Salvation and Protest: Studies of Social and Religious Movements.* New York: St. Martin's Press.

Wentzel, S. 1990. "Charging Religious Movements with Child Abuse as a Social Control Strategy." Paper presented at the annual meeting of the Pacific Sociological Association, Spokane, Wash., April.

Wuthnow, R. 1978. *The Consciousness Reformation.* Berkeley and Los Angeles: University of California Press.

———. 1986. "Religious Movements and Counter-Movements in North America." Pp. 1–28 in J. Beckford, ed., *New Religious Movements and Rapid Social Change.* London: Sage.

Chapter 11

The Precarious Balance Between Freedom of Religion and the Best Interests of the Child

Michael W. Homer

Child custody disputes have often become public or private forums in which unconventional religions are judged. These kind of disputes, involving the overlapping issues of religious liberty, parental responsibility, and the best interests of children, tend to be of a singularly controversial and complicated nature (Atkinson 1992; Beschle 1989). Religious questions have complicated disputes involving the custody of children, particularly when controversial new religious movements are involved. In some cases, children have become pawns in the ongoing struggle between alternative spiritual groups and mainline churches or secular authorities.

By examining various important custody cases in U.S. legal history, I endeavor to show how the courts have sought to apply the current legal standard in their efforts to balance religious liberty with the child's best interest. I review custody cases involving unconventional religions to investigate how this precedent is applied—and challenged—in cases involving new and controversial religious movements. The judgments in these cases clearly demonstrate that, even though the courts can be influenced by popular prejudice against unconventional religions—and are, on occasion, used as arenas for exerting social control over new spiritual groups—the courts have also provided arenas where the concerns and rights of children and parents have been upheld, regardless of the controversial status of their religion.

Religious Compatibility and the Child's Best Interests

In 1994, rural Summit County, Utah, became the focus of national media attention. Judge David S. Young granted a petition to modify a divorce decree and ordered that Alicia Larson, a Mormon convert and the mother of three children, would lose physical custody of the children to her former husband if she moved from Park City, Utah, to Corvallis, Oregon, to marry her fiancé, who was presumably a non-Mormon.[1] The decision was based in part on the judge's finding that it was "unlikely that, if the children were to move . . . plaintiff [the mother] would continue their [Mormon] religious training."[2] Larson decided to appeal Judge Young's decision and complained that during her prior marriage the religious upbringing of the children had never been an important issue. The Utah branch of the American Civil Liberties Union and some national observers expressed the opinion that Judge Young's decision was unfair and reactionary and a breach of the separation of church and state.

Despite these criticisms, the legal standard utilized by Judge Young was not without legal precedent. But although the standard he applied was correct, there were insufficient facts in the case to support the court's finding that Larson should not retain custody. When the Utah Court of Appeals reviewed the trial court's decision, it recognized that "a parent's 'religious compatibility' with his or her children is one factor that a court may consider in determining the children's best interest" and that such "religious compatibility is only a factor when there has been a showing that specific religious beliefs or practices are contrary to the child's general welfare."[3] Utilizing the same standard cited by the trial judge, the Court of Appeals reversed Judge Young's ruling, deciding that there was no evidence in the record to support the assumption that the mother "would not continue her children's religious training" if she moved from Summit County.[4] The *Larson* decision demonstrates that disputes concerning a particular religion's impact on the "best interests" of a child should be evaluated "fact specific" to the child involved and that the court should avoid the temptation to pass judgment on a particular religion involved (Atkinson 1992; Beschle 1989).

The concept of best interests is embodied in the law of most states. When evaluating the best interests of a child, many state courts consider the effect the parents' religion may have on a child's status. By focusing on continuity, courts are recognizing the value and importance of consistency, stability, and security in childhood. Psychotherapists and psychologists are often retained by lawyers to evaluate the parents' ability to care for their children. In 1994, the American Psychological Association published guidelines for child custody evaluations in divorce proceedings. They concluded, "In considering psychological factors affecting the best interests of the child, the psychologist focuses on the parenting capacity of the prospective custodians in conjunction with the psychological and developmental needs of each involved child" (cited in Hagen 1997:198).

In this document, therapists propose three guidelines: (1) capacity for parenting, (2) parenting abilities, and (3) parental values (Hagen 1997:198). An individual's capacity for (1) and (2) includes all the knowledge and skills that help a parent satisfy the needs and provide for the socialization of a child. Values (3), however, open up a complex range of issues affecting gender roles, morals, sexual behavior, education, and religion.

Utilizing these standards, many state courts have been asked to evaluate evidence similar to that presented to Judge Young in Utah. For example, a trial court in New York State modified a divorce decree because the custodial mother was no longer observing or raising the children in Orthodox Judaism. It therefore awarded custody to the father.[5] Presumably, the mother's failure to observe Orthodox Judaism was determined by the court to be detrimental to the children's specific needs and sense of continuity. Similarly, a Minnesota appellate court reversed a trial court's decision to award custody to a father in part because the court found that the mother would continue to raise her children as Catholics, whereas the father had planned to start raising the children as Lutherans.[6] Although these courts took the parents' religious practices into consideration in determining the specific needs of children, they did not make value judgments concerning the religions themselves because to do so is prohibited by the U.S. Constitution.

Government Intervention and the First Amendment

To understand the current legal standard in balancing religious liberty with practices judged detrimental to the well-being of children, one must understand the development of constitutional law concerning the First Amendment. The First Amendment to the Constitution contains two clauses relating to religion: the establishment clause and the free exercise clause. Both clauses are "implicated when government uses religion as a factor in child custody or adoption decisions" (Beschle 1989:416).

The establishment clause provides that "Congress shall make no law respecting an establishment of religion" and lays down "a prohibition of government sponsorship of religion which requires that government neither aid nor formally establish a religion" (Nowak, Rotunda, and Young 1978:850). It was not until 1947 that the U.S. Supreme Court interpreted the establishment clause when it first applied the clause to the states through the Fourteenth Amendment.[7] Further decisions interpreting this clause have usually related to education, to aid to religious institutions by states, and to "activities in the public schools such as prayer or Bible reading" (Homer 1980:1143–1168). The current standard applied by the Supreme Court, first fully articulated by it in 1971, in *Lemon* v. *Kurtzman,* determines that any action taken by the government (federal or state) that affects religion must have "a secular legislative purpose" and a "principal or primary effect . . . that neither advances nor inhibits religion"; the action must avoid "an excessive . . . entanglement with religion."[8] If a state action fails the *Lemon* test, it violates the establishment clause.

Another important factor inhibiting the state's interference with religious activity is the free exercise clause, which declares, "Congress shall make no law . . . prohibiting the Free Exercise [of religion]." Moreover, it "absolutely prohibits the proscription of any religious belief by the government" and "requires the government to make some accommodation for the practice of religious beliefs when it pursues ends which incidentally burden religious practices" (Nowak et al. 1978:871).

The interpretation of the free exercise clause has a long history. Since 1878, when the Supreme Court decided *Reynolds* v. *United States,* the legal standard for balancing the harm of religious conduct against the First Amendment's guarantee of religious liberty has been based on socially accepted, traditional American notions of religious practice.[9] In the *Reynolds* case, which involved a Mormon polygamist in Utah, the Court noted that in "common law, the second marriage was always void . . . and from the earliest history of England polygamy has been treated as an offence against society."[10] The Court found that polygamy "has always been odious" and that it creates "innocent victims," including "pure minded women" and "innocent children."[11] Sarah Gordon (1996:298) has written that these perceived evil consequences were based to some degree on "anti-polygamy fiction and the sentimental campaign against moral diversity in Antebellum America" rather than on legal evidence. Edwin Firmage and R. Colin Mangram (1988:151–159) have noted that the Court's identification of social harm was based on the stereotypes circulated in "penny dreadfuls" and newspaper exposés rather than on substantive evidence.[12] The Supreme Court decided that Congress could constitutionally prohibit religiously sanctioned practices "which were in violation of social duties or subversive of good order."[13] Ultimately, *Reynolds* showed the Supreme Court's willingness to adopt a standard consistent with majoritarian social mores that were often incompatible with the beliefs and practices of minority religions.

Since *Reynolds,* the Supreme Court has continued to protect religious beliefs under the free exercise clause, but it has also circumscribed some religious conduct—including the practice of religious beliefs—at the expense of religious freedom.[14] Because religion is of key importance to many and governs such intimate and personal aspects of our lives, the Court eventually established rigorous standards for interpreting governmental conduct under the free exercise clause. These standards have had the effect of expanding the protection of some religious conduct that is seemingly contrary to civil laws. These standards were articulated by the Court in 1963 in the landmark decision *Sherbert* v. *Verner.*[15] Until 1990, cases involving government action that affected the free exercise clause were decided under these standards.[16]

Adell H. Sherbert was a Seventh-day Adventist whose employment was terminated because she refused to work on Saturday, which was against her Sabbatarian beliefs. The state of South Carolina subsequently refused to pay her unemployment benefits because to be eligible, she had to accept "suitable work when offered." On appeal, the Supreme Court held that the South Carolina statute was unconstitutional because it violated her rights to "free exercise." The Court reasoned that a statute that burdens religious practice must have some other original intention and impact religion only incidentally. Utilizing this standard, the Court found that South Carolina had caused "substantial" interference with Sherbert's religious practice by forcing her to choose between her job and her religion. Furthermore, the Court found that South Carolina had no "compelling state interest" for penalizing Sabbatarians, thereby failing to satisfy the *Sherbert* test and violating the free exercise clause.

The standard articulated in *Sherbert* was eventually applied in cases involving the competing interests of religious liberty and the best interests of children. These cases became a new, intriguing testing ground for measuring the depth of "compelling state interests" when such interests are used putatively to protect the interests of children but also affect religious liberties. Thus, in *Wisconsin* v. *Yoder* (1972), one of the most significant confrontations between religious freedom and the best interests of children, the Supreme Court invalidated Wisconsin's refusal to exempt Amish students (fourteen- and fifteen-year-olds) from the state's requirement that all children attend school until age sixteen.[17] The Court concluded that Wisconsin's compulsory education law would be upheld only if the state could show an interest "of the highest order" in requiring the Amish children to attend public schools that could not otherwise be accomplished. The state failed to provide sufficient rationale to meet this test, and the Supreme Court therefore invalidated the statute. In doing so, the Court relied on experts who testified that the law threatened the Amish religion and lifestyle. If required to go to school, the children would be impaired in their ability to earn a living through farming and agrarian activities. These practical, traditional activities were part of the Amish lifestyle, regardless of the fact that it challenged the state's compulsory education system. Yoder also demonstrated conflicting notions of the best interests of the child. To the Amish, work alongside one's father in the field or one's mother in the household was the most important method of education—socialization; it was the model of what it meant to be Amish. To mainstream America, however, the long-standing tradition of compulsory education superseded contrasting cultural expectations regarding the best interests of the child (Biskupic 1996).

The *Sherbert/Yoder* tests continued to set the standard under which laws affecting the free exercise of religion were interpreted. In 1990, however, the Supreme Court altered this standard in *Employment Division* v. *Smith.* In *Smith,* the Court reviewed a challenge to an Oregon law that prohibited activities claimed to be part of religious rituals by the Native American Church.[18] In deciding the case, the Court departed from the standard, first enunciated in *Sherbert* and *Yoder,* and held that Oregon could deny unemployment compensation to members of the Native American Church who had been fired from their jobs because they used peyote for religious rituals. In *Smith,* Justice Antonin Scalia—who wrote the majority opinion and has recognized that religious beliefs continue to be assaulted in an increasingly secular society—stated that the *Sherbert* test was inapplicable.[19] Even though *Yoder* was not an employment case and was part of the development of the "compelling state interest" standard first enunciated by the Court in *Sherbert,* Justice Scalia wrote that the *Sherbert* test had previously been applied only in cases involving "unemployment benefits" and that it was therefore inapplicable in the context of *Smith.* Instead, he applied essentially the same standard enunciated more than one hundred years earlier in *Reynolds* that laws may not interfere with religious beliefs and opinions, but they may prohibit practices.[20] Under the standard applied in *Smith*, it was not necessary for the state to establish a compelling state interest to properly prohibit the ritual use of peyote as long as the prohibition itself was of general application and only incidentally burdened the free exercise of one's religion.[21]

The *Smith* decision was extremely controversial among both mainstream and nontraditional religious groups in America because it was viewed as a radical departure from the "compelling state interest" standard articulated in *Sherbert* and *Yoder.* These religious groups lobbied Congress to enact the Religious Freedom Restoration Act (RFRA), which President Bill Clinton signed in 1993. The legislation was intended "to restore the compelling interest test as set forth in *Sherbert v. Verner* and *Wisconsin v. Yoder* . . . and to guarantee its application in all cases where free exercise of religion is substantially burdened." In 1997, the Court struck down the act in *City of Boerne* v. *Flores.* Specifically, the Court concluded that in enacting the legislation, Congress had exceeded its "remedial" powers under the Fourteenth Amendment.

In 1998, the Religious Liberty Protection Act (RLPA) was introduced in the Senate; the act would once again require government to demonstrate a compelling interest in order to pass legislation interfering with the free exercise of religion. Like RFRA, this new initiative is supported by traditional and nontraditional religious movement. Regardless of the outcome of RLPA, both the establishment clause and the free exercise clause remain relevant in evaluation of the propriety of government actions and in legal decisions that must take into account religious beliefs and practices. When deciding custody disputes, a court must consult the establishment clause to ensure that a decision is not biased, that it does not have the effect of generally endorsing or repudiating a religious belief or practice, and that it simply evaluates a religious belief's impact on a child. The free exercise clause is applicable when a parent seeking custody must choose between a religious belief and custody.

Family Transition and the Rise of New Religions

Since the beginning of the twentieth century, both the federal and state governments have taken an increasingly active role in protecting children through legislation (Bradley 1987). Government has an interest in protecting juveniles under its traditional role as *parens patriae,* or "parents of the country," which means the government acts as a guardian for people who are under legal disability and therefore exercises the power to restrict any conduct that is harmful to them.

As American society entered the twentieth century, it was marked by changes in family organization and by new assumptions about children in families and in the workplace and about gender roles. For instance, during the late nineteenth and much of the twentieth century, the law, by focusing on social or psychological issues using the "tender years" standard (which attempted to determine which parent was best suited as the custodial parent for each child given the child's particular vulnerabilities), shifted from presuming that a father was better suited as the custodial parent to allowing either parent to prevail. These changes gradually occurred within an increasingly secular and nonagrarian society. In this new type of family, mothers were presumed (in most cases) to be preferable custodians over the children because of the "new" position women played in families during this period. Displaced from a "real" economic role in the farm family, women became the principal transmitters of social values and mores to their children rather than actual participants in the economic order (Degler 1980). At the same time, children moved to the emotional epicenter of the family.

Since the 1970s, a new shift in thinking about family roles has occurred that focuses on the *quality* of parenting rather than the *gender* of the parent. Stimulated by the success of the women's movement, and the increased presence of women in a previously male-dominated workforce, the best interests of the child standard has become firmly established. Under this new way of evaluating the best interests of a child, those interests in relation to the parents are evaluated "gender free," conditioned by "specific facts rather than stereotypes" (Beschle 1989:384).

Religion is only one of the several factors that should be considered by the courts. It should never be the sole factor or even the determining factor (Beschle 1989:397). This has been demonstrated by the *Larson* opinion in Utah, by the *Friederwitzer* case in New York, and by the *Johnson* decision in Minnesota. In another relevant case, a noncustodial Pentecostal father filed an action in the Tennessee Court of Appeals to modify visitation rights so as to allow him to take his son to a different church than that of his mother, who was a Baptist, on alternating Sundays. The court held that "the parties' religious beliefs cannot be controlling in custody cases."[22] Courts are given considerable discretion in determining best interests, and the Tennessee court decided in this case that "in the absence of a showing of harm to the child visitation provisions cannot have the effect of advancing one parent's religion while inhibiting that of the other parent."[23] Since courts are open to accusations of abuse when the religion of either parent is nontraditional or controversial, they must embark on considerations of religion cautiously. Sensitive to this issue, the Tennessee court allowed the Pentecostal father to take his son to church on alternate weekends.

Courts may evaluate the effect a religion has on a particular child, but they may not evaluate the religion itself. But courts sometimes take measures to minimize the emotional harm conflicting beliefs of the parents may inflict on children. In 1988, a father in New Mexico who was a devout Sikh filed a motion to obtain the custody of his children.[24] The basis for his motion was that his children had been raised in the Sikh religion until the parents' divorce and the custodial mother's subsequent remarriage. Following her remarriage, she withdrew from the Sikh religion and discouraged her children from participating in it. The father sought to modify the custody order to give him custody of the children, so that he could control their religious upbringing. The trial court not only denied the father's motion, but also ordered "that the children not participate voluntarily or involuntarily in any Sikh religious activities with their father."[25] The father appealed the trial court's decision, and the Court of Appeals of New Mexico reversed and remanded the case back to the trial court with instructions that its paramount concern be limited to the general welfare of the children and that restrictions on visitation or custody be considered in the context of religion only if "evidence of physical or emotional harm to the child has been substantial."[26] The court specifically held that "there was no evidence that either child was harmed by exposure to their father's religion"; as such, the court, while remanding the case to the trial court for a reexamination of the custody issue, specifically reversed the trial court's decision, which enjoined the "father from encouraging his children to participate in any Sikh activity."[27]

In other situations, however, courts have not hesitated to interfere when it is shown that a child may suffer anxiety and other emotional distress arising from parents' religious differences. The Supreme Court of Montana, for example, in considering whether a two-year-old boy should be raised in the Jewish faith, indicated that it would not debate the merits of religion but noted that any "question of religious education must be strictly limited to the context of the best interests of the minor child."[28] Utilizing this standard, the court upheld the trial court's denial of the Jewish father's request that he be awarded custody or that he be given the legal right to determine the religious upbringing of his child. The court noted that "under the facts of this case, an award of custody for the purpose of religious education should not dominate other elements which comprise the best interests of this particular child."[29] Thus, although the court recognized that Montana law generally allows the district court to appoint a parent as a religious custodian, the facts of this case did not make that necessary. The father's religious and pedagogical concerns were outweighed by other factors, including the finding that the mother had no animosity toward the father, would be unlikely to interfere with the father's relationship with the child, and was more capable of allowing the child to develop his own identity—thus making her a better custodial parent for the best interests of the child.

In battles regarding the religious training of children, even after custody is decided, "the law tolerates and even encourages, up to a point, the child's exposure to the religious influences of both parents even if they are divided in their faiths."[30] Courts do not generally interfere with the religious training a noncustodial parent gives his or her children unless there is "a clear and affirmative showing that these activities and expressions of belief are harmful to the child."[31] Nevertheless, in some cases such harmful effects have clearly been found to exist. Here courts have placed severe limits on the religious training a noncustodial parent may introduce to a child. The definition of "harmful effects" runs the gamut. In a 1989 New York case involving cross-petitions asserting custody and visitation rights, the court noted that the father, a Jehovah's Witness, had stipulated that his ex-wife have custody of their daughter and that under New York law a custodial parent has a right to determine a child's religious upbringing and training but should not prohibit the child's exposure to the noncustodial parent's faith. However, the court found that the father had exerted pressure on his daughter and injected animosity into the relationship between himself and his ex-wife. For that reason, the Court held that he was "permitted to take [his daughter] to Jehovah's Witness services on Sunday but shall not involve her any further except that he may answer casual questions which she might ask him. No other exposure to Jehovah's Witness doctrine and activities will be permitted because it has, and could lead to the kind of strain and conflict [which would not be consistent with the best interests of the child]."[32]

In a similar 1986 Minnesota case involving a Lutheran mother and an Assembly of God father, the Court of Appeals of Minnesota terminated a joint legal custody arrangement and awarded the mother exclusive control over the religious training of their children. In this case, the emotional impact on the children of attendance at five-hour faith healing services, Bible camps, and the intolerant attitude of the father toward other religions determined the judgment.[33] These types of disputes range beyond the issues raised by nontraditional religions and address the issue of the social and emotional environment of the child.

Religious doctrines governing the health and medical treatment of children have become the main focus in many custody disputes between parents of competing religions. The most controversial cases involve Christian Science, a Christian minority church that encourages its members to see practitioners, who heal through prayer, rather than consult doctors or use medicine, and the Jehovah's Witnesses, who do not permit members to receive blood transfusions. In the cases described here, belief alone is not always the determining factor. In 1980, the Supreme Judicial Court of Maine reversed a trial court's award of custody of a minor child to the father because the mother was a Jehovah's Witness and would not consent to a blood transfusion for her son. The court found that in the event of a health crisis a court could order that the child receive a transfusion.[34] Thus, the court held that religious practices cannot determine custody "unless such practices pose an immediate and substantial threat to the temporal well-being of the child."[35] The court relied in this case on previous decisions supporting the principle that, when considering a party's religion, a court "must never assume that a threat to the child's welfare exists."[36]

But a very different outcome occurred in the *Stapley* case the following year, when the Court of Appeals of Arizona took custody of three children away from a Jehovah's Witness mother and awarded it to the father. Although the court recognized that "religious views . . . standing alone [are not] grounds for a change of custody," the religion of a custodial parent may be considered where "there is a serious danger to the life or health of a child."[37] Religious differences between the parents created animosity between them, and the court determined that this animosity exposed the children to emotional turmoil. In addition, the court found that the mother had violated prior court orders, including taking children with her and her new husband to proselytize, and that she had failed to notify the father when one of the children had required medical care.[38]

Child Custody Battles and New Religious Movements

The best interests standard attempts to determine custody by referring to facts rather than stereotypes. The inability, however, of some jurists to distinguish between the best interests of children and the passing of judgment on the "best religion" has led to some unfortunate results that have perverted the legal system. In some cases, this has resulted in "cult bashing" in the judicial forum, particularly when anticult experts have testified about the utopian teachings of a newly founded "cult" regarding sexual relationships and children. In cases involving children in controversial religious movements, it is not uncommon for outsiders or ex-members to highlight the bizarre or pathological nature of nontraditional practices and beliefs in their efforts to obtain custody of minor children (Green 1989). Embittered apostates, aided by anticult groups, are called to testify that their former religion deviates from social norms and has a negative effect on children (Richardson 1998).

The Fundamentalist Church of Jesus Christ of Latter-day Saints, the Branch Davidians, and the Church Universal and Triumphant (CUT) are all examples of religious groups that have been involved in child custody battles in the United States. These groups were targets of intense anticult attacks in large part because of their nontraditional, experimental approaches to marriage and sexuality. They were criticized in the media without any citing of the specific facts or issues relating to the custody dispute at hand. These cases raise important constitutional issues concerning religious liberty.

The Fundamentalist Mormons

The Church of Jesus Christ of Latter-day Saints, which now numbers more than 10 million members worldwide, ceased to practice polygamy in 1890 (at least in the United States) and repudiated its practice throughout the church in 1904 (Hardy 1992; Foster 1984; Embry 1987). This church, which embodies mainstream Mormonism, excommunicates any member who advocates the practice of polygamy (Quinn 1993). In the wake of this rejection of polygamy, dissenters such as John Y. Barlow and Joseph W. Musser taught that when church authorities ceased to support polygamy, they violated a law of God and forfeited their authority to lead the church.[39] Various polygamist communities were established in Salt Lake City and in rural areas, where even today they continue to live in polygamy. These "fundamentalist Mormons" consider themselves to be faithful to the original church led by Joseph Smith, and they have experienced both peaceful and violent standoffs (Van Wagoner 1989).

The "modern era" of the fundamentalist Mormons began in 1953 with a standoff between fundamentalists and Arizona law enforcement officers. The preceding year, Arizona governor Howard Pyle had become convinced that the Mormon fundamentalists were a cult, that the parents were guilty of "profligacy," and that their children were suffering from child abuse (Altman and Ginat 1996:48–53). Fundamentalists were to be charged with "rape, statutory rape, carnal knowledge, polygamous living, cohabitation, bigamy, adultery, and misappropriation of school funds," and certain members of the group were also charged with having "encouraged, advised, counseled and induced their minor, female children under eighteen years of age to actively participate in said unlawful conduct" (Bradley 1993:131). Pyle sanctioned a raid on the fundamentalist community of Short Creek, which was located on the border between Arizona and Utah.

On Sunday morning, July 26, 1953, 120 Arizona peace officers, accompanied by 100 news reporters, drove across unpaved roads to the fundamentalist community of Short Creek to arrest 36 men and 86 women and to take into custody 263 children. Although this was planned as a surprise raid, the families were singing patriotic hymns around a flagpole when the officials arrived in Short Creek at 4:00 A.M. Governor Pyle subsequently announced on the radio that the purpose of the raid was "to protect the lives and futures of two hundred sixty-three children" and that the religious community was "the foulest conspiracy you could imagine . . . dedicated to the production of white slaves" (Bradley 1993:113). Mormon officials (whose church had abandoned polygamy some fifty years previously) applauded the raid and were accused of providing relevant information to the police and other civil authorities. This fueled suspicion among many of the fundamentalists that the Mormon Church had not only participated in but may also have helped instigate the raid (Bradley 1993:132).

Mothers and children were bussed to Phoenix, where they were kept in separate locations, including a crowded rest home and the YMCA, and were told that their children eventually would be placed in permanent foster homes. Juvenile hearings were held in Arizona state courts, resulting in the placement of most of the children in foster homes around Arizona, often accompanied by their mothers. Then, for reasons whose examination is beyond the scope of this chapter, an Arizona Superior Court judge ordered in March 1955 that all of the children be restored to their families, bringing an end to Arizona's efforts to segregate children from fundamentalist parents.

Similar efforts to separate children from polygamous parents were made in Utah, especially in communities in the southern part of the state that bordered Arizona and were also part of the "raid." The most prominent case involved the seven children of Vera Black, who were removed from their home, accompanied by their mother, and were ordered to be placed into nonpolygamous homes. When the Blacks challenged the state's authority to take these actions, the Utah Supreme Court held that parents who enter into polygamous marriages may be deprived of their right to the custody of their children.[40] When it became evident that the Blacks would lose custody of their children, they agreed to sign pledges to "obey the law of the land," including the law of monogamous marriage, and by virtue of this pledge the children were returned to the custody of their parents. However, subsequent to the family's return to its polygamist settlement in southern Utah, the Blacks continued to practice "plural marriage." However, no further action was taken against the Blacks or any other polygamist.

No further efforts have since been made to remove children from any polygamist community in Arizona or Utah, even though there are now an estimated twenty thousand polygamists living in the western United States and anti-polygamy laws are not, for the most part, enforced. In fact, even if the practice of polygamy is still illegal under a federal statute passed in 1862 and the Utah Constitution, the Utah Supreme Court has protected the civil rights of polygamists, including their right, under limited circumstances, to adopt children.[41] On August 5, 1991, the Utah attorney general was quoted as stating, "Unless it's associated with child abuse, welfare fraud or any other illegal act, polygamy for its own sake has not been a crime susceptible of successful prosecution and uses up an awful lot of resources."[42] He further observed that, although the Utah Constitution forbids polygamy, the state's laws do not specifically bar the practice.

A more recent acknowledgment by Utah's governor that many states "have chosen not to aggressively prosecute" polygamy and that the practice may be protected under the First Amendment was recast—within a week—to emphasize that he did not "condone polygamy. I am not sympathetic to its practice" (Rivera 1998b; Fahys 1998). In the midst of this controversy, the Utah attorney general notes that "the claim of religious freedom is no defense to the crimes of statutory rape, incest, unlawful sexual conduct with a minor, child abuse, or cohabitant abuse" (Rivera 1998a). At the same time, groups have organized for the conflicting purposes of legalizing polygamy and prosecuting polygamists (Maffly and McCann 1998; Rivera 1998c).

One of the primary reasons the raid on Mormon fundamentalist communities and the subsequent efforts of Arizona and Utah officials to separate polygamist parents from their children failed was because state officials eventually recognized that polygamous family ties were so strong that all attempts to punish the practice of polygamous marriage through children would be futile. Officials recognized that it would not be in the best interests of the children to be separated from their parents, since there was no evidence of child molestation or deviant sexual activities involving the children. This raid demonstrates how misinformation and stereotyping—as evidenced by Governor Pyle's statement—can and do create the foundation for institutionalized "kidnapping," while suffusing and inundating the judicial proceedings with information beyond what should properly be considered in the determination of custody of children.

The Branch Davidians

Probably the most violent outcome of a custody battle involving cult members was the fiery denouement of the standoff on April 19, 1993, in Waco, Texas, when the Federal Bureau of Investigation (FBI) assaulted the Branch Davidians with armored vehicles and tear gas. Although the raid on the Branch Davidian compound in Waco has been well publicized, it is not widely known that one of the primary catalysts for the tragic events was allegations of child abuse made in the context of custody disputes and that anticult experts were involved in supplying much of the information to the judiciary and to government agents who initiated the raid. At least two of the individuals who provided evidence to the FBI and the Bureau of Alcohol, Tobacco, and Firearms (ATF) were involved in custody disputes with their former spouses, who lived at the Mount Carmel compound.

Attorney General Janet Reno stated that evidence of physical abuse was "clearly" a factor in the ultimate decision to raid the compound.[43] In addition, Representative Lofgren concluded that "agents could easily know from reading those articles [in local newspapers] that 12–year-old girls were being raped repeatedly, that all the male adult members had been removed from their wives and were celibate, so that Mr. Koresh, the Christ figure in his own mind, could have all of the children for use sexually, that there was dire physical abuse underway, with babies, and, there had been kidnappings. There were immigration violations, little girls who had crossed State lines."[44] Despite Attorney General Reno's and Representative Lofgren's suspicions, Catherine Wessinger (1997:127) has noted "that allegations of child abuse come under state, not federal, jurisdiction, and that Texas social workers had investigated and closed the case because they found no evidence of abuse."

Nevertheless, David Jewell was concerned that his nine-year-old daughter, Kiri, might be chosen to become one of David Koresh's plural wives, to bear his seed to restore the House of David. On the basis of information received from Mark Breault, an embittered ex-member, Jewell petitioned the domestic court to obtain custody of Kiri from his former wife, Sherri Jewell, who was a loyal follower of Koresh. Pursuant to a pretrial settlement, the court awarded custody to the father but granted the mother visitation rights if she kept the daughter away from Koresh (Bromley and Silver 1995:65). Following this change in custody, both Breault and David Jewell continued to initiate contact with anticult groups, the media, and, ultimately, the ATF. During these conversations, they alleged that Kiri Jewell had been subjected to physical abuse by Koresh in violation of the court's order. This was one catalyst leading to the ATF's decision to commence the standoff with Koresh and his followers at the compound. Before the ATF raid (excepting a minor incident in 1988), the Branch Davidians (and related predecessor groups) had peacefully coexisted with the local community for more than fifty years. Nevertheless, both the anticult movement and the mass media claimed that David Koresh, a messianic leader who taught communal living, millennialism, military preparedness, and polygamy, had brainwashed his followers into remaining in a compound and was forcing them, through mind control, to adopt practices that deviated from acceptable social mores.[45]

The longer the standoff continued, the more it became apparent that it had been precipitated not only by the rhetoric of David Koresh and his violation of U.S. firearms legislation, but also by the anti-Koresh rhetoric published by the local press and by anticult organizations. To further complicate the confusing situation, the FBI, which developed a rivalry with local police, relied on the advice of Murray Miron, a psychologist, and Rick Ross, a deprogrammer, both of whom were prominent in the Cult Awareness Network, while virtually ignoring the assistance of scholars who offered seminars and educational programs on the nature of new religious movements in general and Koresh's group in particular.

After the standoff, Kiri Jewell testified before a House committee investigation into Waco and spoke of the abuse she had been subjected to in the compound. But according to Kiri's grandmother's statement, the child had not been present in the Koresh compound during some of those occasions when the abuse allegedly occurred, and it has been suggested that she may have been coached in her testimony by members of the anticult movement. The conflict grew out of a custody battle that, like many others in its wake, was "piggybacked" by the anticult movement pushing its own agenda. The result was the tragic deaths of eighty-one people.

The Church Universal and Triumphant

Some new religious movements have been fortunate—or canny—in avoiding sieges and mass raids, but their individual members have nevertheless been subjected to custody disputes in the courts. The Church Universal and Triumphant is a small church (twenty thousand members worldwide) based in Corwin Springs, Montana, where it is organized communally, observes alternative dietary practices, and engages in the chanting ritual of decreeing. Disaffected members seeking custody of their children have described decreeing as "self-hypnosis" and have alleged that it constitutes mental abuse and is emotionally stressful on children (although chanting is a universal and venerable form of religious worship).[46]

Church members have been embroiled in a number of custody battles where arguments have been made that children in the church are subjected to abuse when raised by a parent who adheres to church beliefs and practices. In the *Scheibler* v. *Scheibler* custody dispute (described in Lewis and Melton 1994), four children were removed from the custody of their mother in Indiana in 1992 because "a clear threat to the children's emotional health has been demonstrated regarding the children's presence in underground shelter drills or visits, and in the imposition on them of a fatalistic approach to life and a fear of the end of the world" (Singer 1996:256–257).[47] The judge also considered the impact the church's practice of decreeing had on the children.

The *Scheibler* case was decided on the facts and circumstances specific to that particular case and does not necessarily set a precedent. It is the prerogative of courts with jurisdiction over children and their parents to examine religious practices, but that examination, to pass constitutional standards, must be factually oriented and limited to the impact such practices have on the children involved. CUT members have won other custody disputes. In a custody case in Kentucky, CUT member Melanie Pleasant-Topel was allowed to retain custody of her minor son but was given strict guidelines by the court as to which religious practices she could impose on him.[48] A Washington court awarded custody to Charlene Viau, a member of CUT for approximately eleven years, in spite of the father's contention that the church was an "armed camp."[49] A similar victory was won in the *Milligan* v. *Nardone* case, in which an Arizona court rejected the noncustodial parent's argument that the religious practices of the Church Universal and Triumphant adversely affected the physical and mental health and safety of the divorced couple's minor child.[50] The noncustodial parent, Robert Nardone, wanted the parties' minor child removed from Crestview Academy in Livingston, Montana, which he claimed was affiliated with the church. The court rejected the father's arguments and found that there was insufficient evidence to prove that the religious practices of the church were harmful to the minor child.

Although these results may seem contradictory, individual facts and circumstances often dictate results. Unfortunately, all the relevant circumstances are not always apparent from court records. In other cases, decisions are often result-oriented, and their stated rationale may be misleading.

Parents seeking custody have sometimes relied on experts to testify concerning the abuse of children in the relevant NRM; these experts focus on "creeds" rather than specific "deeds" affecting the relationship between parent and child. Allegations of physical or sexual abuse have often provided a catalyst for the removal of children from parents who are members of NRMs. The most drastic interventions have been raids and standoffs, and these might fairly be termed a kind of *institutional kidnapping*. Many of these raids and standoffs have been reactions to incomplete or biased information supplied by anticult groups. As a consequence, NRMs have become the targets not only of the anticult movement but also of the government and the judiciary because of society's legitimate concern for the best interests of children.[51]

New Religious Movements in Europe

Although new religious movements have been controversial in the United States for more than 140 years, the recognition of the presence of large, well-established NRMs raising their second generations is a comparatively new situation in Europe (Towler 1995; Meldgaard and Aagaard 1997).[52] Just as religious groups that are completely unconnected with David Koresh were ridiculed in the American press during the siege at Waco, and erroneously compared to the Branch Davidians, European new religions have become increasingly marginalized since the mass suicides that occurred in France and Canada (Solar Temple) and in California (Heaven's Gate).

Russian national security adviser Alexander Lebed vowed in 1996 to rid his country of "foreign religions and cults" (Hockstader 1996). He referred to Mormons as "mold and scum" and compared the Mormon Church to Aum Shinrikyo (the notorious Japanese NRM responsible for the sarin gas attack on the Tokyo subway), claiming that Mormons posed a "direct threat to Russia's security" (Hockstader 1996). Lebed's comments indicate that NRMs—even well-established minority churches—are in a precarious situation in the "new Europe." In fact, Lebed's sentiments were translated in 1997 into legislation restricting non–Russian Orthodox religions (Shterin and Richardson 1998). Recent actions taken in France, Belgium, and Germany demonstrate that Lebed's form of cult bashing is not limited to the old Communist bloc countries (Introvigne and Melton 1996). European critics have recently produced a list of "dangerous sects" that includes the Baptists, Jehovah's Witnesses, Quakers, and Mormons. Legislation in France, following a 1996 parliamentary report, was introduced in 1998 that would severely limit NRMs.

Thus, it is not surprising that disputes involving the interests of children in the context of new religious movements have recently become more common in Europe. Perhaps the best-known movement rumored to practice polygamy in Europe (aside from Muslim communities) is The Family, formerly known as the Children of God.[53] Members have been accused not only of raising children in polygamous colonies but also of forcing them to have sexual relations with adults at an early age. The Family's current leaders admit that some radical sexual experiments took place in their "colonies" among adult members in the late 1970s and early 1980s. No longer officially practiced, these included the controversial proselytizing technique of "flirty fishing," which involved offering sexual favors to prospective recruits or patrons, as well as toleration of intergenerational sex.[54] But members of the group now insist that such practices had been abandoned by the late 1980s. According to statements issued by Family leadership in 1986 and 1988 and reaffirmed in The Family's "Charter of Responsibilities and Rights," published in 1995, sexual relations with minors are grounds for excommunication for adults members of the movement. The Family's position on polygamy is somewhat more ambiguous. Although the leaders "do not encourage it among our members," neither do they consider it "spiritually needful in any way or wise." Polygamy is apparently only prohibited "in any country or culture that specifically disallows it."[55] The Family encourages its members "to respect the laws and customs of the countries they live in."[56]

The Family's communal homes were raided in Australia and Spain in 1992 and in France and Argentina in 1993. According to The Family's own literature, these raids were undertaken, in part, to remove children from these communities as a response to allegations of child abuse. In each case where children were removed, no evidence was found to support such allegations and the children were eventually returned to their families.[57]

It is virtually impossible to prosecute polygamists in new religious movements without some evidence of aberrant sexual behavior, even if particular movements have reputations for such behavior. Thus, even if graphic depictions of flirty fishing in The Family's old booklets (which The Family claims are "purged" or no longer circulated) continue to arouse suspicions of illicit sexual activity, The Family's actual current practices have been studied by researchers (see Van Zandt 1991; Melton 1994; Millikan 1994) and found to be quite tame.[58]

Although communal new religions often evolve their own unique, unpredictable forms of marriage and sexuality, they have routinely been—and apparently will continue to be—accused of practicing polygamy. There is a common theme in the opposition to these movements. In the case of The Family, opponents have proposed that children be forcibly removed from religious communities that "teach" unconventional lifestyles or sexual behavior. According to this perspective, it is in the best interest of these children to separate them from their families and place them in foster homes regardless of whether there is any actual evidence of sexual abuse.

The precarious balance between freedom of religion and the best interests of the child is normally evaluated in the United States on a case-by-case basis with a consideration as to how "religious practices and beliefs" can and do affect specific children. The U.S. Constitution does not tolerate either the advocacy or the condemnation of religious beliefs or practices in the context of disputes involving church members. European countries, which are just beginning to experience religious pluralism, would be wise to ensure that accusations of incest and abuse leveled at NRMs be evaluated and proved or disproved in an open forum that permits the different interested parties (cults, anticultists, civil authorities, and professional experts) to examine all of the evidence. In this way the courts will avoid judging NRMs on the basis of past events or stereotypes. If the public is expected to support the possible separation of children from their parents, such legal protections for new religious movements, parents, and children must exist. Furthermore, legal mechanisms must exist for persons to give evidence, at least as a preliminary step. This is preferable to impulsive undercover raids based on hearsay or misinformation, which have in the past led to bloodshed. Improved communications and monitoring of possible cases of child abuse would help avoid confrontations like those in Waco, where it is still unclear whether rumors of child abuse had any basis in fact. Hopefully, the increasingly harsh rhetoric against new religious movements now being heard in Europe and raids on some of these movements stimulated by rumors and past church practices will not be harbingers of violent confrontations in the Old World.

Notes

1. While they were married, Alicia and Marc Larson had raised their children in the Mormon Church. They had previously stipulated in their decree of divorce that they would have joint legal custody but that Alicia would have physical custody. *Larson* v. *Larson,* 888 P.2d 719, 721 (Utah App. 1994).

   The record of the case does not indicate whether Alicia Larson's fiancé, Doug

Pomeroy, whom she met in Corvallis, Oregon, was a Mormon, but it is probable, given the context of the trial court's decision, that even if he was affiliated with the church, he was not a practicing Mormon. See 888 P.2d, at 723–725.

2. Ibid. 888 P.2d 719, at 723–724 (Utah App. 1994).
3. Ibid., at 724, citing *Hutchinson* v. *Hutchinson,* 649 P.2d 38, 4 (Utah 1982).
4. Ibid., at 725.
5. *Friederwitzer* v. *Friederwitzer,* 55 N.Y.2d 89, 432 N.E.2d 765, 447 N.Y.S.2d 893 (N.Y. 1982).
6. In *re Marriage of Johnson,* 424 N.W.2d 85 (Minn. Ct. App. 1988).
7. *Everson* v. *Board of Education,* 330 U.S. 1 (1947).
8. *Lemon* v. *Kurtzman,* 403 U.S. 602 (1971). A portion of the three-tiered test articulated by the Court in *Lemon* was first enunciated in *Walz* v. *Tax Commission,* 397 U.S. 664 (1970).
9. *Reynolds* v. *United States,* 98 U.S. 145 (1878).
10. Ibid., at 164. For a discussion of attempts—prior to the passage of federal antibigamy legislation in 1862—by territorial judges in Utah to prosecute polygamy under the common law, see Homer (1986–1987, 1988, 1996).
11. *Reynolds,* at 167–168.
12. Penny dreadfuls were a British form of popular literature, sold on street corners during the Victorian age, that featured sensational and lurid stories.
13. *Reynolds,* at 164. The Court relied in part on Thomas Jefferson's belief that "religion is a matter which lies solely between man and his God; . . . that the legislative powers of the government reach actions only, and not opinions"; and that government may not opine on the validity of a religion but may only regulate actions that are in violation of social duties or subversive of good order. Jefferson also proposed legislation in the Virginia House of Delegates allowing government to "interfere when [religious] principles break out into overt acts against peace and good order" (at 163).
14. In *Cantwell* v. *Connecticut,* 310 U.S. 296 (1940), the Court acknowledged that religious conduct "remains subject to regulation for the protection of society" (at 304).
15. *Sherbert* v. *Verner,* 374 U.S. 398 (1963).
16. The exception was *Employment Division* v. *Smith,* 494 U.S. 872 (1990).
17. *Wisconsin* v. *Yoder,* 406 U.S. 205 (1972).
18. *Smith,* at 874–875.
19. Ibid., at 884–885. See also Biskupic (1996).
20. *Smith,* at 879.
21. Ibid., at 881–882.
22. *Neely* v. *Neely,* 737 S.W.2d 539, 543 (Tenn. Ct. App. 1987).
23. Ibid.
24. *Khalsa* v. *Khalsa,* 751 P.2d 715 (N.M. Ct. App.), cert. denied, 751 P.2d 700 (N.M. 1988).
25. Ibid., at 717.
26. Ibid., at 720–721 (citations omitted). The Court in *Khalsa* (at 717) relied on two other opinions involving parents who belonged to different religions: *Munoz* v. *Munoz,* 79 Wash. 2d 810, 489 P.2d 1133 (1971) (parent's speculation that six-year-old son, who attended both Mormon services with his mother and Catholic services with his father, was emotionally harmed thereby was insufficient); and *Hanson* v. *Hanson,* 404 N.W.2d 460 (N.D 1987) (mother's testimony that father, a member of the Pentecostal Apostolic Church, had told the children, among other things, that the Catholic

Church believes in cannibalism, which upset the children, was insufficient to prohibit father from taking the children to his church). In *Khalsa,* although not specifically indicated, the mother apparently became a Catholic after her remarriage and was taking the children with her to Catholic services.

27. *Khalsa,* at 721.
28. In *re Marriage of Gersovitz,* 779 P.2d 883, 885 (Mont. 1989).
29. Ibid., at 885.
30. *Neely* (citations omitted), at 542.
31. Ibid. (citations omitted).
32. In *re S.E.L.,* 143 Misc. 2d 455, 541 N.Y.S.2d 675, 679 (Fam. Ct.), *aff'd sub nom., Lebovich* v. *Lebovich,* 155 A.D.2d 291, 547 N.Y.S.2d 54 (1989). The Court relied heavily on the decision in *Bentley* v. *Bentley*, 86 A.D. 2d 926, 448 N.Y.S.2d 559 (3d Dept. 1982). According to the Court, the Appellate Division had noted that the Family Court's order prohibiting a Jehovah's Witness father from instructing the child in Jehovah's Witness teaching, and taking him to Jehovah's Witness religious and social activities, was proper because there had been demonstrated harm to the child (the order would have been improper in the absence of such demonstrated harm). The harm found to exist emanated from the child being emotionally strained and torn because of the parties' conflicting religious beliefs, not from any judicial evaluation of the relative merits of Jehovah's Witness or Catholic doctrine. The basis of this decision was grounded not in any assessment of the respective worth of Catholicism and Jehovah's Witnesses, but in the adverse effect that the conflict of differing religious beliefs had on the child. The Court wished to ameliorate that effect. The purpose of the prohibition was to avoid any further conflict, not to judicially denigrate the validity of Jehovah's Witness teaching. The only way that this harmful situation could be obviated was to allow the custodial parent to determine the child's religious upbringing.
33. In *re Marriage of Andros,* 396 N.W.2d 917 (Minn. Ct. App. 1986).
34. *Osier* v. *Osier,* 410 A.2d 1027 (Me. 1980).
35. Ibid., at 1030, note 5.
36. Ibid., note 6. The Court cited three decisions in this regard: *Lvitski* v. *Lvitski,* 231 Md. 388, 190A.2d 621 (1963) (Mother, a Jehovah's Witness, had recently refused blood transfusion for child with bleeding ulcer; orders of trial court minimizing risk to child affirmed); *Harris* v. *Harris,* 343 So.2d 763 (Miss. 1977) ("Mother belonged to fundamentalist sect believing in snake handling," but no evidence that her attendance at church exposed child to risk of snake bite); and *Smith* v. *Smith,* 90 Ariz. 190, 367 P.2d 230 (1961) (Jehovah's Witness mother; no showing of "circumstances materially affecting" welfare of child).
37. *Stapley* v. *Stapley,* 15 Ariz. App. 64, 485 P.2d 1187 (1981).
38. Ibid., at 1181.
39. On Mormon fundamentalists, see Quinn (1993). For the most comprehensive study of the Short Creek group of Mormon fundamentalists, see Bradley (1993).
40. *In re State in Interest of Black,* 283 P.2d 887 (Utah 1955). See also *Hall* v. *Hall,* 326 P.2d 707 (Utah 1958).
41. See, e.g., *Sanderson* v. *Tyron,* 739 P.2d 623 (Utah 1987) (finding that parent practices polygamy is alone insufficient to support custody award); and *State* v. *Musser,* 175 P.2d 724 (Utah 1948) (a person cannot be prosecuted for expressing opinions of

belief and personal convictions). See also *Matter of Adoption of W.A.T.,* 808 P.2d 1083 (Utah 1991).

42. *Salt Lake Tribune,* August 6, 1991.
43. Statement of Janet Reno, U.S. Attorney General, *Activities of Federal Law Enforcement Agencies Toward the Branch Davidians,* Hearings before the Subcommittee on Crime of the House of Representatives and the Subcommittee on National Security, International Affairs, and Criminal Justice of the Committee on Government Reform and Oversight, 104th Cong., 1st sess., August 1, 1995, Part 3, at 354, 382–383. See also Wright (1995).
44. *Activities of Federal Law Enforcement Agencies,* Part 1, at 320.
45. Even before the American Revolution, unorthodox creeds from Europe, such as those of the Quakers, Shakers, Mennonites, Moravians, and Huguenots, appeared and thrived in the colonies. After the Great Awakening and the first mass revival movement, the Mormons, Spiritualists, Adventists, Christian Scientists, and Jehovah's Witnesses were organized on U.S. soil. In the 1960s when Americans began to look East, new religious movements, such as the Unification Church and Hare Krishnas, spread in the United States. Legal problems concerning new religious movements are often discussed in legal journals both in the United States and Europe. See, for example, Robbins, Shepherd, and McBride (1985). For discussions of new religious movements in Europe, see Messner (1992). See also Del Re (1992); and Braggion (1990).
46. For a study of the Church Universal and Triumphant, see Lewis and Melton (1994). For a critique of Lewis and Melton, see Balch and Langdon (1996).
47. Scott Lee Scheibler and Carol Ann Scheibler, Marion Superior Court, State of Indiana, Civil No. 49D01–8904–DR-563 (1992).
48. *Melanie Gabbard Pleasant (Topel)* v. *Damon Gould Pleasant,* Fayette Circuit Court, State of Kentucky, Civil No. 76–1965 (1981).
49. *Charlene R. Viau and Alexander C. Viau, III,* Superior Court for the County of Spokane, State of Washington, Civil No. 86–3–02805–4 (1989).
50. *Milligan* v. *Nardone,* Superior Court of Tucson, Arizona.
51. Ironically, the anticult movement's brash efforts to legitimize institutional kidnapping proved to be its downfall. In 1996, the Cult Awareness Network, which was the leading anticult movement in the United States, was forced to declare bankruptcy and to liquidate its assets after a judgment won against it by Jason Scott, a member of the Life Tabernacle Church, who had been kidnapped by operatives of CAN. Ultimately, the initial concerns of CAN and its followers (which it had the right to express) crossed the line when the organization ventured into tortious activity as the solution to the perceived problem.
52. The Supreme Court determined that the practice of polygamous marriages was illegal in the landmark *Reynolds* decision. Although Justice William O. Douglas in *Yoder* suggested that *Reynolds* was wrong and would eventually be reversed, subsequent challenges to this prohibition have failed. *Potter* v. *Murray City,* 760 F.2d 1065 (10th Cir.), cert. denied, 106 S. Ct. 145 (1985), and the more recent *Employment Division* v. *Smith* made such a reversal unlikely in the near future.

    Recent European decisions concerning polygamy have involved Muslims rather than fundamentalist Mormons, who do not reside outside the United States, although some nineteenth-century Mormon missionaries in Great Britain, France, and Italy taught the doctrine. In fact, in 1866 a British judge refused to recognize a Mormon polygamist marriage. This decision was effectively reversed in 1972 by the House of Commons when it conferred jurisdiction on the English matrimonial courts concerning polygamous marriages. This jurisdiction was necessary because of the rapidly increasing Muslim population in Great Britain.

53. For the origin of the Children of God and its relation with The Family from an internal perspective, see "Our Families Origins," Bulletin by World Series (April 1992).
54. This practice involved an unknown number of minor females having sex with older males, who were usually in their thirties. For exposés on this practice, see Williams (1998) and the response of The Family ("The Family Responds" 1998).
55. "Position and Policy Statement," issued by World Services (April 1992).
56. This is very similar to the language used in the 1890 manifesto of the Mormon Church, which was intended to prohibit polygamy in the United States but not in Canada or Mexico. See "Position and Policy Statement."
57. "Religious Persecution—in a Democratic Society? Will *You* Be *Next*?" issued by The Family (June 1992).
58. The Family has attempted to explain the publications of the Children of God and prior teachings of its founder, "Father David," in "Our Replies to Allegations of Child Abuse," Bulletin of World Services (June 1992); "Position and Policy Statement."

References

Altman, I., and J. Ginat. 1996. *Polygamous Families in Contemporary Society.* Cambridge, U.K.: Cambridge University Press.

Atkinson, J. 1992. *Handling Religious Issues in Custody and Visitation Disputes.* Chicago: American Bar Association.

Balch, R. W., and S. Langdon. 1996. "How the Problem of Malfeasance Gets Overlooked in Studies of New Religions: An Examination of the AWARE Study of the Church Universal and Triumphant." Pp. 191–211 in A. Shupe, ed., *Wolves within the Fold: Religious Leadership and Abuses of Power.* New Brunswick, N.J.: Rutgers University Press, 1998

Beschle, D. L. 1989. "God Bless the Child? The Use of Religion as a Factor in Child Custody and Adoption Proceedings." *Fordham Law Review* 58: 383–426.

Biskupic, J. 1996. "Justice Scalia Defends Religious Beliefs Against Secular Society." *Washington Post,* April 10.

Bradley, M. 1987. "'Protect the Children, Protect the Boys and Girls': Child Welfare in Utah, 1880–1920." Ph.D. diss., University of Utah.

———. 1993. *Kidnapped from That Land: The Government Raids on the Short Creek Polygamist.* Salt Lake City: University of Utah Press.

Braggion, P. 1990. "I nuovi movimenti religiosi e la libertá religiosa." Ph.D. diss., University of Milan Law School.

Bromley, D. G., and E. D. Silver. 1995. "The Davidian Tradition: From Patronal Clan to Prophetic Movement." Pp. 43–95 in S. A. Wright, ed., *Armageddon in Waco.* Chicago: University of Chicago Press.

Degler, C. N. 1980. *At Odds: Women and Family in America, from the Revolution to the Present.* New York: New York University Press.

Del Re, M. C. 1992. *Culti emergenti e diritto penale.* Naples: Jovene.

Embry, J. L. 1987. *Mormon Polygamous Families, Life in the Principle.* Salt Lake City: University of Utah Press.

"The Family Responds to *Heaven's Harlots . . . My Fifteen Years as a Sacred Prostitute in the Children of God Cult,* by Miriam Williams." 1998.

Fahys, J. 1998. "Leavitt Says Polygamy Might Be Constitutional." *Salt Lake Tribune,* July 24.

Firmage, E., and R. C. Mangram. 1988. *Zion and the Courts.* Urbana: University of Illinois Press.

Foster, L. 1984. *Religion and Sexuality: The Shakers, the Mormons, and the Oneida Community.* Urbana: University of Illinois Press.

Gordon, S. B. 1996. "Our National Hearthstone: Anti-Polygamy Fiction and the Sentimental Campaign Against Moral Diversity in Antebellum America." *Yale Journal of Law and the Humanities* 8(2): 295–350.

Green A. C. III. 1989. "Litigating Child Custody with Religious Cults." *Cultism and the Law* (June): 1.

Hagen, M. A. 1997. *Whores of the Court.* New York: Regan Books.

Hardy, C. 1992. *Solemn Covenant.* Urbana: University of Illinois Press.

Hockstader, L. 1996. "Yeltsin Adviser Blasts Foreign Cultures, Sects." *Washington Post,* June 28.

Homer, M. W. 1980. "The Establishment Clause and Its Application in the Public Schools." *Nebraska Law Review* (59): 1143–1168.

———. 1986–1987. "The Federal Bench and Priesthood Authority: The Rise and Fall of John Fitch Kinney's Early Relationship with the Mormons." *Journal of Mormon History* 13: 89–110.

———. 1988. "The Judiciary and the Common Law in Utah Territory, 1850–61." *Dialogue: A Journal of Mormon Thought* 21 (spring): 97–108.

———. 1996. "The Judiciary and the Common Law in Utah: A Centennial Celebration." *Utah Bar Journal* 9, 7 (August-September): 13–17.

Introvigne, M., and J. G. Melton, eds. 1996. *Pour finir avec les sectes, le debat sur le rapport Guyard et la commission parlementaire.* 2d ed. Paris: Dervy.

Lewis, J. R., and J. G. Melton. 1994. *Church Universal and Triumphant in Scholarly Perspective.* Stanford, Calif.: Center for Academic Publications.

Maffly, B., and S. R. McCann. 1998. "Polygamy: Former Wives Demand Action." *Salt Lake Tribune,* July 28.

Meldgaard, H., and J. Aagaard, eds. 1997. *New Religious Movements in Europe.* Aarhus, Denmark: Aarhus University Press.

Melton, J. G. 1994. "Sexuality and the Maturation of the Family." Pp. 71–96 in J. R. Lewis and J. G. Melton, eds., *Sex, Slander, and Salvation.* Stanford: Center for Academic Publications.

Messner, F. 1992. "Le sétte e le nuove religioni in Europa: Aspetti giuridici." *Libertá Religiosa Diritto e Fenomeno delle Sétte* (special issue of *Sétte e Religioni*) (April-June): 223–258.

Millikan, D. 1994. "The Children of God, The Family of Love, The Family." Pp. 181–252 in J. R. Lewis and J. G. Melton, eds., *Sex, Slander, and Salvation.* Stanford, Calif.: Center for Academic Publications.

Nowak, J., R. Rotunda, and J. Young. 1978. *Constitutional Law.* St. Paul, Minn.: West.

Quinn, D. M. 1993. "Plural Marriage and Mormon Fundamentalists." Pp. 240–293 in Martin E. Marty and R. Scott, eds., *Fundamentalism and Society.* Chicago: University of Chicago Press.

Richardson, J. T. 1998. "Apostate, Whistleblowers, Law, and Social Control." In D. G. Bromley, ed., *The Politics of Religious Apostasy, the Role of Apostates in the Transformation of Religious Movements.* Westport, Conn.: Praeger.

Rivera, R. 1998a. "Graham: Utah to Prosecute Polygamists." *Salt Lake Tribune,* July 30.

———. 1998b. "'I Do Not Condone Polygamy,' Leavitt Says." *Salt Lake Tribune,* August 1.

———. 1998c. "'Polygamy Should Be Legal,' Says Women's Group." *Salt Lake Tribune,* August 1.

Robbins, T., W. C. Shepherd, and J. McBride, eds. 1985. *Cults, Culture, and the Law: Perspectives on New Religious Movements.* Chico, Calif.: Scholars Press.

Shterin, M. S., and J. T. Richardson. 1998. "Local Laws Restricting Religion in Russia: Precursors of Russia's New Natural Law." *Journal of Church and State* 40 (spring): 319–341.

Singer, M. T. 1996. *Cults in Our Midst: The Hidden Menace in Our Everyday Lives.* San Francisco: Jossey-Bass.

Towler, R., ed. 1995. *New Religions and the New Europe.* Aarhus, Denmark: Aarhus University Press.

Van Wagoner, R. 1989. *Mormon Polygamy: A History.* Salt Lake City, Utah: Signature Books.

Van Zandt, D. E. 1991. *Living in the Children of God.* Princeton, N.J.: Princeton University Press.

Wessinger, C. 1997. "Understanding the Branch Davidian Tragedy." *Nova Religio* 1 (October).

Williams, M. 1998. *Heaven's Harlots.* New York: Eagle Brook.

Wright, S. A. 1995. "Two Years After Waco Fire." *Washington Times*, April 19.

CHAPTER 12

Children of a Newer God

THE ENGLISH COURTS, CUSTODY DISPUTES, AND NRMS

ANTHONY BRADNEY

Marriage breakdown not infrequently results in disputes over the care and control of the children. This is just as likely to occur to parents from new religious movements (NRMs) as it is to more conventional parents. Parents may reach agreements about child care that are acceptable to the courts, but if they cannot agree, or when their arrangements are unacceptable, then the courts will intervene.

Under the current English legislation, section 1(1) of the Children Act 1989, English courts are required to make decisions about the custody of children that concern only the best interests of the child. This was also the case in the legislation in force before 1989. Even though the parents may have feelings and wishes about their children's future, the legislation gives them few rights. It is the child who is the focus of the case. Until 1989 the way in which the court reached its decision was within its own discretion. Certain general principles emerged from decided cases. Thus, for example, judges tended to decide that young children or girls of any age were best looked after by their mother. Judges usually tried to avoid decisions that involved splitting the care and control of siblings. However, these principles, and many others that could be adduced, were precisely that: principles, not rules. They were at most presumptions about the disposition of parenting that might be rebutted by the facts in any individual case. The Children Act 1989 changed the powers of the court in custody cases. A new range of court orders was introduced, but the influence on the substantive law that governed the decision as to how custody was awarded was minimal. The new legislation simply took the pre-1989 case-law principles and codified them in section 1(3). Nevertheless, even in this new form they still remain simply factors to be taken into account. Cases were, and still are, decided solely on the basis of what is in the best interests of the child.

When considering a custody case, judges are measuring the relative parenting abilities of two different potential families. To decide which will offer the child a better future, these judges are looking at the mother and father in concert with any new partners they may now have. Judges will also look at the physical care the families can offer, the emotional life they offer, the attitudes that the children manifest towards the two households, and so on. English courts have consistently said that they are not interested in any difference in the religions that the families espouse. Religion is not one of the factors specifically referred to in section 1(3). In *Re Carroll,* a custody case decided in 1931, one of the judges, Lord Justice Scrutton, said that "it is, I hope, unnecessary to say that the Court is perfectly impartial in matters of religion."[1] No English judge has ever resiled from this position. This espousal of neutrality is consistent with a liberal approach to the state's role regarding the values chosen by its citizens. Providing those value choices do not disturb the value choices of other citizens, the state has no interest in them (Sadurski 1990). Notwithstanding these protestations of neutrality, religion can on occasion be an important factor influencing the outcome of custody disputes, and in some instances it can be the determining factor.

Religion and Social Practice

In a case called *Buckley* v. *Buckley* (1973), a Jehovah's Witness mother and the father (who had no religious affiliation) were in dispute over the custody of three girls, aged between five and eleven.[2] At the time of the dispute, the mother had been looking after the children for some two years. In deciding that custody would be awarded to the father, the court noted, among other things, that if custody was awarded to the mother, the children would be brought up differently from other children because of the unconventional nature of Jehovah's Witnesses' beliefs and practices. The children would not celebrate birthdays or Christmas. The judgment in the case described that difference as a "disadvantage."

In another case called *Hewison* v. *Hewison* (1977), the dispute occurred between a father who was a member of the Exclusive Brethren and a mother who had left the sect.[3] The three children, two girls and a boy, were aged seven, eight, and ten and had lived with the father for six years after the parent's separation. In awarding custody to the mother, the court observed that if custody was awarded to the Brethren father, the children would be brought up separately from other children and would be instructed to regard themselves as different and separate. They would be raised in an atmosphere that the court described as being "harshly limiting."

The contrast between the decisions in these two cases and the then-usual practice of the courts is striking. In an empirical study of 652 custody cases in

1972, John Eekalaar and Eric Clive (1977) show that the dominant factor determining the court's decision was usually the question of who had actual care and control of the child at the time when the court's decision was being made. In 94 percent of all cases, parents jointly sought the court's approval for custody arrangements made by themselves. In only 0.9 percent of these cases did the courts make an order that changed the child's place of residence. Only a small minority of the cases Eekalaar and Clive studied involved a dispute between the parents about custody arrangements. In the thirty-nine cases that did involve such a dispute, the court made an order that varied the child's place of residence in only two instances. A much smaller empirical study conducted by Susan Maidment (1984) produced similar results. Most judges took the view that, whatever other factors were present, the child's psychological well-being was best preserved by allowing that child to remain within the stable family environment that had already been established. In both *Buckley* and *Hewison,* the court not only altered the status quo but also ignored a number of the principles, such as girls being the subject of maternal custody, that would normally govern such cases. The court's perception of the social practices consequent on a parent's religion determined the outcome of the cases.

NRMs and Custody Cases

In *Re B and G* (1985), the courts were asked to decide a custody dispute between a father who was a Scientologist and a mother who had once between a Scientologist but was no longer a believer.[4] The children concerned were a boy and a girl aged ten and eight, respectively. The parents had separated in 1978, and the father had assumed custody of the children. The children lived with the father, with visits to their mother, in what the court described as "a warm close family circle" until 1983 when the mother applied for care and control of the children. Mr. Justice Latey, the judge deciding the case, accepted that for the children to leave the care and control of their father and go to their mother would be "confusing and, I think, probably seriously distressing for them for a time." Nevertheless, because of what Mr. Justice Latey considered the "baleful influence" of Scientology and the putative negative effects that it had on its members, as well as what he termed the "immoral and socially obnoxious . . . corrupt, sinister and dangerous" nature of Scientology in general, he awarded the care and control of the children to the mother.

In *Buckley* and *Hewison,* parents lost custody of their children because of the alleged social isolation that their children would supposedly suffer if they continued in the care of these parents. *Re B and G* went beyond this. In upholding Mr. Justice Latey's judgment, the Court of Appeal said that "one of the judge's primary tasks was to assess the nature and extent of the risk to the children if they were brought up as Scientologists." Although Mr. Justice Latey had said in his judgment that the custody case was "neither an action against scientology nor a prosecution of it," the Court of Appeal accepted that "the theory and various beliefs of Scientology in abstract" were central to the case. The court's judgment was not simply that by being brought up by a Scientologist the children would be socially isolated; rather, the court's judgment was that being brought up as and by Scientologists was damaging in itself.

"Social Acceptability" and the Courts

The court's decision in *Re B and G* and the reasoning it used are consistent with previous judgments about other religions. Although judges in custody cases have said that they are neutral about religious beliefs, there has long been a caveat. In a 1981 case, *Re T,* the court said that "it was not for the court to pass any judgement on the beliefs of parents where they are socially acceptable and consistent with a decent and respectable life."[5] In *Re R* (1993), Lord Justice Purchas said that "it is no part of the court's function to comment upon the tenets, doctrines or rules of any particular section of society provided that these are legally and socially acceptable."[6]

In determining issues relating to law and religion, the court's concern with the "social acceptability" of the religion in question is not unique to child custody cases. Under English law, charitable trusts attract considerable advantages, in particular regarding tax "breaks" (Bright 1989; True 1990). Religion is one of the four headings under which a charitable trust can properly be set up. In deciding whether a charity is religious in an 1862 case, *Thornton* v. *Howe,* the judge, Sir John Romilly (then Master of the Rolls), held that "the Court of Chancery makes no distinction between one religion and another."[7] The issue for the court was whether something was religious, not whether it was true. This position reflects that liberal position of neutrality taken up by the court in custody cases. However, just as in custody cases, the courts have added a caveat: although the judge was unconcerned that the subject of the purported religious charitable trust was the writings of Joanna Southcott, a woman whom he described as "foolish [and] ignorant," and whose writings he dismissed as containing "much that, in my opinion, is very foolish," he did investigate whether there was anything in the writings that was "either immoral or irreligious." If there had been such content, then, notwithstanding the fact that the object of the trust was in all other respects religious, it would not have been deemed "charitable." Academic commentators have unanimously agreed that the test of morality would be sufficient to prevent Scientology from being registered as a charitable trust (Picarda 1983).

In child custody decisions, if the parents have behaved in a criminal manner, the assumption is that this behavior might have a direct detrimental effect on children. To be concerned with whether behavior is "socially acceptable" is, however, less clearly the proper business of the courts. It is problematic for three reasons. First, if behavior is socially unacceptable but not criminal, then why should people be penalized by the state? The state defines the limits of permissible behavior through the vehicle of the criminal law. If individuals live within the criminal law but behave in a socially unacceptable manner, other individuals may legitimately make private decisions not to associate with them. However, for the state to institute a second level of quasi criminality that justifies forms of penalty, such as denial of custody of children or failure to achieve charitable status, is to offend against the liberal principle that the state should be neutral about the value choices of its members.

Second, although the rules of criminal law are relatively plain, the notion of social unacceptability is nebulous at best. For example, at least for some people in Great Britain, to be a member of the Church of Scientology is socially unacceptable and even immoral, whereas for others eating meat or voting for a particular political party is socially unacceptable. The concept of social acceptability works best in the context of a consensus vision of society where there is one dominant set of mores. If a society is pluralistic and tolerates diverse worldviews, then the use of a generalized concept of social acceptability has no empirical referent (Bainham 1995:238). Whereas criminal law is the result of a democratic process involving different interest groups in Parliament, within our increasingly global and multiethnic societies, the contemporary court's reliance on notions of social acceptability appears little more than a thinly disguised attempt by one social group to impose its mores on other social groups.

Third, when the courts make decisions based on social acceptability, they assume the dubious role of awarding—or withholding—mantles of respectability to religious organizations. How can judges predict what society will find unacceptable in an unconventional religion? How do judges find out how religions behave?

The Courts and Evidence

English courts, even when they are dealing with custody disputes, are inherently adversarial places. The information that judges have when they make their decisions is such information as the parties have chosen to put before the court. The arguments that judges must respond to are those that the parties, or more usually their lawyers, have raised. In this context, judges search not for a perfect truth, but for the best pragmatic decision, taking into account the circumstances of the case (Atiyah 1987:4).

In custody cases, this dependence of the court on the evidence and arguments advanced by the parties is to some extent ameliorated by the practices of calling for welfare reports and appointing a guardian *ad litem* separate from either parent to act on behalf of any child in legal proceedings. This access by the court to extra evidence and argument in custody cases should not be exaggerated, however. Custody cases are not even included under section 41(6) of the list of proceedings of the Children Act of 1989 concerning the appointment of a guardian ad litem. Guardians ad litem are appointed in only a very small number of cases (Bainham 1993:453). It is more common for courts to call for welfare reports in custody cases. Even here, however, "the proportion of the total is still very small" (Bainham 1993:460). In cases where welfare reports are called for, either a court welfare officer, a qualified probation officer, or a local authority will prepare a report on the child's circumstances. Whereas a guardian ad litem's duty is to represent the child, a welfare report is supposed to provide an objective evaluation of the child and of the child's background (Jackson 1992).

In custody cases involving NRMs, the court's reliance on evidence and argument advanced by the parties is of particular importance. In *Re B and G,* Mr. Justice Latey based much of his judgment on the evidence of Dr. John Clark, a psychiatrist who had made a particular study of Scientology. The Scientologist father chose not to advance expert evidence, though he did call some Scientologists to speak about their life. Mr. Justice Latey not only based much of his judgment on Dr. Clark's evidence; he also said that there was a "large, very large, body of evidence most of it undisputed, supporting Dr. Clark's analysis." Whereas Mr. Justice Latey accepted Dr. Clark's evidence as being "convincing," he described the views of Scientologists themselves as being "subjective and conditioned."

There is a large body of scholarly evidence that, in a variety of ways and to varying degrees, regards Scientology as a destructive influence in the lives of its adherents, but this does not reflect the full spectrum of scholarly opinion. For example, Roy Wallis's study (1976:254), *The Road to Total Freedom*, concludes: "There are beginning to appear signs that Scientology is coming to be recognised as a legitimate and valid religious collectivity. . . . Scientology has . . . increasingly stressed its religious character and subdued its claims to therapeutic efficacy. It may therefore come, in time, to be accorded the same sort of status as is accorded to Christian Science today." Thus, academic opinion can apparently produce a more favorable assessment of Scientology than that quoted by Mr. Justice Latey. Equally relevant is the range of disciplines within which Scientology has been considered. Mr. Justice Latey chose to rely on psychiatric evidence. But because of the nature of the discipline, psychiatric examination tends to find evidence of pathology or aberrant behavior when investigating phenomena such as religious conversion.

Clark's views on NRMs have been the subject of particular criticism. In a 1979 article, Clark (280) described what he called "destructive cults" as "public health problems and a sociopathetic illness," and he noted, "The unique capacity of these absolutist groups to cause harm stems from the central activity of all cults—the sudden conversion through aggressive and skillful manipulation of a naive or deceived subject who is passing through or has been cause to enter a susceptible state of mind."

According to this view, membership in a group labeled a destructive cult becomes almost necessarily an indication of mental illness. Clark has been willing to espouse this view in court even when he has not had the opportunity to closely observe the individuals involved and tests by other psychiatrists have not found any evidence of mental illness (Richardson 1992:240). Because Clark contends that NRMs engage in mind control techniques that allow their adherents to mask the mental damage done to them, concealing this harm from exposure through normal psychological tests, his thesis is almost incapable of disproof (Richardson 1992:237). Clark's views have found a ready audience in groups opposed to NRMs but "have been discredited among most scholars" (Richardson 1992:242).

Elsewhere, judges have noted that the fact that they have had to deal with incomplete evidence might have affected the outcome of the case. In the 1981 *Holmes* v. *Attorney-General* case, which concerned the charitable status of the Exclusive Brethren, the judge, Mr. Justice Walton, observed that evidence about the Brethren practices of "shutting up" and "withdrawal" had come only from the Brethren themselves. Their evidence, he suggested, "may very well put the matter in a much more charitable light than it wears in reality." [8] Given the court's adversarial setting, Mr. Justice Latey cannot be faulted for relying on the only expert evidence cited. Nevertheless, the evidence on which he based his judgment was partial and incomplete.

The Education of the Courts

It is usual to regard exchanges between lawyers and judges in a court case as argumentative or rhetorical discourse (Alexy 1989; Murphy and Rawlings 1981, 1982). In cases involving religious movements, however—and especially in cases involving NRMs—it is helpful to see the presentations by lawyers in court as attempts to educate judges.

English judges rarely deal with disputes involving religion or issues of conscience (Bradney 1990). Their professional lives do not lead them into contact with religions, and there is no reason to suppose that their knowledge about religions is any greater or wider than that of the average person in the street. Indeed, there is no reason to suppose that they do not have the same range of beliefs and prejudices about religions in general, and NRMs in particular, as are found in the population at large. Such beliefs are likely to be, at best, superficial and, at worst, erroneous. Yet these judicial beliefs, whatever their weaknesses, plus whatever evidence and argument are put before the court, must, by the very nature of the court process, form the foundation for the judge's decision.

In some areas of law, the court's decision is based on either the technical analysis of legal rules or arguments concerning abstruse facts far removed from everyday life. In custody cases, however, the essence of the decision concerns the child's everyday life. In passing judgment, judges not uncommonly rely on what is little more than folk wisdom. The judicial approach is well illustrated by a decision made by Lord Justice Griffiths in a 1985 case, *Re P.*[9] In this case the judge had to decide, among other things, what account to take of the wealth of the various families that might look after the child. In dismissing financial considerations as a relevant factor, the judge remarked that "anyone with experience of life knows that affluence and happiness are not necessarily synonymous." Where decisions are based on experience of life, the ordinary beliefs held by the judiciary take on special importance. Unless lawyers can so educate the courts as to lead them to a deeper understanding of NRMs, judgment will be based on that level of analysis.

The Courts and the Children of God/The Family

Both the problematic side of the court's attitude toward NRMs and the results of the wider use of expert evidence are illustrated by *Re ST* (n.d.). This case concerned an application by a grandmother to make her grandson a ward of court and to have care and control of the child taken away from the mother. The only reason that the grandmother had for taking this action was the fact the mother was a member of The Family. The grandmother never suggested that her daughter was an unfit mother or that she had been deficient in her care of her son.[10]

The Family is a paradigm of an NRM that the courts would be likely to view with suspicion in a custody dispute. Members of The Family live communally and separately from society. They have been associated in the media with a variety of different sexual practices, including allegations about the sexual abuse of children. This image of The Family is reflected in the disputed issues that Lord Justice Ward listed for consideration in his judgment: (1) an assessment of The Family; (2) sexually inappropriate conduct; (3) medical neglect; (4) impairment of educational development; 5) impairment of emotional, social, or behavioral development; (6) physical mistreatment; (7) changes made and likely to be made. Each of these issues was addressed separately in the judgment.

The first thing that distinguishes Lord Justice Ward's judgment in *Re ST* from Mr. Justice Latey's judgment in *Re B and G* is the range of evidence that Ward was faced with. He listed seven separate expert witnesses representing a wide range of disciplines: James Richardson was a professor of sociology and judicial studies: Dr. Susan Palmer, lecturer in religion; Dr. J. Gordon Melton, director of the Institute of the Study of American Religion; The Reverend Dr. David Millikan, a minister of the Uniting Church in Australia; Dr. Lawrence Lilliston, a clinical child psychologist; Dr. Michael Heller, a consultant child psychiatrist (described in the judgment as being a "frequent witness in The Family Division"); and Dr. Hamish Cameron, a consultant child psychiatrist. Ward noted that there were ten thousand pages of typewritten evidence and two thousand pages of his own notes of oral evidence. In addition to the expert evidence, the court also heard evidence from the various parties to the case and heard evidence and received affidavits from various members of The Family.

Lord Justice Ward's judgment is a careful attempt to sift truth from rumor. The history of The Family and the various disputed issues are all given separate treatment, with detailed references to the evidence of both expert and other witnesses, together with excerpts from literature produced by The Family. In addition, each of the accounts of the expert witnesses is discussed. On the basis of this evidence, Lord Justice Ward concluded that The Family

(1) had eradicated the sexual excesses of the past.
(2) had begun, but not completed, a ban on inappropriate forms of discipline.
(3) offered wider avenues of education.
(4) had moved from a closed, secret society to one more ready to engage with the outside world.
(5) might be more trusting of the system and perhaps even more amenable to changes required by the system.

Despite this finding, Lord Justice Ward concluded that there was still sufficient evidence of potential harm to the child to justify removing the child from the care and control of his mother. The judge did, however, impose a stay on his order so as to allow both the mother and The Family to reflect on certain suggestions; these he made so that the child might be allowed to remain in the care and control of the mother if she and The Family reacted positively to these suggestions.

Lord Justice Ward insisted on eight concessions from the mother, ranging from her promise to educate the child to university level if he so desired, to her agreement not to live apart from the child for more than two weeks. The judge then made four suggestions to The Family. The first related to the use of corporal punishment and silence as a form of punishment, the second related to education and contact between The Family and local education authorities, and the third related to contact between members of The Family and relatives outside The Family. The fourth suggestion, which Lord Justice Ward described as "the hardest," was that The Family "denounce David ["Moses"] Berg [the movement's founder]. They must acknowledge that through his writings he was personally responsible for children in The Family having been subjected to sexually inappropriate behaviour." Having received satisfactory assurances from both the mother and The Family, Lord Justice Ward permitted the child to remain in the care and control of the mother.

Re B and G v. *Re ST*

In many respects, the contrast between the *Re B and G* and *Re ST* cases and their judgments could not be more striking. Both cases involved NRMs that continue to be subject to adverse publicity in the media. In the case of *Re B and G,* the children were taken away from the care of their Scientologist father and their non-Scientologist mother was both given care and control of the children and given leave to take them to live with her outside of the United Kingdom. In *Re ST,* the mother, a member of The Family, retained care and control. In the case involving The Family, full expert evidence was put before the court. In the other case, the court did not have access to a full range of evidence. It is tempting to conclude that access to more evidence will ameliorate the apparent hostility of the courts toward NRMs. In support of this conclusion, one might compare the statements of the courts about the lifestyle of Jehovah's Witnesses in early cases such as *Buckley* v. *Buckley,* where the living of a restricted and enclosed social life was the subject of criticism, to later court pronouncements, such as *Re R,* where the court held that "it was not necessarily wrong (and I emphasize the word 'necessarily') or contrary to the welfare of children, that they should be brought up in a narrower sphere of life and subject to stricter religious discipline than that enjoyed by most people."[11] It appears that the more evidence is brought in concerning individual cases, or successive cases involving the same religious minority, the more chance the parents from such minorities have of winning their custody cases. Even though the sheer abundance of evidence in the *Re ST* case appeared to work to the advantage of the mother, who belonged to a controversial NRM, a number of disturbing elements emerged in this case, including the court's attitude toward minority religions in general and the suggestions made by Lord Justice Ward to The Family.

The Courts and Moderation

Rex Ahdar (1996:185), in an article analyzing the court's attitude toward religion in custody cases in five separate common law jurisdictions, argues that "there is little doubt that courts are unsympathetic to parents who they perceive as 'fanatics' or take their religion 'too far.'" This attitude is reflected in the judgment in *Re ST.* Early in his judgment, Lord Justice Ward noted, "The mother claims the inalienable right to love her God as she chooses, which is a love she submits brooks no interference from a Court of Law because she is entitled to the fundamental freedom of thought, conscience, and religion." Later, when discussing The Family's attitude toward sexual conduct, Ward scrutinized the mother's evidence:

> NT's [the mother's] closing words to me were to plead with me not to denigrate the Law of Love [The Family's doctrine]. It was an extraordinary observation from her. I would have expected her to plead with me not to remove her son. Many mothers, often totally hopeless mothers, have begged for that mercy. But NT did not. It was as if the integrity of the Law of Love was more important to her than S. Where is her sense of priorities?

Finally, Lord Justice Ward devoted a section of his concluding appendix to the question "Does NT place S's interests first and will she continue to do so?"

A major factor in Lord Justice Ward's decision that the care and control of the child remain with the mother seems to have been the mother's success in convincing him that she had tailored her allegiance toward The Family to suit his views on "moderation." The judge summed up his assessment of the mother's attitude toward The Family as follows:

> I reach the conclusion that NT had come much further along the journey to the truth than I had expected of her. I find her to be more alert

> to risks to S and more intuitive. I find she is conscious of the dangers that zealots within The Family may sacrifice the rights of children on a false altar of misconceived service to the Lord. I am satisfied that NT will protect him from excesses of the group.

Another important factor leading to Lord Justice Ward's decision appears to have been the fact that he accepted the expert testimony of James Richardson, who stated that The Family had become more "domesticated," meaning that its beliefs and practices had become less extreme and more akin to those of mainstream society.

Moderation, Multiculturalism, and Society

Moderation can have two different meanings for the courts. First, it can mean that the believer does not subscribe to all the tenets of the particular religion. Where the court finds the tenets problematic for some reason, a display of moderation will make the believer a more attractive potential custodial parent for the court. Second, moderation, which appears to be desirable in itself as far as the court is concerned, can mean that the believer is more balanced and socially acceptable. Requiring moderation in belief in this second sense is superficially attractive. On closer analysis, it appears contradictory and damaging.

Lord Justice Ward gave his judgment as a Christian. His Christianity did not form the basis of his judgment or lead to any bias. Nevertheless, he used Christian imagery and references in his findings. Understood within this Christian context, it is strange that Lord Justice Ward found NT's devotion to the doctrine and the dogma of The Family unsettling. After all, Jesus Christ, one of the Gospels says, came "to set a man at variance against his father, and the daughter against her mother, and the daughter-in-law against the mother-in-law" (Matt. 10:35). This situation does not apply exclusively to Christianity. Religious beliefs have frequently set the believer at odds with the rest of society and separated him or her from kin.

Religious beliefs are sometimes fundamental beliefs that form the very core of a person's identity. Such persons are not first who they are and only secondarily adherents of a particular religion. They are who they are because they believe. Knott (1986:4) writes that, when examining the attitudes of academics toward religious belief, "one sometimes gets the feeling that religion is like stamp-collecting or playing squash, a minor hobby." If one views religion in this way, it will seem that belief can easily be abandoned or suspended. But belief, and actions arising from that belief, may not, for the believer, be an option. Having accepted a belief, the believer must act accordingly. Viewed correctly, the belief does not take priority over all other things (so that in the case of NT she sets belief in the Law of Love before her desire for care and control of her son); rather, the believer cannot conceive of her- or himself existing apart from belief. Concepts such as "importance" and "priority" have meaning for an individual only within a scale of value.

The same argument has been advanced, albeit within a secular context, by Richard Lovelace in his poem "To Lucasta, Going to the Wars." Explaining the apparent contradiction between protesting love for a mistress and leaving her to go to war, Lovelace writes, "I could not love thee (deare) so much / Lov'd I not honour more." If he refused to go to war, he would not be the man who loved his mistress. Honor does not have priority over the mistress; rather, it allows for the possibility of a worthy love.

It is puzzling that the judge, having understood that the mother feels so deeply about her religious beliefs as to take them to the core of her being, then expresses surprise that for her they are all encompassing. How do we justify rewarding those who, after saying they feel deeply committed to their religious beliefs, will renounce them if they prove socially or personally damaging? To quarrel with the content of someone's beliefs is one thing. To quarrel with the fact that those beliefs are firmly held is another. We may not be capable of being saints or martyrs, but should we not at least acknowledge the superior merit of those who go down that road?

These conceptual arguments have pragmatic consequences. Parekh (1990:68), among others, argues that a multicultural society needs not only individuals but also "lively, responsible and self-disciplinary communities." To encourage moderation will both narrow the range of attitudes that such communities contain and speed up the assimilation of mainstream cultural attitudes into these communities. Those individuals within sectarian communities who are perceived to be "moderate" will be favored. If moderation is the key to success, then The Family cannot hope to retain care and control of children if there is a custody battle; only "moderate" members of The Family will succeed. The court's stance on moderation is equally problematic when judged according to a schemata of individual rights. If individuals have inalienable rights and if these give them rights as parents, then the rights adhere regardless of whether the individuals are moderate (Bradney 1993).

Conclusion

The court's attitude toward NRMs in custody disputes is not fixed and unalterable. Indeed, it may be wrong to construct a court "attitude" on the basis of a restricted number of reported cases. Courts in other unreported cases may have acted differently. Such evidence as we have in this chapter, however, shows an evolving court approach. Within the constraints of a statutory framework, the courts have sought to arrive at a defensible view of the role of religion in custody cases. That view is plainly neither entirely consistent nor entirely defensible within a rhetoric of liberal values nor to the values of flourishing communities. One cannot expect the judiciary, bound by a statutory concern with the needs of the child before it, to rectify this inconsistency. Rather, there is a need for further debate. This debate should begin by acknowledging the real role religion plays in child custody cases and then proceed to consider what the proper relationship is among individuals, communities, society, and the state.

Notes

1. (1931) 1 Kings Bench 317 at p. 336. (All references are to published reports of the judgments where these are available.)
2. (1973) 3 Family Law 106.
3. (1977) 7 Family Law 207.
4. [1985] Family Law Reports 134, [1985] Family Law Reports 493. (Courts sometimes give only initials as titles to cases to conceal the identity of the children involved.)
5. (1981) 2 Family Law Reports 239.
6. [1993] 2 FLR 163.
7. (1862) 31 Beavan 14.
8. *The Times,* February 12, 1981. A full report of the case can be found on the LEXIS database.
9. [1985] Family Reports 635.
10. The judgment in this case has not been commercially published to date, nor is it to be found on the LEXIS database. Given its length, more than three hundred pages, the case will probably never be widely available. This part of this chapter is based on a copy of the judgment supplied to me by members of The Family.
11. [1981] Family Law Reports 239.

References

Ahdar, R. 1996. "Religion as a Factor in Custody and Access Disputes." *International Journal of Law, Policy, and the Family* 10: 177–204.

Alexy, R. 1989. *A Theory of Legal Argumentation.* Oxford: Clarendon Press.

Atiyah, P. 1987. *Pragmatism and Theory in English Law.* London: Stevens and Sons.

Bainham, A. 1995. "Family Law in a Pluralistic Society." *Journal of Law and Society* 22: 234–247.

Bainham, A., with S. Cretney. 1993. *Children: The Modern Law.* Bristol: Family Law.

Bradney, A. 1990. "Making Cowards." *Juridical Review* 129–149.

———. 1993. *Religions, Rights, and Laws.* Leicester: Leicester University Press.

Bright, S. 1989. "Charity and Trust for the Public Benefit—Time for a Rethink?" *Conveyancer and Property Lawyer* 53: 28–41.

Clark, J. 1979. "Cults." *Journal of the American Medical Association* 242: 279–281.

Eekalaar, J., and E. Clive, with K. Clarke and S. Raikes. 1977. *Custody After Divorce.* Oxford: Centre for Socio-Legal Studies.

Jackson, C. 1992. "Reporting on Children: The Guardian ad Litem, the Court Welfare Officer, and the Children Act 1989." *Family Law* 22: 252–256.

Knott, K. 1986. *Religion and Identity and the Study of Ethnic Minority Religions in Britain.* Leeds: University of Leeds Community Religions Project.

Maidment, S. 1984. *Child Custody and Divorce.* London: Croom Helm.

Murphy, W., and R. Rawlings. 1981. "After the Ancien Regime: The Writing of Judgements in the House of Lords, 1979/80—Part 1." *Modern Law Review* 44: 617–657.

———. 1982. "After the Ancien Regime: The Writing of Judgements in the House of Lords, 1979/80—Part 2." *Modern Law Review* 45: 34–61.
Parekh, B. 1990. *Britain and the Social Logic of Pluralism in Britain: A Plural Society.* London: Commission for Racial Equality.
Picarda, H. 1983 "New Religions as Charities." *New Law Journal* 131: 436–437.
Richardson, J. 1992. "Mental Health of Cult Consumers: Legal and Scientific Controversy." In J. Schumaker, ed., *Religion and Mental Health.* Oxford, U.K.: Oxford University Press.
Sadurski, W. 1990. *Moral Pluralism and Legal Neutrality.* London: Kluwer Academic.
True, N. 1990. *Giving: How to Encourage Charity More.* London: Centre for Policy Studies.
Wallis, R. 1976. *The Road to Total Freedom: A Sociological Analysis of Scientology.* London: Heinemann.

Part IV

Hearing the Children

CHAPTER 13

The Ethics of Children in Three New Religions

CHARLOTTE E. HARDMAN

"Robin Hood was right—he was just stealing the riches back."
(Girl at TM school)

"There are no rules, but you should respect others and you should be true to your feelings."
(Girl from Findhorn)

"We need to read and follow the Bible: babies grow from milk, and we grow from the Word."
(Boy from The Family)

The moral order in which children live is made up of a universe of "shoulds": how they should act in the world, how they should exercise willpower, what emotions they should feel or not feel. The universe of shoulds focuses on the self as agent and on appropriate behavior, attitudes and values. In the course of socialization, each child develops a sense of moral rules, a sense of self, and a capacity for independent thought.[1] Sigmund Freud and George Herbert Mead (1934) have been instrumental in pointing out the significance of self-awareness in the process of development. What I address in this chapter is the relationship between the kinds of moral rules that children express (as in the chapter epigraph) and their sense of self and authority as members of The Family, Transcendental Meditation (TM), or the New Age group at Findhorn, Scotland. I want to show how the concept of childhood in the three groups is central to children's construction of morality and their sense of self and authority. Moreover, I argue that the future survival of new religious groups, in the form of a dedicated following in the second generation, is more likely to occur if the self is constructed within a framework of a belief in one absolute Truth, an external source of authority, and a notion of the "child" as essentially fallible and thereby requiring external correction and guidance.[2] The group is less likely to survive when the self is constructed within a plurality of principles and the notion of "child" is one of an innocent or a perfect being with its own innate code of right and wrong.

The context of the three groups—The Family (previously known as the Children of God), Transcendental Meditation, and the New Age group at Findhorn—are distinct.[3] The first group is a fundamentalist Christian one with beliefs in the literal truth of the Bible and the authority of God. The other two are nontheistic, with beliefs in the power of the self and an emphasis on the individual's private experience of spiritual realities. Without entering here into a discussion on what constitutes the New Age, I describe children at Skelmersdale, England, and Findhorn as being raised within New Age ideologies (see Heelas 1996; Perry 1992; York 1995). Both movements focus on ways in which the individual can make inward explorations of the self that lead to increased success in life and harmony in the environment. Both are monistic, underlining the interdependence of all aspects of the cosmos, body-mind holism, and the laws of harmony and balance. Both argue for the possibility of social and cultural transformation (an age of peace, abundance, happiness) as the direct result of personal transformation on a large scale.

That these two groups express such similar philosophies is hardly surprising. J. Gordon Melton (1992:18) describes the New Age as drawing inspiration from Theosophy and Spiritualism and, to a lesser extent, Eastern religions, and he calls the movement a "new revivalist religious impulse directed toward the esoteric/metaphysical/Eastern groups and to the mystical strain in all religions." The language of Findhorn has elements of Theosophy, Anthroposophy (Rudolph Steiner), Alice Bailey, and Christian mysticism. It combines Advaita Hindu philosophy with Pagan nature worship (Riddell 1990:286). Both TM and Findhorn conceive of an "inner knowledge" to be attained by those who follow the path.

Members of The Family—founded by David Berg ("the Lord's Endtime Prophet") in the late 1960s—are fundamentalist Christians with strong millenarian beliefs and a vocation to "serve Jesus."[4] They live in cooperative communal homes because they find that these offer not only spiritual havens but also practical and economic benefits in their aim to serve God on a full-time basis and serve as many souls as they can.[5] Much of the energy of the movement is spent in "witnessing" to win souls, for only the saved will be allowed to live in the New Jerusalem. Members believe that after three and a half years of social chaos and religious persecution known as the "Great Tribulation" (Matt. 24:21), Christ will return to defeat the Antichrist and reign on earth. The group diverges from traditional Christian fundamentalist churches (which tend to denounce it as heretic) in its experiential, erotic understanding of Jesus' love (see Richardson, Stewart, and Simmonds 1979; Richardson and Davis 1983) and in its liberal attitudes toward sexuality (Wallis 1979).[6] Sexual freedom was only one expression of Berg's outstanding doctrine known as the Law of Love: "God's only law is love. There is no other law" (Berg 1978:5010).[7]

Morality

In my interviews with children in all three communities about morality, I had two main questions in mind. The first is whether the children are sensitive to differences between general *moral rules* (hitting, lying, stealing) and *conventional rules* (rules that are applicable for their own system, but perhaps not for other groups, and may be changeable). My second question (if they do understand the difference) is on what grounds they understand it. On what grounds do they accept the authority of some rules but not others? On what grounds can some rules change?[8] Do the children from an authoritarian theistic group have different justifications for the authority of rules, a different understanding of morality, than children of New Age groups with pluralist values where individualism is all important? My theoretical framework can be found in the work of Larry Nucci and Elliot Turiel (1993) and that of Judith Smetana (1981).

Smetana's developmental work with three- to four-year olds investigating their sensitivity to right and wrong produced some very interesting results, especially concerning children's understanding of right and wrong based on their own emotional reactions to other children and to other children's distress at transgression of moral rules. Smetana (1981) told these children about children who engaged in hitting or taking an apple from another child, putting toys away in the wrong place, or not saying grace. Some of these are obviously moral transgressions, whereas others are deviations from convention. What is significant is that those very young children could see the difference. They considered moral violations to be more serious: "very bad to hit," "only a little bit bad to put toys away in the wrong place," "wrong to hit always, even if no rules about it." Acts such as putting toys away in the wrong place, however, they saw as permissible if not proscribed by rules.

On the basis of Smetana's work, we can say that even for young children some actions clearly involve a serious breach of a fixed moral order, whereas others merely breach contingent moral rules. One would expect the distinction between moral rules and conventional rules to vary according to a child's family, community, or religious background. But Smetana found this not to be the case. She interviewed three- to five-year-old children who had suffered from physical abuse, another group who had been neglected, and a control group. All three groups reached similar conclusions: the breaking of local rules, conventional rules (not putting away toys or leaving class without permission), were minor offenses. More serious were instances of not sharing resources, distressing another child, and being physically aggressive toward another child. From this work, we can say that children's judgments about the difference between moral rules and local conventional rules start at three years old and are relatively unaffected by family background.

But how do very young children learn moral rules, if not from their family? Most instructive are the reactions of other children to moral transgressions. The parents are not the main source of information. The children watched by Smetana *never* responded to violations of conventional rules, but they responded to about one-third of moral rule violations. And those reactions to violations of moral rules were made loud and clear! Children who were victims of some other child's aggression, theft, or aggravation responded volubly, and adults who were present reaffirmed the reactions of the children. Young children, if asked why X is wrong to hit or take toys, always refer to the consequences for the victim and the harm or distress the action will cause. Young children's understanding of moral violations can therefore be seen to be tied up with their understanding of emotions (see Harris 1989:chap. 2).[9]

If Smetana is right, then her findings contradict those critics who argue that children will have "no" morality if brought up in a progressive, liberal way—as found in some New Age groups—where there appear to be few strong behavioral rules and boundaries. But absolutes are drawn not from society but from the individual's observations, and children are like scientists. However "liberal" the environment may appear, children do develop *a* morality.

Smetana's work also firmly contradicts any view of children as passive objects or helpless spectators in a pressing environment that affects and produces their every behavior. If this indeed were the case, new religious movements would have no problem with survival; their children would simply replace their parents. Many have argued with subtlety (see Berger and Luckmann 1966:149ff) about how a particular cultural milieu may influence children's behaviors, but other scholars describe socialization as if it deprives children of their own free will; these scholars view children as molds into which the socializing agents just pour their input/culture, including the moral order.

Smetana's investigation supports my own argument that if we are to understand children at all, we have to see them in their own right, not just as receptacles of adult teaching. We must try to understand how they develop their own models of society, often counterpart models to those of adults (Hardman 1973). Children are active participants in the construction of their own social lives (see James and Prout 1990). Central to children's constructions of their ideas of morality, self, and personhood is the group's notion of what a "child" is. Since it is these very notions of self and morality that are the hardest for children and adults to discard, some ideas of childhood/personhood are more likely to produce children that resemble their parents, in spite of children's general propensity to invert adult concepts (see Hardman 1974; Toren 1993).

Children and Morality in The Family

The children (aged four to seven and nine to fifteen) in The Family living in Leicestershire demonstrated a clear understanding of the difference between conventional rules and moral rules.[10] This understanding was expressed by the younger ones in terms of practicalities such as tidiness, cleanliness, and safety: "not running in the house, not going over the line in the kitchen, not to play with dirty get-out balls in the house, not to wear outdoor shoes inside the house, keep nice and tidy, not to play at quiet time."

Moral rule violation was seen as more serious "because it was likely to hurt someone; hitting someone it would hurt; the toy doesn't matter so much, but we have to matter about the body." When asked what the difference was between "playing at quiet time" (a violation of a conventional rule) and "punching someone" (a violation of a moral rule), the children replied along the line of "punching was badder because you hurt someone else." The older children of The Family (those from nine to fifteen) articulated the difference in terms of personal safety and welfare—"not running in the house, doing your jobs in the morning, waking up on time"—as opposed to rules concerning "higher-order matters and spiritual matters": "Bible reading every day; witnessing; no taking without asking—it's stealing; no violence; no drugs; no counterfeit money; no murder; no child abuse." One boy saw the only law as "love": "The Law of Love encompasses all the rules."

That these children had such a clear understanding of conventional and moral rules makes sense in terms of The Family's worldview. The Family model of childhood is based on the belief that, though man was created innocent, through the temptation of Satan he transgressed and fell from the Edenic happy state. Children are thus both spiritual innocents and sinners. As blessings and gifts from God, children are central to The Family, which believes that God takes a very active and personal role and interest in each soul He creates. "We consider a child to be principally and initially a spiritual entity created by God Himself. God then unites this spirit with the physical body of the forming child to become a totally new and eternal living soul, the combination of both body and spirit. A child, therefore, is an act of creation."[11]

But children are also "sinners by nature" in the sense that the infant is fallible and naturally selfish and has to learn how to love. Children are covered by their parents' faith until they can be "saved" themselves, spiritually regenerated, or "born again" at the age of two or three, at which time they can understand how Jesus died for them, how they can take Him into their hearts, and how they can "have Him as their best friend." "Saved" children are nevertheless vulnerable to sin and need guidance. With knowledge of Jesus and the Word, children can start again if they do "sin" (if they persistently sin, He will chasten and correct them). Sinners by nature, children need strong boundaries; they need to be taught self-control and discipline. Without these, children are unhappy and insecure and develop feelings of not being loved. "If the limits and controls are lacking in the early years, a child will not only be at a loss in the later years but will also be more likely to react and rebel against any kind of control. Direct orders are best during the early years."[12]

Children can be led astray by the Devil, who may try to tempt them through the wrong music or unsupervised TV; they may be led astray by not having enough sleep and regular bedtimes. By developing the children's "spirit" with the Word of God, and with prayer, children can protect themselves. "We believe we are engaged in a relentless spiritual warfare. . . . We are in the midst of a great war in which God's Heavenly forces are aiding, supporting and encouraging our efforts, and Satan and his demons are struggling to hinder and halt us."[13] To provide the right spiritual conditions for developing the spirit, The Family emphasizes the importance of keeping children away from mainstream society and with members of the movement in supervised environments.

The Family model of childhood described thus far suggests that The Family creates a "total world"—much as Alan Peshkin (1986) sees the fundamentalist Christian school he studied. Quoting Goffman, Peshkin (1986:261) describes it as a place of "residence and work, where a large number of like-situated individuals, cut off from the wider society for an appreciable period of time, together lead an enclosed, formally administered round of life." Those inside know the Truth, the yardstick for judging music, literature, TV, and the news "to question such Truth, except within the framework of faith, is to question God himself" (Peshkin 1986:261). I propose that the world of The Family has some of these qualities, which contributes to the successful socialization of its children to remain within the group.

Certainly, the strength of The Family children's adherence to the morality of their elders is reflected in their understanding of rule alterability. Although conventional rules change all the time, moral rules cannot. "The rules are changing all the time, but if the rules changed to say you can hit, then I won't." When asked if God said hitting was okay what would they do, the children all affirmed in reply that God *could* change the rules but that He would do so only to make them better: "God wouldn't say that hitting is all right because he's perfect"; "God could change the rules, but not to *bad* rules, only to *good* rules"; "God always changes the Devil's rules to good rules, and now the Lord has more Angels on his side than the Devil."

The children saw the rules in the Bible as unequivocally good. Apart from God, only David Berg, known as Grandpa (the now deceased leader), and Maria (his widow and present leader) could change rules.[14] "Grandpa could give a change of a rule to Mama Maria from Heaven, and she would give it to us." Older children recognized the Bible as the ultimate authority, so they considered that Berg could change the rules only if the Bible supported the change—as, they said, Berg did with flirty-fishing.[15] Even if there are strong trends in society, such as the acceptance of homosexuality, the children insisted they would follow the Bible rather than the rest of society. They felt that if someone had a revelation from God about changing moral rules, and if it fitted with biblical statements, then long debates would be necessary to make sure that it was God talking, and they would take a long time praying.

Children in The Family accepted the authority of the Bible over individual conscience: "The Bible is the ultimate authority"; "Grandpa could only change the rules if it agreed with the Bible"; "The Bible is more of an authority than the rest of society"; "Follow the rules to follow the Lord"; "Babies grow from milk; we grow from the Word"; "We need to read and follow the Bible and do what it says"; "When Jesus speaks to us in the Bible and tells us what to do, we should do it"; "In the New Testament the only law is love"; "The Ten Commandments were not given on a take-it-or-leave-it basis; they are to be obeyed."

Other justifications given by the children had to do with welfare and safety concerns—the harmful effects of not maintaining the rules: "We might eat junk food"; "the rules are to keep us all safe and clean, sane and healthy"; "to stop people being selfish"; "to keep us spiritually healthy." Rules create fairness in the world: "Life is more fair with rules"; "If no rules, half the population could murder the other half."

There was also an awareness of the significance of rules for social relations and the establishment of boundaries and guidelines: "People follow rules to obey and not be punished"; "for the sake of society"; "because if not, you'll be punished"; "would be punished"; "the adults make up the rules and we always agree; the government and the police make rules"; "for the sake of unity"; "to avoid anarchy and chaos."

One further aspect of The Family model of the child helps to explain the second generation's dedication to the authority of both conventional and moral rules and The Family's success in capturing the majority of its children as dedicated members. This is the value placed on the child as "replica," a value in which the individual ego has no place. The community has no time for the individual's desires, freedom, and choice. Children learn to surrender their egos to God and community. "The cut-and-dry rule-keepers bug the teens, but if they break a rule, we just tell them to do better next time." The Family *wants* its children to replicate their adult parents and follow the same Truth. From birth the children study, memorize, and obey the Word to gain wisdom and spiritual strength. They learn to share and be unselfish, to listen to the needs of others, and to put others first. Their sense of self, their identity, is bound up with a consistent, uniform doctrine and with the sense that they are "walking that one mile further than anyone else." Even though it might be a daily battle to follow a life of total dedication, if one knows it is the Truth, then why challenge it?

Although the moral rules and regulations of The Family are constricting and locate Truth and authority narrowly within one domain, the extreme freedom to explore and experience the self *within* that domain make it difficult to challenge. As one boy said:

> There's a secure plan for you: the Lord will bless you when you hold on and if you come through. My teenage friends in The Family have a goal, they seem more fulfilled, but teenagers out there, they're disillusioned with life. I want to help other people find happiness. I've got something to offer. I wouldn't be happy if I lived for myself, and there's a lot of pressure out there to live just for yourself.

The Family's ability to inspire the second generation can also be understood in terms of a successful, dominant meaning system. The importance of looking at the meaning of children's beliefs, which tend to differ from those of adults in any community and tend to be ignored (Hardman 1973), led me to listen for differences in the way children might make meaning of their world. In The Family I could discern few differences. The Family children have wholeheartedly adopted the meaning system of their parents and feel empowered thereby.

Children and Morality in the New Age

For both TM and Findhorn children, the objectivity of rules is far more tenuous.[16] TM children at the day school in Skelmersdale aged between nine and thirteen could not conceive of any *serious* breaches of the conventional code, and indeed several children said that there should not be any rules—"it is only because people become stressed and out of harmony that anyone needs any rules."[17] They clearly distinguished conventional rules from moral rules as having to do with "habit" rather than real consequences (going to prison, making people unhappy); they saw the former as rules that the majority thinks is wrong. Violations of conventional rules (walking on the left, staying in school until told to leave, opening the door) were seen as minor offenses. Moral rules were more important (keeping people happy, not bullying, not teasing, not being hypocritical, caring about others, telling the truth, not killing, not hurting animals). Moral rules also included those laid down by law and by society.

In Findhorn, the children I spoke with could think of few conventional rules, and some flinched at the idea of any rules. They emphasized that there are *no* rules. "I believe in some basic goodness but no idea of religion or religious rules—nothing from outside; from inside maybe, trust in the inherent goodness of others." "There's nothing I *have* to obey." With some humor, one girl said, "It's so safe here you don't lock your door. People here are so nosy—you have to be open—but there are no rules; nothing should be imposed. Parents never imposed anything; it was always my choice and increasingly my responsibility as I got older. If it had been imposed now, I'd be really bitter. Now I can appreciate what they do without having to participate." Some Findhorn children, however, disagreed and thought some conventional rules did exist. "If you look, there *is* a dogma; it has to do with candles and crystals, sitting in circles, meditating, recycling." Such rules included blessing a meal, holding hands, accepting the importance of ecology—saving energy, recycling, and caring for the community.

Rules appear to have a fluid and nebulous nature for New Age children. The key to this fluidity is in the New Age model of childhood, with its focus on individualism and inner potential. Based on the thinking of Carl Jung (1959) and Abraham Maslow (1968), this focus could be called the "self-realization" model. The potential of every individual is to be "the creative center of his activities and of his perceptions, more self determined . . . fully responsible, fully volitional with more `free will' . . . more spontaneous, more expressive, more innocently behaving, more natural" (Maslow 1968: 106–107). Since self-realization is central to the model, experience and experimentation are important, whereas doctrine and complacent acceptance or repetition are to be avoided. Children are encouraged to develop their own tastes and values, to look within and find in themselves the answers to questions—including moral questions. There is little need for rules because authority and responsibility lie within the children themselves. Parents I interviewed did not see any reason to lay down the law:

> They decide for themselves—I don't decide for them—basic morality is inside them; there are no rules, no strict rules, we all just muddle along; because we have no doctrine, there's nothing to follow—so it's all spontaneous—in the moment. We don't celebrate anything. We're in an unfolding/evolution of consciousness—life is a journey, every moment is a learning so how could we give them some static dogma?

Children are empowered to challenge their elders, to "stand up for what you believe in. Rebel against that which you do not. The world is in need of change. As long as we remember that a process of love may only be created by an act of love, whatever we do is right" (Brockbank and Raymont 1993:10).

An example of the expression of the self-realization model is the Findhorn Youth Project, which was established in 1984 to provide an outlet for the children's self-expression in the community. Two members, Jennifer Brockbank (twenty) and Tom Raymont (fifteen), said the Youth Project was "to use our talents as supporters of ourselves and our world, through communication and creation, to build respect and belief in ourselves, others and our planet, with love, gratitude and fun!" (Brockbank and Raymont 1993:10). The impetus behind the project was some petty thieving and vandalism, which were perceived not as indicating the sinful or fallible nature of those involved, but as expressing their boredom and frustration about fulfilling their own purpose in the community. The Youth Project, working on the notion of catharsis—that once expressed, anger is partially resolved—allowed all anger and dislike to be aired. The aim was to encourage children to experiment with their identities and "real selves," to be responsible for themselves and develop their own support system. It was to provide them with a place to air their emotions, their grief, and their anger without harming anyone or anything, so that they could understand themselves better. In this way, they could work toward the self-realization that is the key to the New Age concept of childhood.

Both TM and Findhorn children had a relativistic attitude toward moral and conventional rules that was unthinkable to those in The Family. TM children wondered whether moral rules would be the same for every culture and made such comments as "How you've been brought up makes things right," "Once slavery was right," and "Nothing is absolutely wrong." There was disagreement concerning whether there was any context in which stealing or murder could be considered right—whether Robin Hood could be considered right to steal from the rich. After all, he was stealing it back and King John did not need the money. Some felt that there were times when "they had the right to take the law into their own hands." They proposed that it was the moral majority that makes something right: "If the majority feel it's right, then that's how you see it." Some insisted, however, that there was *no* context in which stealing or murder is right. Like the TM children, those at Findhorn held a relativistic view of morality: "Different people have different oughts, and it depends on your personality"; "Morality depends on the person, the culture." Moral rules had to do with acting nonviolently, respecting others and the earth, expressing emotions, and being responsible for oneself: "shouldn't be violent"; "Listen to everyone and not just what you want"; "Say what you want and what you need"; "Be truthful, honest—I can't lie—I always feel guilty"; "You shouldn't hold in anger"; "Everyone *should* get angry because when you hold in anger, you get bitter." The only moral rules that they thought could be interpreted as "religious" in some sense were those having to do with the earth, seen as divine and requiring respect and reverence—although some children questioned whether this view was morality, preferring to see it as common sense.

What was striking about the description of moral rules among Findhorn children was the focus on *affect as morality*. The children generally agreed that for a community to work, those involved *have* to get on, must do their best, and must have some knowledge of what to do with emotions in a community. Expressing emotions is seen as part of the natural process. I was told that everyone cries at Findhorn, quite often in the hall "You get used to seeing people in tears—mostly the adults—it's good for you; then people also get really happy." People also get angry, and one common technique when angry is for the person to punch a pillow and scream and scream and let it all out. The cathartic strategy goes alongside taking responsibility for emotions, knowing what to do with them, when to express them, how and on whom, "learning to center oneself when upset." The New Age self is an emotional self. Similarly, for Findhorn children expressing emotions is not only an indication of a healthy, open individual; it is also a way to facilitate the social process. Part of what is wrong with the world outside is that "outside the Foundation people are closed. At school in Forres everyone was like a closed box."

When asked about justifying rules, TM and Findhorn children made no uniform reference to any nonhuman authority as The Family children did to biblical authority. They saw actions as a matter of individual, personal choice. This was sometimes mixed with an understanding of the personal usefulness of the action—an important justification for expressing emotions at Findhorn and for meditating for TM: "It's *harmful* not to meditate."

TM children were especially concerned about the harmful effects of not following the rules to relieve stress, since this is what "makes people want to do bad things"; Findhorn children mentioned the consequences of not taking care of the earth. At times, what Nucci and Turiel (1993:1479) describe as "obligation" featured in the justifications, in which the wrongness is self-evident; all the ecological rules were seen as a matter of common sense—the wrongness of not following them must be self-evident and obvious to any rational being.

Both groups also emphasized social relations and social consensus as justifications: "What people say is powerful—the laws are what most people think is right—it should be the majority." Findhorn children said, "If everyone has had their say and everyone agrees, then it must be right."

There was no reference to any religious authority and indeed what was stressed was "system contingency"—that nonmoral rules would differ from culture to culture. The location of authority was very firmly in the hands of parents and children, with some going to government. "Authority?—I have some myself but wouldn't put it all within me"; "My parents are my authority, but I am responsible for myself, and as I get older, I can be increasingly responsible for myself." A few TM children mentioned karma, as in "Hitting is bad karma" or "Whatever I do comes back later."

What emerged from all the New Age children's comments is the degree to which the evolving dynamic of the self is highly individualized, with rights to make choices, define reality and assert relativism. They understood the self as being full of natural emotions of anger and love, which require expression. They had a sense of the relativity of self and their own world, with its multiplicity of opportunities. As a result, many Findhorn children rejected much of their parents' spiritual endeavors: "When I was thirteen, I saw the foundation as a lot of old hippies"; "There is no *should* about meditating, and most of us don't"; "I'm not spiritual"; "We talk about our weird hippie parents and tell them, 'You're so spiritual—get off it!'"

Members of TM and Findhorn believe that a child's true potential and individuality can be expanded through meditation. In the school at Skelmersdale, all the children meditate twice a day. The pedagogical significance of meditation is emphasized in New Age literature.[18] One New Age religious education textbook, for example, offers a methodology for reintroducing spiritual development into religious education using meditation and guided fantasy (Hammond, Hay et al. 1990) through which children can explore the natural realms of personal experience without the imposition of any particular value system. Religious education practitioners are beginning to accept these practices as an important corrective to the emphasis on the purely external, public, and institutional aspects of religion in which the spiritual development of pupils has little relevance. Not surprisingly, the practices are particularly attractive to those who have no single set of values, no single conception of "the good" and a pluralist attitude, as is reflected in the ideology of both TM and Findhorn (see Kevin Mott-Thornton 1996:85).[19]

One implication of this emphasis on experience and children's intuitive spirituality is that conventional education is seen as being a block, rather than an aid, to development—hence the creation of schools like the TM school at Skelmersdale. Adults at Findhorn and Skelmersdale are, therefore, concerned to provide an environment that will encourage spiritual development. The argument is that if children live in harmony with nature and other people, they will not want to break rules or create problems. TM children, for example, receive what is called "culturing behavior" in the school. That is, teachers create a school culture that encourages discipline from within so that children do not want to do wrong, and punishment is minimized. Teachers set good examples by meditating regularly; they develop good relationships with pupils and convey a strong message of what is acceptable behavior and what is not, directing children to be guided by five key rules: (1) listen to the quiet voice inside; (2) treat toys and the material world with love; (3) treat each other with love; (4) speak the sweet truth; (5) raise your hand before you talk. This view of schooling is not child-centered, as in Montessori, but is aimed at uplifting, at starting from where the children are and enhancing the five fundamental principles of teaching: *receptivity*—cultivating fine feelings in children; *intelligence*—improving the orderly functions of children's minds; *knowledge*—selecting and presenting the children with suitable content and methods; *experience*—allowing the children to integrate the new knowledge with their own experiences of life; *expressing*—ensuring that the children have sufficiently grasped the new material that they can teach it to someone else.

According to the head teacher, "We always come back to the self—their consciousness." He added that the ultimate aim of the school is to teach children that sweetness is uplifting. As the Maharishi Mahesh Yogi, the founder of TM, said, "Education is a programme which enables an individual to do maximum justice to himself and in the same stroke of operation—the same stroke of silence—bring fulfillment to his obligation to society."[20]

The concern that public education not block children's potential is found at Findhorn as well. Most parents choose the Findhorn Steiner school because the "central role of spiritual education in the Steiner system is close to the philosophy of the Foundation" (Riddell 1990:196), encouraging autonomous, creative children who are sensitive to others.[21] The young child's imaginative and emotional life is emphasized in the Steiner method through artwork, drama, and poetry. The development of rational, critical, and clear thinking in the child is postponed until after age fourteen. After age eleven, Findhorn children go on to the local academy in Forres. Most of them described some problems in the shift:

> It's when you're older that problems start: it's hard going to school with normal children—we didn't have TV, we lived in caravan, had no car, they teased us about our hippie parents. When they started asking questions, I felt different. They asked why my mum didn't have a normal job. I didn't really understand myself, so it was hard to explain. They thought they were hippies—airy fairy, flowery skirts, and flowers in their hair, people holding hands to bless the land. . . . The bullies tease you and call you hippies, and [at] the bus stop the "hippie stop," they'd shout, "You goin' back to your wigwam?" and some parents won't let their children up here—others think it's cool. We're not like everyone else.

Some children reflected that their experiences at the foundation and at the Steiner school had at least given them the necessary emotional equipment to cope with the bullying at the Forres Academy. One boy described the teasing as rolling like water off a duck's back.

Thus, in spite of the individualism expressible in the libertarian environment at Findhorn—or perhaps because of it—the children do have a grasp of binding prescriptions. But they also have their own desires and visions—different from those of their parents.[22] As one girl said: "One of the main things I learnt was to express myself verbally, learn to stick up for self, learn to express emotions; and I was angry with the foundation—I felt different and wanted to be normal. I wanted a car, a TV, a normal house, and not a caravan."

Few children expressed a wish to remain long term in the community: "I definitely don't want to live here—I want to go to university." For adults at Findhorn, the most crucial relationship is with the God within, the Divine Self. In contrast, very few of the children even meditate, and those that do are considered "weird." The spiritual world of the adults is barely approached by the second generation, although the parents claim that the children do not need to, having naturally gained the spiritual development so painstaking sought by the parents. One mother said: "They do it so normally, they can't see it. . . . They have a bigger heart, a bigger space inside, a bigger understanding, a bigger appreciation of context than any of us. . . . They have a clarity about who they are—where they're going as individuals—and they don't like interference."

Childrearing at Findhorn is fairly unstructured. There are no rules—but during my visit I noticed a growing resentment among those without children who had come to Findhorn for their own spiritual development at the degree to which children were "taking over" adult space. The turnover within the community is very rapid, with people leaving and couples splitting up. The children who stay have to readjust constantly to new people. Funding for staffing positions in the Children and Family Department is still uncertain; there are problems in defining who is responsible for children. Adults are beginning to ask, what is the reality for children in the community now, and should children be fully integrated into all aspects of community life? Children have never been included within the core of the spiritual work. Most children belong to members working in the "open community," as opposed to members of the Findhorn Foundation, who have committed themselves more intensely and undergo "Experience" and "Orientation" programs to develop their "true selves" and their spirituality. For Foundation members, the key focus is on their own spiritual ambitions. A different kind of ideology that would develop their concern for the children of others is absent.

The peripheral nature of the children's existence may be a contributing factor in the high defection rate of teenagers in the community. Although the children share certain values with the adults, their symbolic world is their own, and they often make their own meaning by not identifying with the spirituality of their parents.

The children in The Family form a sharp contrast to these New Age children. They share a strong morality and sense of mission with their parents, and they aspire to follow in their parents' footsteps.[23] Even though Family children view some conventional rules, such as saving souls and selling literature and witnessing, as prescriptive and binding, they are more likely to see nonmoral religious rules as applying to everyone than New Age children are, who stress moral relativity. The one rule these New Age children "generalize" concerns humanity's correct attitude toward the environment. The implication of these findings is that Family children have a hard time conceiving of someone as being a "really good person" without being a member of The Family, having "been saved," and adhering firmly to Family rules. Yet for children in TM or Findhorn, moral discourse comes from within, and they wholeheartedly accept the notion that someone can be a "good" person *without* being a member of their respective communities. Indeed, many of the Findhorn children did not meditate, chant, or have any spiritual practice. They did feel it was important to take responsibility for themselves, care for others, and express their emotions—but someone could still be a good person if she or he did not.

Conclusion

These findings fit with Peter Berger and Thomas Luckman's (1966) hypothesis that success in socialization occurs under conditions in which identities are socially predefined and profiled to a high degree, in which every individual faces the same institutional program for life. "Identity is highly profiled in the sense of representing fully the objective reality within which it is located. Put simply, everyone pretty much *is* what he is supposed to be"; "unsuccessful socialization may be the result of heterogeneity in the socializing personnel" (Berger and Luckmann 1966:183, 187).

In terms of the survival of the three groups described here, the children in The Family have been most successfully socialized into the ethics and worldview of their parents. They have a significant role to play in the future of the movement as the leaders of the new millennium, the "Lord's Endtime children." The world outside The Family badly needs saving; however attractive its forbidden fruits might be, Family children have a strong sense that what is right is biblically based. Listening to these children, we can hear their absolute trust in an external authority. Whatever their own feelings are, their understanding of self and ethics is such that they must ultimately seek guidance from the Word of God. In fundamentalist Christian groups, children's moral views must conform with those of their parents. Those who deviate will either struggle to conform or leave.

The New Age children of Findhorn or of TM find themselves in a very different situation. They have powerful, individualized notions of self in which personal choice and the expression of emotions are central to their ethical understanding. The moral views individually created by the New Age children may well lead them to reject the world they were brought up in.

Notes

1. Socialization, as I mean it here, is best defined by Berger and Luckman (1966:150) as the "apprehension of the world as a meaningful and social reality" in which the complex form of internalization means that "I not only 'understand' the other's momentary subjective processes, I 'understand' the world in which he lives, and that world becomes my own"; the ontogenic process through which this is brought about is a "comprehensive and consistent induction of an individual into the objective world of a society."
2. The Family uses the term *sinful,* meaning not "wicked," but "falling short"—"all of the sins that come short of the glory of God" (Rom. 3:23).
3. The children from The Family were observed and informally interviewed by me during 1993, 1994, and 1995 at Dunstan Bassett, Leicestershire; the children from Transcendental Meditation, at Skelmersdale, Lancashire; and the New Age children, at Findhorn, Scotland.
4. David Berg is known within the movement as "Father David," "Moses David," "Dad," and "Mo," as in the MO Letters through which he communicated with members of the movement.
5. Much has been written on The Family, particularly in the last few years. Interest in The Family increased when it came under attack from the anticult movement and governments in France, Spain, Australia, and Argentina made accusations of child abuse. All the cases have been acquitted.
6. Sex and drugs were part of the culture that followers of Berg left when they joined his Jesus Movement. The authors argue that participants did not completely drop the desire for the experiential when they joined and welcomed the openness toward sexuality that developed in The Children of God/The Family.
7. Melton (1994:94) gives a full analysis of the Law of Love and its development from a doctrine of positive sexuality, to its practical application in flirty-fishing, to the view of it as "radical freedom in which extramarital sexual contact between adults within the family became common," to the relatively conservative attitude today. The latter emerged, in part, because of the large number of children in their teenage years and a growing sensitivity to women and children and the laws of other nations.
8. See Nucci and Turiel's (1993) work looking at the generalizability and alterability of rules among Amish and Dutch Calvinist children.
9. Young children brought up in communal situations are aware of each other's emotions. In kibbutzim communities, for example, "we see, very early, the first signs of the children's give-and-take: . . . a one-and-a-half-year-old child wanting to play with a toy that is in the possession of a girl of the same age; the girl holds the toy very tightly in her hands, whereupon the boy finds a large yellow leaf and gives it to the girl, who then gives him the toy. . . . A two year old is crying bitterly, and another of the same age stands next to him and cries with him, silently. The children receive their directives from the nurse or the metapelet, but *they identify with their peers.* This is really a regulating factor. . . . I think that under conditions of group living, group identification and sharing, as well as group control of individual behaviour, can be learned by very young children. . . . The children learn from others' reactions the real character of their surroundings, and share their feelings about it" (Neubauer 1965:74).
10. At the house at the time were four teens, nine children aged nine to thirteen, three aged five to seven, four aged about three, and three babies.

11. From The Family's publication *Our Statements* (1992): 17.
12. From The Family's collection *Raise 'em Right—A Guide to Raising Happy Children* (1989): 8.
13. From the Family's publication *Our Statements* (1992): 4.
14. "Maria" and Peter Amsterdam were Berg's chief assistants and after his death in 1994 succeeded him in the leadership of the movement.
15. Flirty-fishing was practiced between 1977 and 1984. It was seen as a new form of witnessing whereby women could have a more godly and unlimited view of love and, in a sacrificial way, use sexuality to save souls.
16. The children at the TM Maharishi School of Age Enlightenment live with their parents. Skelmersdale is a small village in Lancashire to which many TM members moved to create an open TM community.
17. Since the TM children were seen at school, we talked informally in their classroom settings, unlike the other children, whom I talked with more informally one at a time or in twos.
18. Although meeting some of the needs of a liberal and pluralist society, schools in Britain rarely attend to the spiritual development of children.
19. Opposing the New Age approach, Thatcher (1991) argues that this experiential approach cannot be used in schools, since it leads to a radical and unacceptable individualism (quoted in Mott-Thornton 1996:85).
20. From a document entitled *Here's Health* circulated by TM.
21. The school is now independent of the foundation and has five classes for children aged six to eleven years old. Most of the children who attend are linked in some way to the open Findhorn community.
22. I was unable to ask the TM children at Skelmersdale about their criticisms of TM and about their own desires and visions. Nevertheless, since the community is loosely structured, and since the children are offered the same kind of individualism as at Findhorn, I would expect TM children to be as selective about what they take from TM as are the children from Findhorn.
23. Those children in The Family who want to make their own meaning of the world, experimenting with what society outside has to offer, must remain outside of the "core army" (see Hardman 1994).

References

Berg, D. 1978. *Is Love Against the Law?* Mo Letter.

Berger, P., and T. Luckman. 1966. *The Social Construction of Reality.* London: Penguin.

Brockbank, J., and T. Raymont. 1993. *One Earth.* Findhorn, Scotland: Findhorn Publication.

Hammond, J., D. Hay et al. 1990. *New Methods in RE Teaching: An Experimental Approach.* Harlow, U.K.: Oliver and Boyd.

Hardman C. 1973. "Can There Be an Anthropology of Children?" *Journal of the Anthropological Society of Oxford* 4(1): 85–99.

———. 1974. "Playground Fact and Fantasy." *New Society.*

———. 1994. "Keeping the Faith and Leaving the Army." In J. Lewis and G. Melton, eds., *Sex, Slander, and Salvation.* Stanford, Calif.: Center for Academic Publication.

Harris, P. 1989. *Children and Emotion: The Development of Psychological Understanding.* Oxford, U.K.: Blackwell.

Heelas, P. 1996. *The New Age Movement: The Celebration of the Self and the Sacralization of Modernity.* Oxford, U.K.: Blackwell.

James, A., and A. Prout, eds. 1990. *Constructing and Reconstructing Childhood.* Basingstoke, U.K.: Falmer Press.

Jung, C. G. 1959. *The Archetypes and the Collective Unconscious.* London: Routledge and Kegan Paul.

Maslow, A. H. 1968. *Toward a Psychology of Being.* New York: Van Nostrand Reinhold.

Mead, G. H. 1934. *Mind, Self, and Society.* Chicago: University of Chicago Press.

Melton, J. G. 1992. "New Thought and the New Age." Pp. 15–29 in J. R. Lewis and J. G. Melton, eds., *Perspectives on the New Age.* Albany: State University of New York Press.

———. 1994. "Sexuality and the Maturation of the Family?" Pp. 71–95 in J. Lewis and G. Melton, eds., *Sex, Slander, and Salvation.* Stanford, Calif.: Center for Academic Publication.

Mott-Thornton, K. 1996. "Experience, Critical Realism, and the Schooling of Spirituality." In R. Best, eds., *Education, Spirituality, and the Whole Child.* London: Cassell.

Neubauer, P. B. 1965. *Children in Collectives: Childrearing Aims, Practices in the Kibbutz.* Springfield, Ill.: Thomas.

Nucci, L., and E. Turiel. 1993. "God's Word, Religious Rules, and Their Relation to Christian and Jewish Children's Concepts of Morality." *Child Development* 64: 1475–1491.

Perry, M. 1992. *The God Within.* London: SPCK.

Peshkin, A. 1986. *God's Choice.* Chicago: University of Chicago Press.

Richardson J. T., and R. Davis. 1983. "Experiential Fundamentalism: Revisions of Orthodoxy in the Jesus Movement." *Journal of the American Academy of Religion* 51(3): 397–425.

Richardson J. T., M. Stewart, and R. B. Simmonds. 1979. *Organized Miracles.* New Brunswick, N.J.: Transaction Books.

Riddell, C. 1990. *The Findhorn Community: Creating a Human Identity for the Twenty-first Century.* Findhorn, Scotland: Findhorn Press.

Smetana, J. G. 1981. "Preschool Children's Conception of Moral and Social Rules." *Child Development* 52(13): 33–36.

Thatcher, A. 1991. "A Critique of Inwardness in Religious Education." *British Journal of Religious Education* 14: 1.

Toren, C. 1993. "Making History: The Significance of Childhood Cognition for a Comparative Study of Mind." *Man* (NS) 28: 461–478.

Wallis, R. 1979. "Sex, Marriage, and the Children of God." Pp. 74–90 in R. Wallis, ed., *Salvation and Protest: Studies of Social and Religious Movements.* New York: St. Martin's Press.

York, M. 1995. *The Emerging Network: A Sociology of the New Age and Neo-Pagan Movements.* Lanham, Md.: Rowman and Littlefield.

Index

About the Contributors

Helen A. Berger is an associate professor of sociology at West Chester University in Pennsylvania. She has been involved in a participant observation study of Witches and Neo-Pagans in New England for the past ten years. She is also working with Andras Corban Arthen, the founder of the largest Neo-Pagan organization in New England, on a survey of Neo-Pagans throughout the United States. She has published articles in major scholarly journals.

Anthony Bradney is a senior lecturer in the faculty of law at the University of Leicester. He is a member of the executive committee of the Socio-Legal Association and past vice-president of the Association of Social and Legal Philosophy. He has written widely on the relationship between legal rules and religions in Great Britain. His publications include *Religions, Rights and Law.*

Simon Coleman is a lecturer in the department of anthropology of the University of Durham, England. He has written extensively on the globalization of evangelical Christianity and is currently also engaged in two other projects researching Creation Science and pilgrimage respectively. He has carried out fieldwork in Uppsala, Sweden, since 1986; in Walsingham, England since 1993; and in Durham, England, since 1996.

Judith Coney received her Ph.D. from the School of Oriental and African Studies, London, England. Her doctoral dissertation was on the Sahaja Yoga movement.

Charlotte E. Hardman is a lecturer in anthropology, religion, and contemporary Britain at the University of Newcastle Upon Tyne. She was the deputy director and research officer for INFORM (Information Network Focus on New Religious Movements) between 1990 and 1993. She has published numerous articles on new religions, the anthropology of children, and Nepalese communities in anthropology and religion journals, and has worked as researcher on two documentary films.

Michael W. Homer is a practicing trial lawyer at the law firm of Suitter, Axland & Hanson in Salt Lake City, Utah. He has published dozens of articles on new religious movements, the law, Mormon history, spiritualism, and on the life of Sir Arthur Conan Doyle.

Massimo Introvigne is professor of history and sociology of religious movements at the Pontifical Athenaeum Regina Apostolorum in Rome, and managing director of the Center for Studies on New Religions (CESNUR) established in 1988 in Turin, Italy. He is the author of twenty books and the editor of another ten in the field of new religious movements and contemporary magic.

Susan J. Palmer is an adjunct professor and lecturer in the department of religious studies at Concordia University, and teaches full-time at Dawson College in Montreal. She is the author of *Moon Sisters, Krishna Mothers, Rajneesh Lovers* and *AIDS and the Apocalyptic Vision*. She coedited *Millennium, Messiahs and Mayhem* with Tom Robbins, and *The Rajneesh Papers* with Arvind Sharma. She has worked on documentary films, most recently as associate producer of *The Endtime*, with DLI Productions.

Elizabeth Puttick did a doctoral dissertation on the Osho movement at King's College, University of London, and now teaches a course on alternative spirituality at the City University, London. She is the author of *Women in New Religions* and the coauthor of *Women as Teachers and Disciples in Traditional and New Religions*.

James T. Richardson is a professor of sociology and judicial studies at the University of Nevada, Reno. He has been researching new religions for over twenty years and has published *Organized Miracles* and four other books and nearly seventy-five articles in journals and books.

E. Burke Rochford Jr. is a professor of the department of sociology and anthropology at Middlebury College, Vermont. He is author of *The Hare Krishna In America* and has published articles on ISKCON in *Sociological Analysis*, *Journal for the Scientific Study of Religion*, and other journals.

Gretchen Siegler received her Ph.D. degree in sociocultural anthropology from the University of Nevada, Reno, in 1992. She is an assistant professor at Westminster College in Salt Lake City, Utah.

Amy Siskind received her Ph.D. in sociology from the New School for Social Research in New York in 1995. Her doctoral dissertation was on the Sullivan Institute.